THE TWILIGHT YEARS

ALSO BY WILLIAM WISER

THE TWILIGHT YEARS

PARIS IN THE 1930s

William Wiser

CARROLL & GRAF PUBLISHERS, INC.
NEW YORK

First Carroll & Graf edition 2000

Carroll & Graf Publishers, Inc.
A Division of Avalon Publishing Group
19 West 21st Street
New York, NY 10010-6805

Library of Congress Cataloging-in-Publication Data is available.
ISBN: 0-7867-0786-0

Manufactured in the United States of America

FOR ORIANE

NEWCOMER TO RUE STENDHAL, PARIS, 2000

ACKNOWLEDGMENTS

I AM GRATEFUL to the following instiutions for assistance with the research and writing of this book: Bibliotèque Nationale, Paris; Centre Pompidou, Paris; Humanities Research Center, Austin, Texas; Denver Public Library, Denver, Colorado; University of Colorado Library, Boulder, Colorado.

I offer particular thanks to Kathy Zipp, Kitty Kolody and Jim Foyle at the Penrose Libarary of the University of Denver, Colorado.

For information, texts, suggestions, hospitality and moral support, I would like to express my thanks to Veronique Briquet-Laugier, Hugh and Judy Bostic, Leo Bukzin, Noel Riley Fitch, Diane Harlé, Crystal Lindfors, Jon and Eva Lundberg, Jean Newman, Bin and Linda Ramke . . . along with a large *merci* to my patient and supportive family: wife Micheline, son Paco, and daughter Anne.

For the warmth and welcome to their abundant shelves at the bookstores in Paris: The Village Voice (Odile Hellier) and Shakespeare and Company (George Whitman); in Denver, The Tattered Cover.

PHOTO CREDITS

CONTENTS

THE TWILIGHT YEARS

1

ENTER LAUGHING, TRISTE ADIEU

I

*I*N THE WAKE of a homebound return for legions of the 1920s expatriates, a balding exuberant Brooklyn boy of near-ly forty years—ten dollars in his pocket and ship's passage paid, one-way—set forth for France to write the book "of the man that I am." It was March of 1930 when Henry Miller arrived in Paris at the raw beginning of an uncertain spring. The legendary expatriate scene had shifted dramatically: the former easy, free-wheeling invasion of Montmartre and Montparnasse had ended with the stock-market crash of 1929; an American exodus now flowed across the Atlantic in the opposite direction, but Miller was not one to drift on the outgoing tide.

For the next decade Paris was to become Miller's icon city in ways no predecessor had experienced. By personal inclination and hard necessi-ty he sought out the darker side of the city of light, the lower depths unrecorded by Hemingway, Fitzgerald, or Gertrude Stein, an idiosyncratic view from the underside, a Paris unknown or ignored by the café terrace set. Writing from grim acceptance and Rabelaisian humor, even rapture, he intended to create a picaresque masterpiece. To accomplish his *Tropic of Cancer* Miller would revive an extreme bohemianism closer to the tradition of Rimbaud and Baudelaire than to the posturing of a previous generation of American expatriates.

"God damn it, it's wonderful!"

His first room was in the heart of the Latin Quarter five flights up, nestled under the eaves of the Hôtel St.-Germain des Prés, with a view of medieval church towers at the corner and a façade opposite where artists hung their freshly painted canvasses to dry attached to the window-ledge grillwork like a bright panoply of flags or Persian carpets on display. Below his dormer window the street vendors of rue Bonaparte each cried a different chant punctuated by auto horns from the chaotic traffic on the boulevard St.-Germain.

"The streets sing," he wrote, "the stones talk."

Too excited to continue this letter to his Brooklyn friend Emil Schnellock (the first of a series of letters, actually a tentative first draft of *Tropic of Cancer*), Miller rushed down to savor a Pernod in the café below; then, unable to linger in that congenial ambience he dashed on, edged his way through the animated shoppers at the rue de Buci open-air market, then along the rue Saint André des Arts in search of the ancient crumbling Église de St. Severin.

This Paris Sunday was like no other Sunday he had ever known. (The Protestant ethic, he believed, was responsible for the pall cast over the traditional Sunday in America.) Mass was in progress but Miller was too elated by the street panorama to mingle with churchgoers and puzzle through a sermon in French. He rushed on, as if the devil's pitchfork prodded him forward to cross the pont Marie to Notre Dame on the opposite bank rising tomblike from the Seine. He stumbled across a sad collection of homeless women sleeping on newspapers in a tiny triangular park in the shadow of the great cathedral, a vision of the social milieu he would become more and more familiar with, and part of. Looking up he was reminded of Quasimodo's Paris: "The gargoyles leaning far out from the white façades, grimacing fiercely, hanging there like an idée fixe in the mind of a monomaniac." The monomaniac was Miller himself, and the city of Paris his idée fixe.

The language eluded him, a music he was determined to master however crudely with his glutteral Brooklyn accent. At a restaurant he could not remember the word for beans and was obliged to engage in a grotesque apelike dumbshow with the waiter when he tried to order. Would he ever find the key to communication with these people, share their ineffable spirit, verily penetrate the mystery of the place? He had missed out on the larger excitement of the decade just past, when the creative fervor was at its height; he was too late for the time when everyone was a James Joyce or a Picasso, or soon would be. Never mind, the newcomer felt he had shed twenty years on arrival full of fresh impressions of this great good place. He was bombarded with sensation, overcome with new attitudes and strange insights reacting instantly to the Paris of the moment. The book of his life had begun, and express himself he must despite whatever puerility of thought—and Miller's linguistic exuberance would often run away with him—the written record would at least be *his*.

"A year, six months ago, I thought I was an artist. I no longer think about it, I *am*."

THE TWO HUNDRED francs monthly Miller was to pay for his picturesque room (even the five-franc supplement for a bath was a major consideration) became far beyond the means of a man financially dependent on a wayward wife (June, the Mona of *Tropic of Cancer*) who had promised to cable money to meet his living expenses. When Miller met her at a dance hall off Times Square, June was a taxi-dancer and, appropriately enough, or so he said, he seduced her in a taxi. Soon they were living together, and eventually married when Miller finally secured a divorce from his first wife. At first Beatrice refused, but then divorced from sheer outrage at having discovered her husband and June in flagrante delicto in her bed.

June was as free-spirited as Miller, and as unreliable and impractical. One of their money-making schemes was to open a speakeasy in a Greenwich Village basement, June to be the alluring hostess while Miller tended bar. The speakeasy failed, but June continued to exploit her charm and sensuality. Miller was uneasily aware of his wife's sexual restlessness, but if she was unfaithful by sporadic impulse he pretended not to know or to believe the fleeting attachments were platonic only. Whether platonic or not, June's serial liaisons produced loans or gifts of money, for she was still a taxi-dancer at heart—time spent with her must be paid for in cash—and the Millers became dependent on this largesse, an income more substantial than anything he earned from dishwashing, working in his father's tailor shop, door-to-door sales, or as a streetcar conductor. None of his jobs lasted more than a week (some less than an hour) except for the position as personnel manager for Western Union. The job would offer rich material for a future novel, *Tropic of Capricorn,* but allowed for little time to write. It was the one responsible position of Miller's lifetime, until June convinced him to give it up: "I'll find a place where you can write. You won't need to earn money. I'll soon be making lots of money."

She was planning to become a film star; the place she had in mind where Miller could write was Paris.

Throughout the trials and turbulence of their marriage, June professed great faith in Miller's literary gifts; she believed he would, with her help, make a name for himself as a man of letters. First, he would need the stimulus and inspiration of Paris in which to create his Great Book. The dream was Miller's own, and Paris was about to be realized with June's moral and financial support.

Before she could put together the money for his departure, a disturbed and disturbing third partner drifted into their already unstable household. This was Jean Kronski, called Mara (Stasi, in *The Rosy Crucifixion*), a mentally unbalanced poet and painter dressed in boy's clothes, "a face neither male nor female," according to June; to Miller she resembled Rimbaud.

Mara attached herself to June, and June to her while Miller remained a hapless third partner in the lopsided arrangement. Perversely Miller acquiesced in this bizarre ménage à trois even when it became apparent June preferred Mara to himself. Because of his sexual bondage to his wife, Miller endured the humiliation of second-string lover in the triangle, the role of masochist-voyeur, observing Mara and June "undressing one another, licking one another all over, like calves in the meadow."

Miller threatened suicide, and did make an attempt to poison himself, but the friend who provided the necessary pills made certain the dosage was not fatal. June was greatly impressed by the suicide letter declaring that if he could not have her he preferred death. But the affair with Mara had not yet run its course, and would end only when June left with Mara for a Paris sojourn. They quarreled violently, apparently requiring a third-party rival (the insanely jealous Miller) to add spice to their affair; and June returned alone. A final act of morbid masochism in this strange arrangement was when Miller worked as a grave digger to be able to send June and Mara money for the stay in France.

It was now June's turn to send Miller abroad. He had a novel in progress she fervently believed in, since it was mainly about her, called *Crazy Cock,* and she proposed to finance Miller's solo venture to Paris with money she inveigled from a doting suitor. The affair with Roland Freedman may well have been platonic, as June maintained— Freedman later committed suicide while still in thrall to her, a death inspired by the same frustrations June aroused in Miller.

With June's promise of support, passage paid by Freedman's generosity, and a ten-dollar bill shoved into his pocket by Emil Schnellock at the pier, Henry Miller embarked on his long-anticipated odyssey.

EVERY MORNING MILLER made the pilgrimage to the American Express on rue Scribe in expectation of the funds June promised but rarely sent. The walks from Left Bank to Right were nevertheless inspiring. This critical lack of cash would help set the pattern of alternating desperation followed by euphoria, a manic-depressive reaction to this new life in Paris, survival on the narrowest of edges in the world's most fascinating city.

Those first mornings of hopeful monetary expectancy (sometimes rewarded, more often not) he chose a different bridge over the Seine each trip, from the pont Royal to the pont Neuf, a selection of four magnificent spans over the same somber gray river. The most immediate thoroughfare to his destination was by the pont du Carrousel, then through the precincts of the palais du Louvre. He timed these daily excursions in order to arrive at the American Express when it opened at nine, the first eager client at the mail desk.

"Nothing for Mr. Miller."

He sometimes made as many as three disappointed trips across the Seine in a day and once went five days without food when there was "nothing for Mr. Miller" for weeks. This crossing and recrossing of the Seine was not without reward of another kind: "All along the banks the trees lean heavily over the tarnished mirror; when the wind rises and fills them with a rustling murmur they will shed a few tears as the water swirls by it. No one to whom I can communicate even a fraction of my feelings . . ."

True, he was exceedingly lonely. He could have called on the sculptor Ossip Zadkine but hesitated to get in touch with him, jealousy outweighing loneliness, for he was convinced June and Zadkine had been lovers on June's venture to Paris.

He wrote fan letters to the poet Cocteau and to filmmaker Bunuel, no answer. Could they have deciphered his neglible French? He attempted to speak to strangers on the street, but the French have a low tolerance for a halting, imperfect command of their beloved language. June sometimes responded to his letters, and Emil Schnellock often wrote; he kept copies of Miller's jottings, later to be incorporated in *Tropic of Cancer*. June kept none of his letters. Lacking a companion to whom he could speak, Miller poured out his impressions on paper.

"I start tomorrow on the Paris book: first person, uncensored, formless—fuck everything!"

FROM THE HÔTEL St.-Germain des Prés Miller was obliged to move to the Hôtel Central on the avenue du Maine, at 125 francs (about five dollars by the month), but even that rate was more than he could afford. He moved from hotel to hotel ". . . looking for a good cheap hotel the last three days. Have visited over *100* so far!"—and until he acquired a circle of friends and cronies who might lend him a spare bed overnight, or let him sleep on the floor of their rooms, he often had no place to stay the night. Miller moved around Paris so frequently and possessed so little to transport, he could declare, "When I move I have only to pack a few condoms and I'm off!"

The condoms became a leitmotif. Everywhere he encountered the grim skull-and-crossbones warnings: DEFENDEZ-VOUS CONTRE LA SYPHILIS, and at first the constant reminders imposed on the hot-blooded Miller a vow of celibacy. The notices were posted in every streetcurb *pissotière*, the open-air public urinals that initially disturbed his American sensibilities along with other quaintly impossible toilet facilities. (He could always avail himself of the civilized facilities at the American Express.) Eventually French plumbing became less and less a concern, and the famed *pissotières* (or *pissoirs*, his term) a veritable object of art.

Despite his vow, Miller soon enough gave in to the urge to sample the commercial sex so flagrantly available. Unable to resist a whore with a story, his first encounter cost 177 francs, an amount he had calculated to last the next ten days, "and I'm probably contracting syphilis in the bargain." The fear of infection rendered him impotent. He pleaded a sudden case of melancholy, dismissed the girl, and fled by cab (another five francs blown), appalled and depressed by the evening's folly.

His next adventure, with Germaine Gaugeard, was closer to the Paris experience he was writing in his mind. He confessed to Germaine from the start that he wasn't flush enough to pay her standard fifty-franc fee, and she readily accepted his offer of twenty francs, though the reduced rate placed her closer to the *poules* of the lowest rank, the ten-franc girls—prostitutes, Miller discovered, had social status according to the price one would accept.

Germaine considered Miller chic in his odd American knickerbockers and loud golf socks. Her territory (strictly defined, but subject to dispute between pimps) was the boulevard Beaumarchais, a characterless spoke leading from the place de la Bastille. Soliciting this district, she insisted, was merely a sideline. Actually she was a model, or so she told Miller. Since he was a writer and she a model, they were both artists, *n'est-ce pas?* Miller thought she might have been a factory girl, but if the script called for a twenty-franc tumble with an "artist's model," so be it.

More than a one-night stand, they became friends and Germaine was truly flattered to be seen with her American. When they met at her way station, the Café l'Éléphant, she insisted he wear his authentic costume, the knickerbockers. Often when Miller was out of funds—he was more often broke than not—Germaine would admit him to her room on the rue Amelot (her pimp was not to know of this) and there offer her favors *pour l'amour* only.

Initially Miller made it a point not to associate with "the insufferable idiots of the Dôme and the Coupole," the dilettantes and poseurs of the boulevard Montparnasse. He did not intend to be affiliated with the dregs of the 1920s scene; however, stark necessity finally drove him to frequent the café terraces and loiter over a drink in the hope of putting the touch on some visiting American. Not long after Germaine had succumbed to the Miller charm—for all his thick-lipped balding homeliness and verbal overflow, Miller generated a certain charm—he began to acquire a circle of American, Russian, and French acquaintances, strays and intimates who could be counted on for a loan, a dinner, a drink—even a bed for the night if he could be smuggled past a watchful hotel concierge.

When Miller was evicted from the Hôtel Alba on the rue Vanves, he could have, as so often before, curled up on some cobbled quayside under the shelter of a bridge over the Seine, lying on a pad of newspapers like the destitute women he had seen asleep in the shadow of Notre Dame, but a sympathetic cinema owner, Monsieur Girardot, allowed him to sleep in his office at the Cinéma Vanves. Here was a long-term solution to Miller's pressing need for sanctuary—ideal, except that Monsieur Girardot was obliged to lock up the premises for the night.

From the time of the last film showing until nine in the morning, Miller was a prisoner in the empty movie house, all doors locked from outside and the window in the office barred. At first he could not sleep at all, and when he did sleep he suffered crushing claustrophobic nightmares. He would awaken in the small hours or at dawn to the street sounds that so fascinated him his first day in Paris, but now the streets of Paris stirred beyond his reach outside the bars of his cell.

Mornings, a prisoner still, he endured the remaining hours of incarceration suffering pangs of obsessive hunger. When Miller did eat, he ate exceedingly well: he had come to share the French passion for *la bonne cuisine*: he now knew the term "haricots verts," but as yet could not pronounce the throaty "r" in *beurre*, and was adding to his vocabulary, and taste, daily. He dreamed up hearty American breakfasts as the breakfast hour passed, then imagined a five-course French lunch, with wine, squeezing his stomach to suppress the rumblings of hunger. He recalled with horror a Frenchman feeding paté de foie gras to his poodle.

Enough! When next he was freed by Monsieur Girardot promptly at nine, Miller thanked his benefactor, and jailer, but chose not to return that night or any night thereafter. His address was no longer Cinéma Vanves; he now headed his correspondence: "Henry V. Miller, Man of Letters, c/o American Express, 11 rue Scribe—Vive la France! Liberté Egalité Fraternité—Pax Vobiscum."

For the artist-nature, security he decided was a kind of cage not unlike the locked and barred Cinéma Vanves. America represented another kind of cage, one he had successfully fled, so why submit to imprisonment in Paris? (Miller actually risked literal imprisonment when he wandered certain suspect quarters at night; he was liable to arrest if a gendarme demanded to inspect the *permis de séjour* he did not possess.) Eagerly he returned to the uncertainty of the streets and the irregular charity of friends, a free agent whose vagrant existence brought Paris into the closest possible focus and a state alternating between anguish and delight. He would accept the inevitable elusiveness of the city, the disillusionment and depression that accompanied its pleasures. Beyond the façade, Paris was a whore: "From a distance she seems ravishing, you can't wait till you have her in your arms. And five minutes later you feel empty, disgusted with yourself. You feel tricked."

Tricked and disgusted, but rewarded by an accumulation of insights making possible "the struggle of the human being to emancipate himself, that is, to liberate himself from the prison of his own making."

II

IF ONLY MILLER had contacted Zadkine earlier, or when he did, had been willing to see him more frequently ("Henry," the sculptor complained, "why do you stay away from me?"), he would doubtless have been drawn into the charming and congenial company of Jules Pascin, the painter who throughout the 1920s was considered the Prince of Bohemia. Miller and Pascin were much alike in temperament, an indifference to material attainments, dedicated to Paris as the city supreme, and both in bondage to their relentless sexual needs.

In his journal for July 4, 1930, Zadkine sadly noted: "Here it is a month since Pascin died. The decision must have been taken long ago, the idea matured, the act carried out in obstinate determination. . . . No one, none of his many friends nor of his harem of women realized the man was on his last legs. Not a soul with whom he could confess before a witness. God, what a life of an abandoned dog is this Parisian existence."

Not long before Pascin's death, Ernest Hemingway sat with him at his favorite table on the rue Delambre side of the Dôme, Pascin "looking more like a Broadway character of the nineties than the lovely painter he was." As always Pascin wore his hard black bowler perched at a jaunty angle on his mop of black Levantine hair, his heavy-lidded eyes moving from one young model to the other; the two women sat flanking the painter, restless as kittens, having posed through the long afternoon while the light lasted. The model Pascin had been least attentive to he offered to Hemingway, "to bang."

"You've probably banged her enough today," Hemingway replied.

A friend to all, and a generous one, Pascin was known throughout the quarter for his parties, his dinners, money lent and spent on acquaintances as recent as that day's aperitif hour. He was the softest of soft touches and so casual about his work, once completed, that when he saw in his atelier mirror a visitor slipping watercolors into his jacket, he said to him: "Not from that pile, please. I need those for a show," and indicated with an offhand gesture another selection from which the thief might help himself.

He was a casual but consistent voluptuary: his interest in models, preferably the very youngest, was as much sexual as painterly. There was nothing intentionally predatory in this; Pascin was, like so many of the habitués of Montparnasse, sharing in the largesse of available flesh. The sensualist in Pascin was evident in the temperament and attitudes expressed in watercolor or in paint: languorous poses of the nude, perhaps two or three together in soft-focus deshabille. The expression on a model's face could well have reflected his own, a detached stare into the middle distance of postcoital contentment of the sadder variety. Unlike Toulouse-Lautrec, who was surely an influence (fellow explorers of the same nether regions, the subterranean terrain of the bordello), Pascin intimates a sad blasé acceptance of sex in contrast to Lautrec's hard-line approach to the ravaged depravity of his brothel scenes. Pascin was exposed to this exotic underworld at an early age.

HE WAS BORN Julius Mordecai Pincas in Vidim, Bulgaria, of an Italian-Serbian mother; his father was a Sephardic Jew. Little is known of his childhood on the Danube at the frontier of Bulgaria and Romania; he never spoke of his origins to friends, nor submitted to interviews when success came. The Hungarian painter Tibor Polya knew him as a young man, and tells of his liaison "with a Fanariota woman" (never named) twice his age, madam of a brothel in Bucharest. By way of "this woman" the young Julius was introduced to the inmates of her *maison close*, a wide-eyed teenage spy admitted to the seraglio who began a clandestine record of this licentious setting with a series of drawings, his first sharply observed sketches of women.

The boy's talent was evident, especially to this unnamed woman of the world who encouraged his artistic endeavors as well as his sexual pursuits. In his early drawings he showed a flair for satire and wit that caught the attention of the editors of *Simplicissimus* in Munich. In classic opposition to his father's wishes—Julius was to follow in the Pincas family grain trade—he slipped out a window and escaped his home in Vidim to become a satiric cartoonist in Munich. At this first stopover in his wanderlust along the wayward path of art, Julius became Jules and he made an anagram of his surname, Pincas to Pascin.

From Munich he went to Berlin, then to Vienna, Budapest, and, finally (his destination all along), to Paris. No sooner had he arrived in the home of his heart than the Great War broke out and his adopted Paris was under threat of invasion. He was obliged to take up the way of the Wandering Jew again; he fled first to England, then to America—where he spent the war years, found middling success at New York galleries, and even became an American citizen. Pascin traveled through the southern states, crossed to Cuba, and ventured from island to island in the Caribbean making drawings and watercolors of the black-skinned

A drawing of two women by the voluptuary and artist Jules Pascin.

Creoles he found so exotic. To draw unobserved, he worked out a cramped method of preliminary sketching executed in his coat pocket on stiff paper with a pencil stub: his models remained unaware of being sketched.

DURING PASCIN'S FIRST sojourn in Paris he had been living with Hermine Cartan—also known, with considerable irony, as Hermine-Lionette Cartan-David-Hapsbourg, for her mother insisted that Hermine was the natural daughter of a Hapsburg prince following *"une nuit de folie"* during which she allowed the prince "every indulgence."

Perhaps the Hapsburg bloodline or her belief in aristocratic origins led Hermine to make free with Pascin's earnings. Also, she aspired to more lavish live-in arrangements than the seedy Hôtel Beauséjour offered, situated at the lower end of rue Lepic. But this disreputable section of Montmartre appealed precisely to Pascin's bohemian sensibilities: the boulevard Rochechouart, which became the boulevard de Clichy at the rue de Martyrs, from one end to the other was a realm of pickpockets and prostitutes, the Paris that flourished so vividly after dark.

Why, implored Hermine, could they not take a flat with studio in the Other Montmartre, the upper region of winding streets where at the higher levels one had magnificent views of all of Paris? (Pascin did not paint "views" but people, particularly women.) Their close friend Suzanne Valadon, painter and former model, Maurice Utrillo's mother, lived on the heights of rue Cortot. (One often saw the aged ailing Degas struggle up the steep rue Lepic to pay an old man's court to Suzanne, his former model and painting protégée.) Or they might find suitable quarters on the rue des Trois Frères where Pissarro once lived, near the summit of la Butte—or on rue Hegesippe-Moreau, near the Moulin de Galette where Cézanne had lived.

Pascin was disinclined to any such move or any move at all. Besides, Hermine's domestic motives were suspect. The Hôtel Beauséjour was where common-law couples lived; an apartment meant marriage. Before she could convince Pascin to move, the Great War had broken out and the painter abandoned Paris altogether.

Hermine followed Pascin to New York, and there worked her will on him at last. They were married—or, as Pascin explained the circumstance, they were obliged to marry because their prudish American grocer refused to deliver to a couple "living in sin."

When Pascin returned to Paris after the war he looked up another love of his life, Lucy Vidil, his model (whom he had not seen for a decade), now married to the painter Per Krogh. Neither Pascin's marriage, nor Lucy's, prevented the two from taking up the liaison again, a quarrelsome affair that nevertheless endured in the troubled fashion of the day.

ALL OF THAT first day of June 1930, the stones of the boulevard de Clichy had baked under a relentless summer sun, and by nightfall Pascin's fifth-floor studio had become a suffocating corner of purgatory. The *volets* were closed, drapes drawn, and the floor littered with drawings the artist had simply let fall from his work table, stepped upon with indifferent footprints. On the mantelpiece was a crowded collection of squeezed-out paint tubes, cigarette butts, and wineglasses with lipstick stains, but despite certain festive traces, Pascin had been alone for the last three days. The concierge saw him go out for a breath of air, but oddly enough without his trademark derby perched tilted on his head.

He was seen passing the Cabaret du Néant, a name surely appropriate to his contemplations: *non-être*, or not to be . . . nothingness. As his friend Hemingway had written in an existential short story, "It was all a nothing, and a man was nothing too."

The artists he knew, certainly the Eastern Europeans like himself—Kisling, Zadkine, Lipchitz, Brancusi, Chagall—arrived anonymously in Paris, most often destitute, and now were recognized. They were sought by dealers and many were selling well or, like Soutine, supported by a patron. The group was beginning to be called a school. L'École Juive (most were Jews) had surely flourished, none more than Jules Pascin. He could look forward, oddly with dismay, to a well-publicized retrospective at Galerie Bernheim Jeune where returns would be lucrative, priced according to contract "by the square inch," for the market. "I sell," he said to friends, *"au numéro,"* which was a way of saying, "I sell out."

Money could be spent, given away, lavished on women, and stuffed into the pockets of old friends and new acquaintances at parties, at the Dôme or the Cabaret du Néant, but what of the quality of his work and the purity of intent he had brought with him from Vidim to Paris? Was he repeating himself, painting only what would please his public? How had he acquired this public with its demand for product at the loss of mystery and discovery in the artistic process?

Pascin deplored an evident decline of quality in the work of such painters as the Dutchman Van Dongen who had been one of the original Fauves (the Wild Ones), now tamed and grown fashionable. Kisling too had discovered that his hollow-eyed portraits became appealing and collectible the larger and more sentimental the model's wistful stare. The decadence had set in; what was once daring had become commercially chic.

At a time when newcomer Henry Miller was shouting aloud, "I have no money, no resources, no hopes. I am the happiest man alive!" Jules Pascin was brooding desperately on the opposite.

He was seen to pause at his favorite Montmartre café, the Maison Rouge, but did not stop for a nightcap as was his custom. Nor did the distraught painter venture by cab to the Left Bank, where a long-established clan of admirers would have applauded his return and cheered, "Bravo, Pascin!" after the three-day absence from his favorite table.

Around the corner from the Dôme, at the Falstaff Bar, the inimitable Kiki was no doubt perched on the zinc *comptoir* to exhibit her fine legs to the crowd: the legs were still worth looking at though the rest of her was no longer worth the paint on canvas except as a portrait in caricature. (Perhaps we all become cartoon characters in decline.) Kiki held court at the Falstaff nightly now, there to promote her so-called memoirs describing how picturesque was the poverty in those days of obscurity and good times . . . what rapture to be critically neglected and down to the last ten francs, and how *delightfully* crazy were *les années folles* when posing for Pascin among others, and sleeping with him gratis, among others. And now for eighty francs a copy (a sum that back then would have purchased paints and canvas and bread and wine for a month) you could savor Kiki's mythmaking autobiography and a kiss from the unforgettable author herself—with an introduction by Hemingway to guarantee sales, if the promotional kisses didn't work.

Foujita would be at the Falstaff as well. You couldn't miss him for the trademark Japanese bangs that stood out in any crowd scene where a publicity stunt was on. His yellow Ballot parked in the prime spot in front of the bistro, its hood ornament a copy of Rodin's *Man with a Broken Nose*. Whoever heard of a painter who never drank? But that was Foujita. Never as much as a pastis passed his lips, though all of Montparnasse was welcome to drink at Foujita's private bar at home, the furnishings sold to him by Simenon the Belgian writer. Foujita didn't drive, but the yellow Ballot was for Youki, his mistress, a toy and symbol to show how successful Foujita had become painting "society" portraits of such as—he complained of her falling asleep during the pose—the aging comtesse de Noailles.

They all wanted automobiles now, a machine that could be polished to a shine that reflected success. *"Cinq chevaux! Cinq chevaux!"* Kisling had crowed boasting of the five-horsepower Citröen he bought after the "successful" show at Paul Guillaume's. Success! Success!—and success it was, or was it?

On this night of nights their pal Pascin was a missing detail to the colorful tableau at the Falstaff or on the Dôme's animated terrace. Pascin's nonchalant wit was a much celebrated element of that scene. Who else, since Nerval himself, could utter with casual insouciant seriousness, *"Je veux une mort rigolotte,"* "I want a humorous death"? It was exactly in the style of Gerard de Nerval who would promenade through Montparnasse with a lobster on a leash, the Prince of Bohemia a century ago, the crown inherited by Amadeo Modigliani at Nerval's death, and by Jules Pascin when Modigliani died. De Nerval committed suicide by hanging himself still wearing his "crown," a top hat. The gendarme who discovered the formally attired body on the rue de la Vielle-Lanterne thought at first the man had frozen to death.

AT THE DÔME that night, Lucy Krogh sought out Kisling, a friend close enough to confide in: "It's over between Pascin and me, and for good. He asked for his key back." Lucy implied that the break was just as well; the two had always quarreled, but the fights had become even worse of late.

"He has gone away for a few days," Kisling explained, as if to account for Pascin retrieving his key. "He takes one of his trips to the Midi."

"I think not." Lucy was beset by forbodings she could not define. "He has a big show coming up. He wouldn't leave Paris before the show is hung."

They discussed Pascin's illness, a deteriorating liver ailment—but cirrhosis was endemic in the bohemian community of Montparnasse; a "liver problem" hardly explained Pascin's detached mood of late.

"Jules had his demons," she told Kisling, suggesting that not even she could know what his present bedevilment was.

Pascin was not one to confide in either wife or mistress, but both women had become acquainted with the artist's "demons" firsthand. Kisling was now beginning to share Lucy's anxiety: something was surely amiss with her lover. Lucy was closest to him, and the one to inquire.

"Go see him," Kisling advised.

"How can I? He took back my key. He doesn't want to see me again."

"Go to him anyway!"

FROM THE STREET Lucy could see that the fifth-floor shutters were closed. The concierge was uncertain if Monsieur had left on a journey or not; he came and went at *n'import quelle heure*. Banging on Pascin's door brought no response. Lucy was certain he had not left for the Midi, but she did not want to force an entry without the help of a friend. A neighbor, Charlotte Gardelle, was known to both Pascin and her, and the two women sought a local locksmith who was unable to accompany them but sent his young apprentice, a mere boy. The apprentice was able to open the door. A faint light from the bedroom penetrated the gloom.

"Are his suitcases here?" Charlotte Gardelle asked, for that would prove if he had left Paris or not. Lucy entered the bedroom, let out a terrible shriek, and backed out again.

"Il est là!"—"He's there!"

Pascin was crouched beneath the knob of an inner door as if he had fallen to his knees and slumped against the door. A cord was wound round his neck, attached to the knob. Nearby were two basins of water streaked with carmine, as if he might have been cleaning his brushes in them.

The two women had become hysterical; only the young locksmith kept his head, saying, "You have to get help for this man."

Of course.

Charlotte Gardelle went in search of Dr. Tzanck, Pascin's doctor, while Lucy waited, sobbing in the concierge loge. Dr. Tzanck climbed to the fifth-floor atelier alone, for neither woman dared enter the scene of horror with him. Pascin had been dead from strangulation for many hours. The doctor also discovered the artist had slit his wrists with a straight razor, and had dipped the bleeding wounds in water—however, the cold water slowed the flow of blood and the suicide, impatient to be done with these last moments of life, had contrived to hang himself from a doorknob.

Among his drawings was found Pascin's last will and testament, directing that his worldly goods and works of art were to be equally divided between his wife Hermine and his mistress Lucy. On the studio wall Pascin had painted in blood flowing from his wrist the inscription: ADIEU LUCY.

2

BEACHHEAD IN BOHEMIA

To SUSTAIN HER celebrated bookshop, Shakespeare and Company, Sylvia Beach depended on the Anglo-American trade so abundant in the tourist twenties but in steep decline as the thirties turned somber. It was as if the Parisians had recaptured their city from the American visitors: the Montparnasse cafés were now populated by a predominant French clientele and fewer Americans found their way up from the place de l'Odéon on boulevard St. Germain to the literary landmark at 12 rue de l'Odéon, the street—"as restful as a little street in a provincial town"— Shakespeare and Company had "Americanized." So popular had the bookshop become that Americans departing for France gave 12 rue de l'Odéon as their forwarding address and writers known to Sylvia Beach were given credit and loans in French francs (until their dollars came through) at what Sylvia began to call her Left "Bank," or the Odéon Bourse. Although the Depression was slower to reach France, Shakespeare and Company was feeling the effects of the Wall Street crash well in advance of other Parisian enterprises, and Sylvia Beach might be said to seek credit and loans herself.

Sylvia had long enjoyed a certain commercial overflow and decided cultural overlap from a French bookshop at number 7 on the same narrow thoroughfare. This was Adrienne Monnier's La Maison des Amis des Livres; the proprietor and Sylvia were devoted to one another. Their long-standing affair of the heart dated from the first encounter, when plump Adrienne in a skirt down to her ankles (her traditional costume "a cross between a nun's and a peasant's") chased Sylvia's Spanish hat down the rue de l'Odéon, blown off by the wind.

"J'aime beaucoup l'Amérique," declared Adrienne, to which Sylvia replied, *"J'aime beaucoup la France."* Thus the Franco-American liaison was forged, an attachment as substantial and enduring as that of Gertrude Stein and Alice Toklas.

Adrienne had first introduced Sylvia to the book business, and encouraged and helped her establish Shakespeare and Company, first on nearby rue Dupuytren, and then opposite her own shop on bookish rue de l'Odéon, a duplicate bookshop across the street.

Now that the American trade had diminished so drastically, Shakespeare and Company depended on attracting a French following, but a Frenchman (like Erik Satie, who called Sylvia Beach "Mees") was there to absorb the literary atmosphere, to browse or borrow from the lending library but not buy. One prominently displayed item did draw French and American alike—this was James Joyce's monumental novel *Ulysses,* in 1930 still banned in England and America but openly available at Shakespeare and Company. *Ulysses* was now in its eleventh edition, proudly published by Sylvia Beach.

Throughout the 1920s James Joyce had surrendered his literary affairs (as well as many domestic and personal responsibilities) into the willing hands of his publisher. Little could Sylvia have known the consequences of her spontaneous offer, after having known Joyce only a few days: "Would you let Shakespeare and Company have the honor of bringing out your *Ulysses*?" Having suffered persecution and prosecution for many years over his completed masterpiece, Joyce accepted this opportunity "immediately and joyfully." The novel was a work of genius, Sylvia knew, but she could not have known the sacrifice genius demands in its service, or the all-consuming requirements of those enlisted in the "Joyce industry." Most likely Sylvia would have proposed

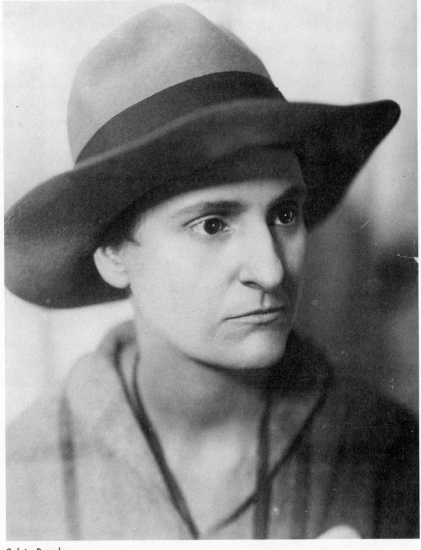

Sylvia Beach.

to publish *Ulysses* even if she had known (except for the sad deceptive ending to her relationship with Joyce) what she was in for. Perseverance, loyalty, devotion were fixtures of her nature. Joyce was equally persevering, but he reserved loyalty and devotion for his immediate family.

As the 1930s got under way, Joyce entered his most demanding phase, the self-interest covered by a show of impeccable courtesy (after ten years, Sylvia was still "Miss Beach," or, in a playful mood, "Madame Shakespeare," while Joyce remained forever "Mr. Joyce") when issuing a barrage of demands in the form of requests, usually for funds "by 'tomorrow,' 'by express,' 'by return of post.'" Sylvia's working hours at Shakespeare and Company were from nine A.M. until midnight, the larger part of her responsibility concerned with the care and feeding of her *enfant terrible*, Mr. Joyce.

Since *Ulysses* had proven so successful a publishing venture, it was assumed that the proprietor of Shakespeare and Company earned a substantial profit after paying the author's twenty-five percent royalty. If Sylvia had been a shrewd enough accountant and could have resisted Joyce's constant and excessive needs, she might have earned considerably from *Ulysses*, but the profits seemed to be drawn from her cash drawer as if by "a magnet in Joyce's pocket." A typical note from Joyce might read: "Thanks for the cheque . . . Have you paid my florist?" As the money came in, more than earnings went out; from the penury of his struggling years, Joyce became flagrantly extravagant. Hemingway's earlier report that it appeared "[Joyce] and all his family are starving but you can find the whole celtic crew of them every night in Michaud's . . ." was an indication of Joyce's penchant for dining out, and in the thirties the restaurant was Les Trainons, across from the gare Montparnasse, where Joyce dined regularly with family and friends. Joyce himself was an indifferent gourmet, but insisted that guests enjoy the most expensive dishes and vintage wines while he himself would be content with "a plate of lentils" and *vin de table* (Alsatian whites preferred, the cheapest would do as long as the supply was unlimited). His tips, in the F. Scott Fitzgerald manner, were legendary.

When word reached Sylvia of Joyce's casual spendthrift ways, she defended his profligacy as one having been denied even the necessities of life during the hard years, and "when you think of Joyce's labors, he was certainly underpaid." Joyce now traveled extensively, usually *en famille*, and invariably first class. Meanwhile Sylvia and Adrienne journeyed to their weekend retreat by the cheapest means, with "a mountain to climb" before reaching their rustic abode to sleep in a hayloft. Nevertheless Sylvia maintained that Joyce, "with his reputation and achievements was entitled to a certain material ease."

Another put-upon supporter was Harriet Weaver who generously bestowed upon Joyce the inheritance she received from her aunts, a settlement from which he could live off the interest. Her socialist belief was that wealth should not exceed "personal need," and her own wealth was sufficient that she might share with the Irish genius. Joyce might have lived modestly on the interest from this windfall, but he continually drew from the principal, thus reducing his income. When in need of one thousand pounds to join his daughter (Lucia was suffering from schizophrenia) and pay his hotel bill at the Carlton Elite in Zurich, Miss Weaver used the often cited accusation that Joyce spent "like a drunken sailor." Joyce then appealed to her that he needed false teeth and had to pay for the gravestone for his recently deceased father. She sent the money.

Robert McAlmon, like Sylvia Beach, supported Joyce in every possible way—with money from his wife, the poet Bryher (heiress to the Ellerman fortune—her marriage to McAlmon was in name only) while serving as general factotum and sometime secretary. Their friendship suffered a series of setbacks because of McAlmon's light-minded flippancy in matters Joyce considered sacred and from an increasing disillusionment, on McAlmon's part, with the obeisance expected of the Joycean acolytes. Sylvia Beach considered that Joyce had "earned" this undivided devotion of his followers, but McAlmon in the 1930s began to stray.

Joyce's Irish sense of humor could condone such incidents as the stir McAlmon caused at the reading of *Anna Livia Plurabelle*, a lyric section from Joyce's *Work in Progress* (*Finnegans Wake*). The reading was held at Adrienne Monnier's bookshop since the ALP section, as it was known in short, had been translated into French (already difficult enough in the original English) by Valery Larbaud and others, the audience, naturally, predominantly French literary dignitaries. McAlmon was a reluctant participant to what he considered a secular version of High Mass and at one point, as the audience sat in hushed reverence, McAlmon raised his hands, palms together, in a gesture of mock prayer. Immediately a Frenchman rose from his seat and slapped McAlmon's face. It turned out that the Frenchman (Edouard Dujardin, who was said to have originated the technique of "interior monologue" Joyce had adapted so brilliantly in *Ulysses*) was not protesting McAlmon's irreverence toward the séance but thought McAlmon was mocking his wife's thick ungainly ankles, about which he was sensitive to the point of obsession.

James Joyce reading, 1938.

Even though Joyce may have relished the farcical misunderstanding for what it was, he viewed McAlmon with growing annoyance that culminated in the memoir McAlmon wrote in 1934, *Being Geniuses Together*. Joyce objected to the boozy portrait of himself—Sylvia Beach thought it an honest enough portrayal—which he called "the office boy's revenge." Briefly he considered suing McAlmon for defamation of character, but *Being Geniuses Together* was not published until 1938 due to editorial shifts and quibbles, and by then McAlmon was no longer of any concern to Joyce.

The author of *Ulysses* was possessed of and by a compulsive litigious nature and was forever entangled in lawsuits he initiated whose outcomes accomplished little or nothing. Legal fees, of course, were a further drain on his fluctuating resources. One lawyer who worked for

James Joyce with Sylvia Beach and Adrienne Monnier, the two publishers of *Ulysses*, in Shakespeare and Company, 1938.

Joyce without pay (taking on many of the tasks formerly assigned to McAlmon and a series of unpaid assistants), Paul Léon, was asked to involve himself in legal action seeking an injunction against a Japanese publisher who was illegally publishing *Ulysses* in 1932. However, when Léon got in touch with the British consul in Tokyo he learned that the book's European copyright was valid for ten years only by Japanese law, and had recently expired.

The scandal of *Ulysses* being banned in the United States, for all the frustrations this represented to author and publisher, was largely responsible for the book's extraordinary success, the eternal attraction of forbidden fruit. But the interdiction left the way open for pirated editions, since the banned book could not receive copyright protection in the United States, where the literary piracy was most flagrant and damaging to Joyce. The most notorious pirate was Samuel Roth who produced a bogus volume often mistaken for the original. Sylvia Beach was already engaged in a heroic effort to challenge Roth, sending out dozens of personal letters to eminent literary figures worldwide asking their shared indignation at Roth's blatant piracy. A formal protest was drawn up by Ludwig Lewisohn, revised by Archibald MacLeish, to be signed by supporters of Joyce, among whom Ernest Hemingway's name appeared erroneously as a member of the Académie Française. This mistake may have prompted Roth's angry suggestion that the "vicious virago" Sylvia Beach had even added names of deceased writers to the protest (several had died since signing). In *Shakespeare and Company* Sylvia wrote, "The only writer who refused to sign was Ezra Pound," adding, "That was just like Ezra." Pound was one of Joyce's first supporters and ardent defenders, responsible for bringing Joyce to Paris in the first place, but the two men were fast growing apart, ostensibly over Pound's disagreement with Joyce's current *Work in Progress* (*Finnegans Wake*) and Joyce with Pound's latest cantos.

Despite the time and energy-consuming campaign Sylvia waged in Joyce's behalf—letter-writing, telephoning, searching *Who's Who* for those she might solicit in defending *Ulysses*—her efforts fell short of Joyce's expectations. (As Nora Joyce expressed the personal services her husband demanded, "If God Almighty came down to earth, you'd have a job for him.") At one point Joyce even tried to convince Sylvia to reestablish Shakespeare and Company in New York rather than Paris, where she could more immediately pursue Roth through the American courts.

Perhaps the most quixotic lawsuit Joyce contemplated was against the *Frankfurter Zeitung* for having published a detective story by "James Joyce." When the story came to Joyce's attention he immediately initiated legal proceedings; he notified his London lawyers to prepare to sue, but his political friend in London, Harold Nicolson, suggested he simply demand a correction and apology from the newspaper with the possibility he would sue if the *Frankfurter Zeitung* did not print a retraction and apology. As it turned out, the newspaper had done just that, under the title "Michael und James," which explained that the translator, Irene Kafka (Joyce failed to see the comic implications of the name Kafka in the affair) had confused the name Michael Joyce with the far more celebrated James. Both Michael Joyce and Irene Kafka wrote Joyce personal letters of apology, but once on the hot trail of litigation, Joyce was not easily dissuaded. He insisted that Lionel Monro, Harriet Weaver's lawyer, pursue the matter in Frankfurt through a German lawyer, Willi Rothschild (Joyce also failed to react ironically to the lawyer's name in seeking a damage settlement). Rothschild wisely discouraged any further procedure by informing Joyce the most to be gained from a court settlement was twenty-five pounds. Joyce had already invested far more than that sum in legal fees, as had the ever-supportive Sylvia Beach who helped fund the hopeless cause and devoted more time than she could spare on letters seeking support. (Joyce himself wrote thirty-six letters and sent eleven telegrams.) Finally, to Sylvia's profound relief, Joyce was persuaded not to sue.

In what appeared to be a beneficent and considerate gesture, Joyce presented to Sylvia Beach a contract that offered her what had been their de facto agreement all along: "the exclusive right of printing and selling throughout the world, the work entitled ULYSSES." The friendly understanding between them, the bond that had survived the twenties was now—December (the ninth spelled as "nineth") 1930—made official, or so it would seem, with the three-franc sixty *République Française* stamp on the upper left-hand corner and the signatures of both author and publisher inscribed below the formula *"lu et approuvé"* (read and approved). This "strange Jesuitical document," as Janet Flanner called it, may have sounded dryly legalistic and formally binding, but was neither

27

James Joyce strolling with Adrienne Monnier on rue de l'Odéon, 1938.

witnessed nor notarized. Since Sylvia Beach had never requested an official contract between them, satisfied with Joyce's word from the beginning, she saw no reason to question the terms offered in the document.

If "after due consideration" the publisher wished to relinquish her
right to publish *Ulysses,* then the rights could be purchased from her "at
the price set by herself." This sounded fair enough, and the phrase "in
the interests of the AUTHOR" aroused no suspicion—the interests of
the author had been uppermost in Sylvia's dealings with Joyce all along.
Thus Sylvia Beach was granted world rights to the work entitled *Ulysses,*
but as she discovered, that world belonged to Joyce.

At long last (November 25, 1933) Judge John M. Woolsey of the United
States District Court delivered his famous statement on *Ulysses,* that the
book was not obscene by the standards of the day, "And may, therefore, be
admitted into the United States." The way was now clear for author and
publisher to reap the benefits of English-language copyright and sales long
denied them because of the obscenity ban and outright piracy.

AS THE DEPRESSION years reached France in late 1932–early 1933,
the effect on Shakespeare and Company was drastic: Sylvia found herself in much reduced circumstances, and consequently Joyce could
count less and less on her benevolence and the largesse of the Odéon
Bourse. By way of the agent J. B. Pinker, a number of publishing firms
were making offers for *Ulysses* now that its existence had been certified
and made legal by Judge Woolsey, and Sylvia realized she was being kept
in the dark concerning these negotiations. Apparently Joyce had
informed Pinker that Sylvia Beach was his *representative* rather than his
faithful publisher (and benefactress) for the past ten years. Neither
agent nor author considered the clause stating that *Ulysses* "shall be purchased from the Publisher at the price set by herself," according to the
contract Joyce himself had originated. Now that Joyce could no longer
count on a steady income from Shakespeare and Company, and far richer rewards appeared at the foot of the rainbow, he surreptitiously withdrew from their long-standing arrangement with no consideration of
Sylvia's rights or welfare in the transaction. The so-called contract was
in part a ploy on Joyce's part to shift responsibility and expense of litigation. When the lawyer in the case against Roth's piracy demanded a
two-thousand-dollar balance due, Sylvia was expected, as "owner" of
Ulysses, to pay the legal fee.

"This didn't seem to me the correct way to do things," was Sylvia's mild admonishment. "Then I began to be exasperated at being ignored. I told Joyce so . . ."

Who really "told Joyce so" was Adrienne Monnier, who effectively ended the Joyce-Beach relationship with a strongly worded letter in which she refuted the myth that Joyce was unconcerned about success and money: "—you are, on the contrary, very concerned about success and money." She also let him know that while he lived extravagantly during these hard times, "We're traveling now third class and soon we'll be riding the rods." (Maria Jolas, still loyal to the halo placed upon Joyce's head by his followers, was outraged by the letter and thought it reflected Adrienne's sapphic jealousy, and that she wanted to "rid Sylvia of an importunate suitor.")

Sylvia believed, and was encouraged by Adrienne and others to believe, that she was surely entitled to "something for relinquishing my rights." In a moment of pique she suggested to the literary agent Pinker that she should receive the exaggerated sum of twenty-five thousand dollars. Neither Pinker nor the lineup of interested publishers took her request seriously (Sylvia did not take it seriously herself: "I explained to Joyce that [twenty-five thousand dollars] was only proof of my esteem for the book.") One publisher, Heubsch, did offer to pay Sylvia a royalty on sales: "But there was no question of my accepting it, because it would have come out of Joyce's royalty."

The final blow came in a confrontation with an old friend of Joyce's (unnamed by Sylvia, it was Padraic Colum) who tried to persuade her to withdraw any request for compensation for the sale of *Ulysses*. Sylvia brought up the contract that specifically granted her the right to name her own price in the event of a sale to another publisher.

"That's no contract," said Colum. "It doesn't exist, your contract."

True, the contract would not likely have withstood legal challenge, and in any case—which both Colum and Joyce well knew—Sylvia would never have gone to court over the issue.

"You're standing in the way of Joyce's interests."

As soon as Colum had left and her heartbeat subsided, Sylvia phoned Joyce to inform him that she would release all claim to ownership of any rights to *Ulysses*.

The association, and friendship, was over, but in the aftermath of the break, whenever anyone criticized or belittled Sylvia Beach in his presence, Joyce might rise to her belated defense: "All she ever did was make me a present of the best years of her life."

Meanwhile Joyce had charmed and impressed an eager replacement, Paul Leopoldovich Léon, a White Russian émigré he recruited to fulfill many of the duties formerly assigned to Sylvia Beach. "Taxifuls of Joyce business were transferred from Shakespeare and Company to Paul Léon," Sylvia wrote—neither relief at having shed the "Joyce industry" nor bitterness implied. With her customary modesty and a philosophic shrug, Sylvia endured the betrayal over *Ulysses* saying, "A baby belongs to its mother, not to the midwife, doesn't it?"

Shakespeare and Company remained a shrine for visiting Americans in Paris, though missing one of its central attractions, the near-blind Joyce seated cross-legged among the collection of Sylvia's books, and his own, under the portraits of the literary elite taken by Man Ray, or by his assistant Berenice Abbott. Now only the Man Ray photograph of Joyce marked the spot where once the writer himself sat holding court or stood crookedly "like a question mark" caressing a volume he had taken from the bookshelves, trying to make out the print through his thick glasses.

It was inevitable that Henry Miller would eventually find his way to Sylvia Beach's doorstep on the rue de l'Odéon, seeking the same literary ambience as those eager tyros who had preceded him—but Miller's errand was more immediate and pressing than to browse and soak up the bookish atmosphere. In his bumptious forthright way and with the raw confidence of the neophyte, he was offering his *Tropic of Cancer* for publication by Shakespeare and Company.

Since Sylvia Beach was known as a risk-taking publisher of an unpublishable book, more than one author of an "obscene" work had come to her with a manuscript likely to be banned or that no one else would touch. Most recently, Frank Harris had stopped by with *My Life and Loves,* followed by D. H. Lawrence hoping to convince Sylvia to publish his *Lady Chatterly's Lover.*

Miller arrived in the company of an exotic beauty, the very "Japanese-looking" (thought Sylvia) Anaïs Nin, Miller's latest love.

Sylvia was more interested in his companion than in Miller himself. Anaïs Nin had become Miller's sexual and intellectual obsession, rival to his wife June as the love of his life—and the threesome would later form a jangling ménage-à-trois when June eventually arrived in Paris. Anaïs Nin had written a study of the work of D. H. Lawrence, an essay that first attracted Miller's attention to her, written out of a surge of self-discovery and sexual awakening that Lawrence inspired in the woman long smothered by her stifling bourgeois background. Miller had entered her life at just this critical and propitious moment.

Sylvia Beach's answer to *Tropic of Cancer* was no. Shakespeare and Company was no longer a publishing enterprise, she informed Miller—but did not add that the "Joyce industry" and recent collapse of that commitment had cured her of publishing forever. He might, she suggested, try Jack Kahane whose Obelisk Press favored works of "a certain forthright sexiness." Miller followed her advice and did find publication with Obelisk; Sylvia heard little more from him after that first visit, since Miller had established his own literary coterie at his bohemian headquarters on rue Villa Seurat, though she continued to be interested in the passionate diarist Anaïs Nin.

Other writers from America came her way. Maxwell Perkins had just handed Thomas Wolfe a check for the successful *Of Time and the River*, "put him on a boat bound for Europe," and directed him to Shakespeare and Company where he made an early call. He impressed Sylvia as "a young man of genius, and perhaps very unsatisfactory as a social being."

George Antheil was back in Paris, with funds for musical composition awarded by the Guggenheim Foundation. Naturally he looked up Sylvia: in the 1920s he had lived in the studio above the bookshop; when he lost the key, he heaved himself up to the second-story window by way of the Shakespeare and Company sign. James Joyce was an admirer of Antheil's radical compositions and was trying to convince him to write an opera, to be adapted from Byron's *Cain*, primarily as a vehicle for his favorite tenor and protégé John Sullivan. Antheil was at first willing to consider the scheme, thinking Joyce would contribute to the libretto, but Joyce, as he explained, "would never have the bad manners to rewrite the text of a great English poet." Furthermore, Joyce expected Antheil to write the composition in such a way that only Sullivan could sing the title role. Antheil may have learned from Sylvia's unfortunate association with Joyce, and managed to withdraw from the project before the crisis stage.

But newcomers and returned expatriates were not clientele enough to reestablish the fiscal imbalance brought on by the *Ulysses* debacle and the Depression years. Lean years could be endured, but Sylvia faced penury.

To the rescue came Adrienne Monnier, a rally from her side of the rue de l'Odéon where the French congregated. Shakespeare and Company was on the verge of closure when Adrienne passed the word to her clientele. As soon as André Gide learned of Sylvia's distress he helped form a committee of rescue that included such literary lights as Georges Duhamel, André Maurois, Jean Paulhan, Jules Romains, and Paul Valéry. The French were not always on the best of terms with their American neighbors in Paris (or with one another), but Sylvia Beach was a notable exception.

Jean Schlumberger composed a proposal asking two hundred subscribers to pledge two hundred francs a year for two years. The committee for Les Amis de Shakespeare and Company inaugurated a series of readings at the bookstore to attract the "two hundred"—subscriptions were limited to that number, for that was as many as could be squeezed into Shakespeare and Company. The readings were successful. The highlight was the one and only reading ever given by Ernest Hemingway who overcame his aversion to public speaking for this performance to benefit his dear friend Sylvia.

FROM THE MOMENT he had stepped across the threshold of 12 rue de l'Odéon in 1923, Hemingway remained a faithful friend to Sylvia Beach. Through Sylvia he had met many of his contemporaries on her premises—not always to such enduring *amitié* as this one exceptional, noncompeting bond he forged with "Madame Shakespeare."

"I managed somehow to have them all get along with each other," said Sylvia of her subtle diplomacy. "—Rather difficult when you mix writers."

One writer of beautifully crafted stories, new to Paris in 1932, was Katherine Anne Porter, who moved into the flat abandoned by Ezra Pound when he settled in Rapallo. This was also Hemingway's old neighborhood, the rue Notre-Dame des Champs, and from there, as Hemingway had discovered, it was an easy and pleasant promenade through the Luxembourg Gardens to the Théâtre de l'Odéon and a few more steps to the door of Shakespeare and Company. (Hemingway's stroll through the Gardens supposedly included his shooting of pigeons

Sylvia Beach encouraging George Antheil in a climb to his apartment at 12 rue de l'Odéon.

with a slingshot, hard up for the evening meal—an apocryphal adventure not entirely believable by Sylvia or anyone else.)

Sylvia found Katherine Anne "a thin twiggy sort of woman, quick-tongued, quick-minded and light on her feet," and was delighted to enroll the newcomer as a member of the lending library and welcome her into the congenial circle associated with the bookshop.

Porter in turn described Sylvia as "not pretty, never had been, never tried to be; she was attractive, a center of interest, a delightful presence not accountable to any of the familiar attributes of charm."

The two women shared very few personal attributes except a tendency to migraine headaches (Sylvia's intensified by dealings with James Joyce) and a fondness for cats. There was always a reigning feline at Shakespeare and Company; no dogs were allowed on the premises because of Joyce's aversion to canines. Katherine Anne Porter related to Sylvia how she lowered her cat from the second-story

ABOVE: T. S. Eliot reading to the cosmopolitan crowd at Shakespeare and Company, 1936.

RIGHT: Sylvia Beach and Ernest Hemingway in front of Shakespeare and Company.

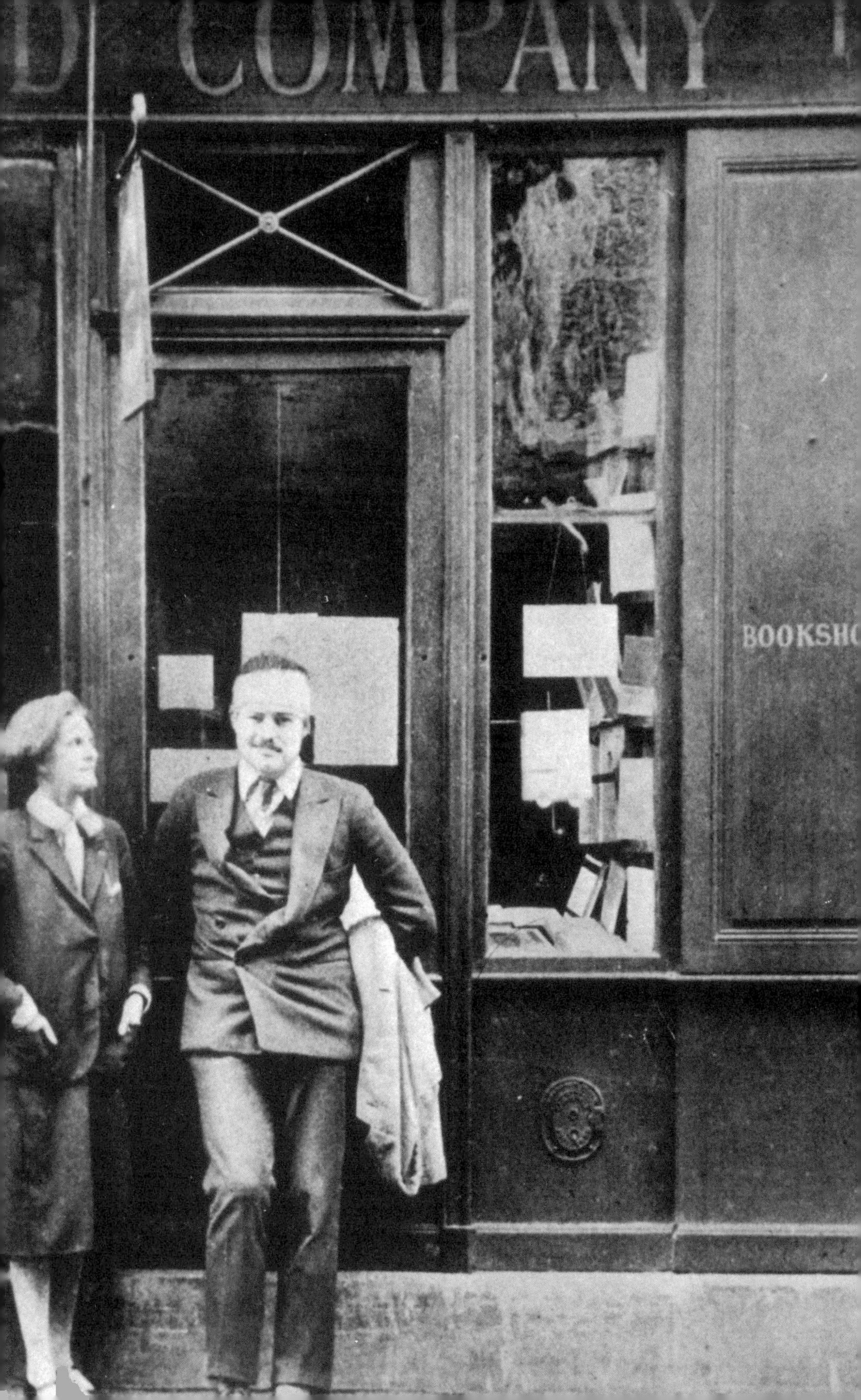
COMPANY
BOOKSHO

window in a basket, and once interrupted a cat-snatching woman about to make off with her pet. Frenchwomen, Porter decided, must be inordinately fond of cats to want to steal one.

"Yes," agreed Sylvia, and warned, "They make such excellent rabbit stews."

KATHERINE ANNE PORTER'S stories and novellas, set in Texas and Mexico, were admirable works of art, and equal, Sylvia believed, to the famous stories of Ernest Hemingway working in the same genre. The two must meet.

One rainy afternoon when Porter was in the shop, the bulky Hemingway loomed in the doorway wearing a shabby raincoat and rain-soaked hat. On entering he immediately wrapped Sylvia in a wet bear-hug. It was the perfect moment to arrange for "the two best modern American writers to know each other." Saying this to them, and holding each by the hand, she presented them by name, then hurried away to answer the telephone. (Not taken into account was Hemingway's notorious rivalry with his contemporaries, especially with writers of short stories, female, like Dorothy Parker.) "The two best modern American writers" stood facing each other in awkward silence for some weighty seconds; then Hemingway turned abruptly away and hurtled through the door into the rainswept rue de l'Odéon.

3

PARIS BY NIGHT—I

*A*T HIS FAVORITE table on the terrace of the Dôme, Henry Miller nursed a café-crème—"fishing," which was to expect a crony to join him and pay for it—and asked the waiter for stationery, one of the civilized amenities of a Parisian café. Instead of scribbling notes for his *Tropic of Cancer,* Miller was inspired to compose an upbeat begging letter, copies of which he would send to a selected assortment of newfound friends. Each was asked to volunteer a convenient evening when he might share "your homely repast" on a regular basis. In return, the fortunate host would be treated to the writer's outspoken wit and wisdom (the wit might take a sarcastic or insulting turn, but Miller's friends were tolerant of this)—along with the self-gratification of supporting Art. Beds he could find, often enough with an obliging woman, or at last resort he could sleep in the WC at the Dôme, the sawdust still pressed to the back of his jacket when he took his morning café-crème. However, the risk of starving in Paris was a constant.

Surprisingly, the scheme for a round of dinners was enthusiastically taken up. Miller reasoned, correctly, that no one friend wanted full-time responsibility for a penniless parasite, but would offer a charitable meal one night a week. And there was the reward of the writer's lively monologues. With Wambly Bald, for example, there was the added advantage of inviting Miller for lunch on the day of his deadline for the Paris edition of the *Chicago Tribune*, when he might glean an odd item or two from the latest colorful bohemian for his column *"La Vie de Bohème."* (The column about Henry Miller was in fact written by Miller himself, when Bald was too hung over to meet his deadline.)

The alternating round of dinners succeeded so well that Miller could afford to drop any host whose cuisine was not up to the culinary standard

Café le Dôme at 108 boulevard de Montparnasse, where Henry Miller composed his begging letters.

of the others, or of those whose conversational remarks were too banal in reply to his own passionate discourse. Henry Miller began to live by the code that beggars can be choosers.

The openhanded painter Pascin was Miller's predecessor as master-of-ceremonies at the Dôme; now Miller replaced Pascin with a droll style of his own. Pascin had been generosity personified, while Miller placed himself at the receiving end of any café windfall. Miller's extrovert charm and unyielding frankness, a city-bred worldliness combined with childlike innocence, attracted many into his widening coterie of acquaintances.

Of his numerous pals and cronies, he had been slowest to warm to Ossip Zadkine. June had known Zadkine on a previous visit to Paris, before Miller's own solo voyage, and Miller—painfully aware of June's promiscuous nature—could well imagine the carnal entwinings of his wife with the sculptor. However, in spite of Miller's persistent suspicions of a sexual liaison with Zadkine, he allowed Zadkine to join the list of seven hosts who provided the scheduled meals. Zadkine would have relished more of Miller's company than his one allotted dinner a week: "Henry, how do you make so many friends here?? . . . I am very lonely. . . . I never think of speaking to someone unless I know him . . . why don't you take me with you when you go on your folklore expeditions?"

Miller's private response to the appeal was, " 'Folklore expeditions.' Cripes!"

SINCE HIS RELEASE from the prisonlike confinement at the Cinéma Vanves, Miller could again take up his night-prowling rounds and record his impressions for the skewed version of a city's raw underside in the autobiographical *Tropic of Cancer*. He intended to catch "a glimpse of the life which the French deny us foreigners by erecting their Chinese wall of cafés." No, he would not take Zadkine with him on these "folklore expeditions" but he did share his passion for voyeuristic tours of nighttime Paris with a strange little Transylvanian photographer, Gyula Haldász, who called himself Brassaï for his native village Brasso.

Brassaï was part of the wave of Russian, Hungarian, Romanian, Polish, and Czech artists drawn to Paris in the 1920s, and he originally intended to be a painter. It took him ten years to discover the more direct art of photography with "a very old camera with a cracked lens hood, a tripod which kept kneeling down like a camel," as Lawrence

Durrell once described Brassaï's "really amazing equipment, but as cherished as it was venerable."

Miller's memory conflicts with Brassaï's in how they met, but both agreed that the first meeting was at the Dôme.

"I seem to see you standing in the gutter at the Dôme," said Miller, "at the angle of the rue Delambre and boulevard Montparnasse. The spot where you stood I see so vividly I could draw a circle around it."

Brassaï's recollection of the meeting was that Louis Tihanyi, a deaf Hungarian painter (unofficial public relations man at the Dôme), introduced the two men.

"I will never forget the sight of [Miller's] rosy face emerging from a rumpled raincoat," was Brassaï's remembered impression, "the pouting lower lip, eyes the color of the sea."

Each noted the other's intense gaze and unforgettable eyes; Miller began to call Brassaï the Eye of Paris, a title that might just as accurately apply to himself as the city's visionary. The deaf Tihanyi mumbled an incomprehensible introduction (no one at the Dôme could understand his gibberish Hungarian-French): Miller's French was at a crude beginning phase, not much less gibberish than Tihanyi's . . . and Brassaï knew no English. At that first meeting neither Eye of Paris could properly communicate, though they established instant rapport. What they initially shared was an almost mystic perception of the city, especially Paris by night. Miller, who subscribed to the revelations in horoscopes, would have said their stars were in conjunction.

"WE [MILLER AND Brassaï] explored the 5th, the 13th, the 19th and the 20th arrondissements thoroughly. Our favorite resting places were the lugubrious little spots . . ." None was more lugubrious than the 20th, where the two could explore Père Lachaise cemetery.

From the Café Wepler of *Quiet Days in Clichy*, which Miller considered "the vaginal vestibule of love," he nightly observed the prostitutes casting their nets (their own version of café "fishing"), or outdoors installed at curbside in front of some unimposing *maison de passe*, whispering the invitation, *"Tu viens?"*

He confessed to Brassaï he was fascinated by the prostitute with the wooden leg whose way station was at the entrance to a dark blind alley next to the Gaumont Palace cinéma—intrigued by the exceptional success her deformity attracted. Another of Miller's voyeuristic outposts

A *maison close* in the 7th arrondisement.

was La Fourche (the fork, where avenue Saint-Oeun branched off from avenue de Clichy), a concentration of vice after dark equaled only by the narrow streets adjacent to the gare Saint-Lazare, or the streets off boulevard Rochechouart in Montmartre, where semen, he declared, ran thick in the gutters.

Meanwhile Brassaï managed to penetrate the commercial seraglios, the *maisons closes* scattered across Paris, depicted in paint and pastels by Degas and Toulouse-Lautrec, now vividly exposed to Brassaï's blunt black-and-white photographs. Brassaï's method was direct and unadorned: "I don't bother with psychology. I photograph everything—one doesn't need psychology."

Miller's observations would be distilled in the passages of *Tropic of Cancer,* his revelations stark and disturbing, his style equally direct: "a gob of spit in the face of art."

BRASSAÏ APPEARS AS a character in *Tropic of Cancer:* "Then one day I fell in with a photographer; he was making a collection of the slimy joints of Paris for some degenerate in Munich. He wanted to know if I would pose for him with my pants down, and in other ways."

Untrue, insisted Brassaï: "Never did I use him as a model for any pornographic pictures. For one thing, I did not do pornography; I was doing a photographic study of human behavior, and that was why I frequented the centers of pleasure and vice that had so captured Miller's imagination." (Miller may not have posed for "filthy pictures" sold to tourists along boulevard Rochechouart, but he very likely wrote the English-language brochures for the Sphinx, a notorious brothel on boulevard Edgar Quinet, where, for his literary contributions, he was awarded an occasional *coupe de champagne* or a *passe* with one of the girls.)

Miller's vivid impressions of these "centers of pleasure and vice" were being distilled into the heady mix of *Tropic of Cancer* while Brassaï, exploiting the same sources, was assembling his first collection of photographs, *Le Paris secret des années 30*. The two nocturnal voyeurs of the Paris scene might prowl until dawn, "the day sneaking in like a leper," and Miller often making the steep climb to the Sacre Coeur to witness

Inside the Sphinx, among the *filles de joie*.

the city coming awake in the first light. He learned to get to sleep before the birds began to screech; otherwise it was hopeless.

Later, Miller was eager to see the harvest from the night before, Brassaï's developed prints spread across the bed at the Hôtel des Terrasses on the rue de la Glacière. Brassaï could not read Miller's work at that time, or he would have discovered his images confirmed Miller's own predilections: bare-breasted backstage nymphs at the Folies-Bergère, Kiki of Montparnasse lifting her skirts on the bandstand of the Cabaret des Fleurs, the reclining clients at an opium den gazing in stunned indifference at the photographer, a transvestite prostitute soliciting the butchers at La Villette abbatoir. Both Brassaï and Miller were willing to explore the Parisian netherworld and study those nocturnal tribes no anthropologist had as yet discovered.

One series of photographs illustrated Miller's own unceasing obsession with the cloacal waste of Paris, the city's picturesque systems of accommodation to bowel and bladder. "To relieve a full bladder is one of the great human joys," Miller declared in *Black Spring*. "There are certain urinals I go out of my way to make—such as the battered rattletrap outside the deaf and dumb asylum, corner of the Rue St. Jacques and the Rue de l'Abbé-de-l'Epée." As if in response to Miller's fetish-object, Brassaï included in his collection one such curbside *vespasienne* like some Art Déco monument illuminated from within, a solitary men's lighthouse of the night. With its multiple advertisements for Byrrh, a tonic-apéritif *"Recommandé aux Familles,"* it served as a double attraction to Miller who delighted in the trickling waterflow down the mossy zinc partitions of the circular enclosure. Miller also favored the seatless Turkish-style toilets, two raised footprints on either side of an open sewer-hole in the cement where "one is alone with oneself" squatting in glorious solitude. He often lingered in a Paris privy as a reading nook. Among the list of his essay topics appear two significant titles: "The Legend of the Pissoirs" and "Toilets on the Right Bank and Toilets on the Left." He noted that Proust frequented a certain lattice-enclosed *pissotière* on the Champs-Elysées undaunted by the odor within, a known rendezvous station for homosexual encounters.

For Brassaï's part, the interest in excrement extended to a quaint interview with close-up photographs of a team of *vidangeurs,* the cesspool cleaners. Brassaï met with this unusual crew at midnight in the rue Rambuteau, the all-night les Halles market district, and from there accompanied them in their horse-drawn rig through the ancient quarter of le Marais. Over the racket of a steam-driven Richer pump, the crew boss explained how dangerous the work was for the man who handled the hose down inside the tank: he could be asphyxiated by hydrogen sulfate, and because of the risk the inside man drew double pay. Later, at a café that catered (because of their smell) only to those of the métier, Brassaï learned that the quality of *merde* varied from tank to tank: the waste from an office building, for example, was harder to extract, almost rock solid, compared to an apartment building where the constant household waterflow served to liquefy the *merde* in advance.

Regrettably, Miller did not accompany the photographer on this particular Rabelaisian adventure, for he would have found his kind of poetry in the pungent exercise.

THE BRITISH WRITER Lawrence Durrell was an early fan and literary protégé of Henry Miller (his *The Black Book* was inspired by Miller's *Tropic of Cancer*) and came to know Brassaï in Paris. Durrell recounts Brassaï's confession that he came late to photography, and "indeed I rather despised it." Originally Brassaï was part of the diaspora of painters and sculptors like Pascin, Zadkine, Kremegne, Chagall, Lipchitz, Soutine, and Brancusi who were drawn from their desolate shtetls and villages in the east to the exciting capital city of Art, lending their particular Slavic flavor to the School of Paris. Brassaï lived at night. His preference for Paris after dark led him to question by what medium he could convert into an artistic vision the inventory of images that haunted him from his nocturnal excursions. He had never held a camera in his hand, "until my friend André Kertesz broke the spell by lending me a camera; I followed his advice and his example."

The friendship with Miller had been equally fortuitous. Like Durrell's discovery of a literary soul mate in Miller, Brassaï had found an affinity with a fellow "noctambulist." There was something calming and reassuring in Miller's company. Miller, in his serenity, "reminded me of an ascetic, a mandarin, a Tibetan holy man."

But Brassaï did not know the Brooklyn boy, the American Miller confronting the one great passion of his life, June. For all the pleasure Paris offered, and the many small wonders of the city asleep, Miller yearned for a reunion with his wife. June constantly promised (or threatened) to join her husband in Paris, but like her cables "Money follows," and nothing followed, June languished—in whose arms? Henry wondered—in Manhattan.

BY STAGES MILLER had actually penetrated that bourgeois world he had been so curious about, from his narrow cranny in the lower depths, observing the other France denied foreigners like himself by the formal, off-putting social manner of the French that stood in the way of intimacy with the middle class. Café acquaintance prevented casual friendships from maturing too swiftly, if ever. (Social custom allowed for a drinking acquaintanceship on a café terrace; an invitation to a Parisian home was slow to come, or came not at all.)

Miller's most recent benefactor maintained a studio in the chic district around place Dupleix, an adjacent quarter to Montparnasse and, like most of fringe Montparnasse, "strangely charmless and unpicturesque corner of Paris," as Brassaï described the quarter, "surrounded by wealthy apartment buildings altogether lacking in character."

The new friend and patron was Richard Osborn (Fillmore in Miller's *Tropic of Cancer*), a young lawyer in the legal department at the Paris branch of National City Bank. A bohemian at heart, Osborn relished Miller's unorthodox company, and Miller was happy to share Osborn's bourgeois comfort—albeit American-style—for a change. Each morning before his thoughtful host left for the bank, Osborn left ten francs beside the typewriter where his guest would be sure to find it. Miller would awaken to the sound of bugles, aware of the morning's stiff erection (a matinal hard-on he compared to the sight of the Eiffel Tower). From the window where he typed (after pocketing Osborn's ten francs) Miller looked down on the barracks of l'École Militaire, observing the lunatic morning maneuvers of cavalry recruits, "floundering around in the mud, the bugles blowing, the horses charging—all within four walls . . . A madhouse, it seemed to me. Even the horses looked silly."

Osborn's superior at National City Bank was another American, Hugo Guiler, whose wife had written "an unprofessional study" of D. H. Lawrence that Osborn was certain Miller would want to read, and would, all the more, want to meet the extraordinary woman herself—a type Miller was unlikely to encounter cruising the meaner streets of Paris.

The "extraordinary woman" was Juana Edelmira Antolina Nin y Castellano, called Anaïs, born in France of a Danish singer, Rosa

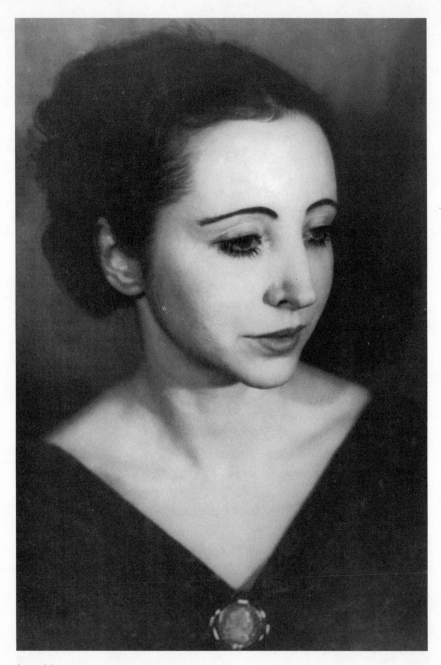

Anaïs Nin.

Culmet, and Spanish father, Joachin Nin. Her father was a pianist and composer of middling success and fluctuating fortune; more successful as an inveterate Don Juan, Nin abandoned his family when Anaïs was eleven, a trauma she attempted to assuage by keeping a diary in English, one of her several languages. The diary was psychologically or symbolically meant as an extensive "letter" to her errant father, a scrupulous and poetically expressed record of mood and minutiae that had reached forty-two fulsome volumes by the time she met Miller—and would not stop there; in fact, it blossomed with this new experience.

47

The meeting was arranged by Osborn. The enthusiastic go-between regaled Anaïs with tales of the free-spirited American writer with whom he shared his studio, and to Henry he described the exquisite Anaïs, a "Madame Bovary" (as she described herself in the current volume of her diary) cloistered in loveless limbo in medieval Louveciennes, a suburban village forty minutes by train from the gare Saint-Lazare.

It was the gray-misted raw autumn of 1931 when Anaïs expressed her household frustration and anguish: "I have days of illuminations and fevers. I have days when the music in my head stops. Then I mend socks, can fruits, polish furniture. But while I am doing this I feel I am not living."

Not one to pass up the promise of an excellent meal in the confines of the bourgeois citadel (at last!), Miller took the train to Louveciennes where he was charmed by the formal elegance of the ancient house enshrouded in ivy—once part of the estate of the comtesse du Barry—and intrigued by the exotic apparition at the open door. She resembled June! Osborn did not exaggerate.

As for Anaïs, she was suddenly restored to "illuminations and fevers" by the arrival of this unusual dinner guest: "When I saw Henry Miller walking toward the door where I stood waiting, I closed my eyes for an instant to see him by some inner eye. He was warm, joyous, relaxed, natural." Like Brassaï, Anaïs Nin saw in Miller the image and essence of an Eastern sage: "He looked like a Buddhist monk, a rosy-skinned monk, with his partly bald head aureoled by lively silver hair, his full sensuous mouth."

The meeting was an accomplished success. The two sensed, even at that first dinner, that they were destined partners, in literature and in love.

By some perverted fate—a horoscope Miller had never known or entertained—his wife June now decided to make the long-promised voyage to Paris, and was determined to rejoin her missing husband as soon as she could inveigle ship's passage money from some likely source, preferably male.

Henry Miller at Louveciennes, 1932.

4

PARIS BY NIGHT—II

*B*LACK REMAINED BEAUTIFUL on the nightclub circuit of Paris: Josephine Baker throughout the thirties was black queen of the night. A brief vogue for *peau rouge* came into favor in 1931, but lasted not long, nor was the fad sensational enough to replace the Queen by an Indian Princess.

A troupe of American nightclub chorines appeared in Montmartre led by Texas Guinan, the New York club owner whose "Hello Sucker!" greeting defined her attitude toward her free-spending clientele (and whose equivalent in Paris was Bricktop, the orange-haired mulatto hostess of Bricktop's in Montmartre). Guinan had brought her chorus line from New York, all white except for one dark exotic in the center of the line, a Penobscot Indian. Texas Guinan was to discover she was the sucker herself for a change: she failed to anticipate the new French work permits required for entertainers from abroad.

Black jazz musicians had dominated the nightclub scene throughout the 1920s, but now, as the Depression approached, French musicians wanted a fair share of performance time, and pay. The entire Texas Guinan team was rounded up and installed in a third-class hotel the dancers called the Hoosegow Hotel, where they awaited deportation.

As an authentic "redskin," Molly Spotted Elk could defect from the white dancers at the Hoosegow and find a dancing gig at the International Colonial Exposition in the bois de Vincennes dancing a tribal solo at the fairgrounds. She was discovered by *Le Petit Journal* and her photograph in feathered regalia appeared on its front page. Molly was part of the "social Darwinism" the Exposition purported to represent, though considered by some as more of a demeaning and exploitative spectacle despite its billing as a human showcase of an enlightened colonial rule.

France is said to be color-blind, but could more accurately be termed color-conscious. It is true that the French find their dark-skinned *indigènes* of Caribbean, Polynesian, and African origin as exotic fruit of empire. They are in essence the mysteriously attractive primitives, the "noble savage," celebrated by Rousseau. In the 1920s a wave of black jazz washed over Paris as the *dernier cri* of sophisticated entertainment; the black musicians were part of the mystique of the exotic Other, and as *entertainers* were welcomed as no other Americans were ever to be. When not in performance they were mostly confined to cheap-hotel ghettos bounded on the north by the porte de Clignancourt and on the south by the boulevards Clichy and Rochechouart—as removed from Paris's common cityscape as were the grass and mud huts of the fairgrounds in the bois de Vincennes.

MOLLY SPOTTED ELK may have felt shamed and exploited by her show-biz stunt at the International Colonial Exposition, but the instant public success allowed for a sojourn in France while the others of Texas Guinan's troupe were deported in a bureaucratic decision of racial prejudice in reverse.

Actually Molly had other and higher aspirations than to perform a choreographed rain dance in redskin costume, or to display her brown legs on the music-hall or nightclub stage. She was a protégée of Ruth St. Denis, and if dance she must, she chose to be a modern dancer in the style of Isadora Duncan (who had died in France four years before, strangled to death by her long trailing scarf, which caught in the wheel of a speeding motorcar). Her other ambition was to join the literary community of Paris as a novelist—she had already made a serious beginning on a novel that drew from her Native American background.

What Paris wanted of Molly was an uninhibited "squaw dancer" of Josephine Baker's sensual suggestiveness. In appearance the Penobscot appealed to the French fantasy of the primitive exotic; in substance her agenda was as civilized as their own.

Her future was decided at an interview by a French journalist from *Paris Soir* at the Café Rotonde. Their dialogue amounted to no more than casual newspaper chat—"How do you find Paris?" "Too noisy, I

The Moulin Rouge at night, 1935.

prefer the woods"—but the banal encounter established an instant rapport between the unlikely couple. The seductive Frenchman, Jean Archambaud, fell in love with the visiting Penobscot, and immediately after their first Left Bank meeting Molly moved in with Jean. Archambaud eventually proposed, but Molly would not marry him, even when she became pregnant; marriage would make her a Frenchwoman. "Our people," she replied to Jean's proposal, "never needed a ring, or paper, to be united."

The novelty of a Penobscot Indian dancer was but the sensation of a season, though Molly would find occasional work in the French cinema; an inauthentic tribal dance was no rival to the natural (but shrewdly calculated) pagan gyrations of a Josephine Baker at the Casino de Paris. It was the sight of black flesh in motion that so enthralled the sophisticates of Paris: Josephine stripped down "au poil" to a garterbelt of bananas, or the lesser spectacle of Panama Al Brown, retired world champion bantamweight, a success not so much for his *claquettes* (tap-dance) routine at the Cirque Médrano but for skipping rope to a jazz combo in his boxing shorts.

(Aware of the *dernier cri* for colored entertainers, the transvestite Barbette—originally a white cowboy from Round Rock, Texas—tanned himself in the bois de Boulogne as body makeup to enhance the concluding *frisson* to his tightrope-walking act when all was revealed.)

Josephine Baker's first interview was an uninhibited contrast to Molly Spotted Elk's response to Jean Archambaud: "*Très* sweet *le public*, and it's *grâce à les journalistes* that I have a life *aussi agréable*, understand?" Along with learning French, Josephine was learning the art of personal publicity that the Penobscot failed to profit from. Both dancers entered long-term relationships with men and both dodged the prospect of a marriage contract, Molly with Jean and Josephine with "Pepito."

THE BLACK AMERICAN colony in Montmartre remained a compact community that Sidney Bechet remarked upon: "You couldn't walk down rue Fontaine without seeing five more colored, and you knew them all."

"It took only two nights to see just about every Negro American in Paris," said Bricktop, so it was inevitable that Josephine and Bricktop would meet in the lively night world of black Paris.

"She was just a kid [of seventeen, when first in Paris] and one of the

A poster by Pico for a revue at Folies Bergère.

most vulnerable stars I've ever met." (Josephine was more calculating than Bricktop realized, and capable of turning the odds—illegitimacy and racial prejudice—in her favor.) "She could hardly write her name and, suddenly, everybody wanted her autograph."

Bricktop "adopted" the waif from St. Louis who sought advice on everything from stage presence to personal comportment. Josephine was known to eat spaghetti with her fingers, and crunch into a *salade de crevettes* unpeeled shrimp and all. Bricktop was her guide and mentor in every problematic challenge except for men.

There was a string of unsatisfactory affairs that older and wiser show-business queen Bricktop might have spared her protégée. An early love was Georges Simenon, the Belgian author of the Maigret detective novels, and Josephine subjugated Simenon to the extent of making him into her private secretary and general factotum. Simenon confessed to having been so smitten by the black dancer that he was on the verge of proposing marriage—except that he was already married.

The most unsatisfactory alliance, in Bricktop's judgment, was with a gigolo who frequented Bricktop's known as "Pepito": Giuseppe Abatino, who called himself the Count di Albertini, an assumed title that Bricktop translated into "the no-account count." When Bricktop's disparaging remarks got back to Pepito, he contrived to steer Josephine away from the "deadbeats" (as he characterized the rue Fontaine crowd) and into the company of the "right people" like himself and the Montmartre gigolos.

Pepito became Josephine Baker's manager as well as lover, though Bricktop would have substituted the term *"maquereau"* for Pepito's role in Josephine's life, her pimp. This was unfair to the no-account count, for Pepito, while taking predatory interest in the outcome, truly sought to enhance and advance Josephine's career. Like Bricktop, he advised her about how to carry herself onstage and off (his experience with women made him an expert tutor to the St. Louis love child) and what occasions to take advantage of, when to withdraw—professionally and socially. Pepito was the one to advise constant change, and to add singing to her repertoire, thus responsible for her trademark success, the song *"J'ai Deux Amours."*

As manager and agent, Pepito accomplished several lucrative bookings for the "Ebony Venus," which included—though the bankroll was suspect—the successful investment in a nightclub of her own, Chez Josephine, an establishment on rue Fontaine in competition with Bricktop's cabaret. (The origins of this *placement* could be traced back to funds allegedly drained off from French insurance companies, possibly part of the wider corruption scandal that would rock the state in

On stage at Folies Bergère, ca. 1937.

1934, involving the notorious swindler Serge Stavisky, a show-business czar among his other illicit schemes.)

CHEZ JOSEPHINE DID not displace the venerable Bricktop's, and Josephine, who appeared to dominate the French public, had no chance of winning over Bricktop's devoted following, the American colony of expatriate renown. The author Anita Loos, who wrote *Gentlemen Prefer Blondes* (though caramel-colored Josephine did not prefer gentlemen), spread the unkind word that Josephine Baker's prime endowment was her "witty rear end," a backside paddling meant to sting, but such observations, especially whitebread comments, rolled off that same celebrated derrière. Maria Jolas—"who's she?" would be Josephine's response (Jolas with her husband edited the expatriate journal *transition* and were close friends to James Joyce)—added to Loos's spiteful mot: "She just wiggled her fanny and all the French fell in love with her."

In his short story "Babylon Revisited," Fitzgerald's disillusioned protagonist wanders into Chez Josephine on a nostalgia trip for the twenties, but fails to find the dancer's "chocolate arabesques" an enchantment in the thirties—but then, F. Scott Fitzgerald was at heart a devoted Bricktop's fan, more drunkenly at home in her Montmartre cabaret, a preferential client whose wallet Bricktop expropriated for safekeeping when the inebriated Scott began scattering franc notes to the musicians, and to the wind.

(One memorable night at Bricktop's a wealthy American woman tipped the members of the band ten dollars each to play jazz in the nude: nighttime Paris allowed for equal time to women imitating the privilege of a male audience paying to see Josephine Baker naked at the Folies Bergère.)

Bricktop's was the celebrity rendezvous catering to a range of "dukes" (from Ellington, who sat in with Bricktop's band when he passed through Paris on tour, to the Duke of Windsor when he was still Prince of Wales and introduced his mistress Wallis Simpson to Bricktop), a ragout of aristocrats, the well-heeled, and several bogus titles and deposed royalty, along with such legitimate celebrities as F. Scott Fitzgerald and Cole Porter, the *gratin* of the expatriate Smart Set.

A passing challenge to Bricktop's lasting popularity was Frisco's on the rue Florentin (no one ever called Jocelyn Bingham anything but

Josephine Baker in 1939.

attract such a celebrity collection as Bricktop's steady clientele: the comte de la Rochefoucauld, the marquise de Polignac, and Bricktop's favorite crowned head (but to lose his crown for love of Mrs. Simpson), the Prince of Wales, clinging desperately to his mistress on the crowded dance floor.

LOUIS ARMSTRONG, ACCEPTING a celebrity engagement at Bricktop's, was the idol of French jazz guitarist Django Reinhardt who performed regularly there, but the visiting Satchmo failed to acknowledge the presence of the French guitarist, to the dismay of Django, perhaps because of the white-black ratio imposed by the French quota system (Django was white: five French musicians must be employed for every "foreign" jazz player) . . . but French jazz was an oxymoron to African-American musicians: Louis Armstrong had probably never heard of Django Reinhardt.)

COLE PORTER HAD written a song for Bricktop, "Miss Otis Regrets," which became her theme song in the way that *"J'ai Deux Amours"* was a song belonging to Josephine Baker, associated with her only. Bricktop hobnobbed with the Smart Set elite at her club, but she was well aware of the social boundaries between black and white, even in "color-blind" Paris. She was invited to the Colporteurs (as the French called Monsieur and Madame Porter, but which means street vendor) at their *maison de ville* at 13 rue Monsieur, a tiny street tucked behind the imposing Invalides: "It didn't look like much on the outside," was Bricktop's impression of the ancient edifice. "In fact it looked like it might come tumbling down any minute—but inside it was spectacular." "Spectacular" to Bricktop meant the zebra-skin rugs, chairs painted mandarin red, and a room "wallpapered" in platinum. (One austere monk's cell was Cole Porter's composing room.) Bricktop was under no illusion that she was a guest among guests in that set, but was invited as an entertainer. Whether she sang "Miss Otis Regrets" or not, she would still be expected to sing for her supper.

The story went around Paris—probably originating with Cole—that he had escorted Bricktop to the Paris Opéra Ball dressed in the same Molyneux gown as worn by Princess Marina of Greece. It was a stunt Porter was capable of, but Bricktop denied the event had ever taken place: "I knew my crowd and it wasn't at the Opéra."

AN AFTER-HOURS rendezvous for expatriate blacks was known as The Flea Pit, and was the particular haunt of a black journalist who collected enough gossip there to fill columns of newsprint for African-American newspapers back home. He called himself the Street Wolf of Paris and one story he could not have missed, for it originated in the jazz-club territory, he considered his bailiwick.

Violette Nozière defied the authority her middle-class parents exerted, by tradition, over their adolescent daughter who took stray sequential lovers and financed her jazz-club night life by stealing money from her mother's corset drawer. Despite a strict bourgeois upbringing, Violette was dominated by desires her parents knew nothing of nor were responsible for. If they had known they would no doubt have heeded the Bishop of Paris's injunction against jazz—following an earlier ban on the tango as an immoral dance. Not that their daughter would have submitted to restrictions concerning jazz and sex (in her mind the two were concomitant), for Violette led a most secret life at night.

Apparently she was a caring daughter to Papa and Maman Nozière. Knowing how addicted her parents were to patent medicines, Violette introduced them to a tonic to imbibe with their evening coffee, her father the stronger dose, but an increasing prescription for her mother. The "tonic" was meant perhaps at first to lull both parents to an earlier than usual bedtime, but as the evenings passed (Violette passed hers in the jazz clubs of Montmartre and Montparnasse) expenses mounted for the delinquent *gamine* beyond the slim pickings from the corset drawer. As her monetary needs increased, so did the powders of the tonic . . . known as barbital, containing a powerful and dangerous hypnotic, veronal.

When the daughter's dosage reached the number of twenty powders for Papa, and almost as many for her mother, her parents fell into a coma manifesting all the symptoms of death. Calmly Violette set fire to the curtains, expecting to burn all traces of her crime and its victims, then called *"Au secours!"* to fabricate a scenario of panic and attempt to seek aid. Her cry was answered by a neighbor who called the fire brigade, the conflagration was suppressed in time, and, moreover, both mother and father recovered from the tonic meant to kill.

Violette had fallen in love with a fellow jazz enthusiast; a member of the Camelots du Roi, the radical Rightist militants whose expressed goal was to restore the monarchy to France and whose unexpressed strategy was to riot often enough to disgrace and undermine the Third Republic then in power. In his spare time Jean was a respectable law student at the Sorbonne, but at night he entered an apprenticeship as pimp, with Violette as his sole *fille de joie* so far. He sent his loving *petite amie* in search of clientele at her jazz-club rendezvous and along the dark streets familiar to her, for she had prostituted herself since age thirteen. As her lover and *maquereau,* Jean was the recipient of expensive gifts, and he had grown fond of the English leather goods from the place de la Madeleine and silk neckties from Charvet—though he offered Violette nothing in return but the pleasures of his bed. If Violette could not afford to keep him in style, Jean intimated that their affair was at an end.

Violette grew desperate. She was not pretty enough to attract a well-paying clientele, and many nights scored not at all. And the competition at the jazz clubs was ferocious.

Father Nozière had by dint of French thrift accumulated a nest egg from his salary as locomotive engineer on the Paris-Vichy line of the *chemin de fer,* savings meant to augment his pension at retirement time, not far off. But his errant daughter needed that money—if she was to hold on to Jean—and right now.

The second attempt to do away with her parents was a replay of the first, except that this time Violette served up a surely lethal dose of tonic, beyond measure; and when mother and father apparently succumbed, Violette cried *"Au secours!"* again. In mock distress, she had opened the gas burner, filling the house with gas.

The same neighbor who had summoned the *pompiers* the time before responded again, but this time smelled more than gas in the Nozière ménage and reported his suspicions to the commissariat of the 15th arrondissement. The father had indeed expired, yet Violette's mother still lingered in critical condition at the Hôpital Saint-Jacques. By the time Madame Nozière recovered, and a criminal investigation was under way, the suspect parricide had disappeared.

Posted on kiosks across Paris, the photo of Violette Nozière, Wanted, appeared alongside the advertisements for music-hall concerts and the schedule of performances at the Comédie Française. Violette brazenly continued her rounds of the nightclubs and embarked on a new course of serial lovers. One such, recognizing Violette's photo in *Paris Soir,* ungallantly went to the police. The latest lover agreed to an entrapment rendezvous, and before Violette could enjoy the pleasure of a second tryst, an *agent de police* came from behind the drapes and another, with a pair of handcuffs, entered from the hallway.

THE SENSATIONAL NOZIÈRE trial began sedately enough, with call by the *hussier* for five minutes of silence to honor King Alexander of Yugoslavia who had been assassinated the day before in Marseilles. Before the last minute passed, Violette's outraged mother began to hurl imprecations at her murderous daughter and had to be silenced. (An anomaly of French law allowed for the mother to instigate a parallel lawsuit to the state's original indictment, charging her daughter to submit to *"dommages et interests,"* payment of damages and interest, for having deprived Madame of a beloved spouse.)

The wayward daughter was found guilty—she had in fact confessed, with some arrogance, to the crime—and the judge intoned the ancient liturgy relating to the verdict: "that Violette Nozière is to have her head severed from her body by guillotine, in a public place in the city of Paris, being led there barefoot, clad only in her chemise, a black veil covering her head."

By 1930 the sentence of death was not applicable to women, and was automatically reduced to life imprisonment. Violette responded to the sentence by screaming the vilest curses, picked up in her errant street life, at her mother and at her dead father.

Before being led away to La Santé prison, Violette instructed the bailiff to look for her handbag, which she seemed to have misplaced in the prisoner's box during the trial, for it contained her lip rouge and compact.

THE CULTURAL INFLUENCE of jazz was not altogether corrupting in the way the Bishop of Paris feared, though the laissez-faire moral ambience of the nightclub circuit might contribute to the delinquency of an adolescent Violette Nozière (and the establishments themselves attracted investment by a criminal element), for the new rhythms emanating from the black jazz scene inspired Django Reinhardt to create influential music for the guitar . . . and jazz found its way into the modern compositions of musicians known as Les Six, who frequented their own club, Le Boeuf sur le Toit, a coterie that included Darius Milhaud. Milhaud (with Jean Cocteau) composed an opéra bouffe and circus-ballet celebrating both jazz and surrealism at the same time, and called it *Le Boeuf sur le Toit*, a title that suggested the paintings of Marc Chagall (*The Cow on the Roof*).

As for the sprawling fairgrounds in the bois de Vincennes, its influence was notable for the effect the Colonial Exposition had on Pablo Picasso. So impressed was he by the primitive art he found in the African exhibits, he adapted the motifs and style in his seminal canvas, *Les Demoiselles d'Avignon*.

5

THE SIBYL OF MONTPARNASSE AND
THE BOOTBLACK OF MONTMARTRE

Picasso only sees something else, another reality.
Complications are always easy but another vision than
that of all the world is very rare. That is why geniuses are
very rare.

—GERTRUDE STEIN, *PICASSO*

*I*N THAT RARE species of genius Gertrude Stein naturally
included herself, as well as the Spanish painter who first
appeared to her as a "good-looking bootblack," Pablo Diego
José de Paolo Juan Nepomuceno Maria de los Remedios Crispin
Crispiano Santisima Trinidad Ruiz y Picasso. She had "discovered"
Picasso—or her brother had, accord to Leo Stein's report—at the top of
the steep climb along rue Ravignan, living and working in that bohemian hive of artists known as the Bateau Lavoir in the heart of
Montmartre. In partnership with her brother Gertrude made a first purchase of *Jeune Fille aux Fleurs* despite the "rather appalling" drawing of
the legs and feet when eventually Leo's insistence won out—though she
herself "did not want it in the house" they shared.

In time Gertrude grew accustomed to Picasso's other reality and
came to share his other vision. From 1906 through the 1920s she
bought more of his work while at the same time publicizing the "bootblack" with wit and extravagance (to her own advantage as well, for this

confirmed her discernment and increased the value of her growing collection of Picassos). Eventually she sat for him, resulting in the famous portrait that viewers complained Gertrude resembled not at all.

"She will," replied Picasso, and she did.

Earlier Gertrude and Leo had taken up another genius, the painter Henri Matisse, under altogether different circumstances and in stark contrast to the background and appearance cultivated by the bootblack of Montmartre. At his easel Matisse wore a spotless smock over his sober business suit; only his knotted necktie risked paint stains, while Picasso animated and vociferous, cavorted about the Bateau Lavoir in his "monkey suit," a garage mechanic's one-piece overalls.

Matisse in his well-ordered atelier led a bourgeois life of *mesure* with a sensible wife who worked at millinery to support her artist husband. Never would Matisse have indulged in such vulgar hijinks as Picasso pinning an explicit cartoon to his atelier door so as not to be disturbed, a caricature of himself seated on the toilet.

At Picasso's studio his mistress of the moment, Fernande Olivier, was very much in evidence, even part of the décor. She would read aloud the fables of la Fontaine to amuse Gertrude during the tedious sittings for the portrait. Whether at the Bateau Lavoir or chez Matisse, Gertrude delighted in the company of the two very different painters. Picasso and Matisse were alike in one respect, that of being undiscovered until Gertrude Stein discovered them.

The first Matisse the Steins purchased was in 1905, *La Femme au Chapeau*, being ridiculed at the current Salon d'Automne. Matisse and his wife agonized over the question of accepting less than the asking price of five hundred francs (one hundred dollars), but the Steins paid the full price without a murmur, which made the difference of a winter coat for their daughter Margot. At any price the purchase was considered a major folly, but not by Gertrude and Leo.

By the 1930s Matisse could remark: "One likes one's paintings less when they are worth money than when they are worth none—when they are poor children." Like Picasso, Matisse had become successful, and the time when he had painted with gloves on in the unheated studio was no more than a bittersweet memory. In their early poverty Madame Matisse had sold her only piece of jewelry so that her husband could purchase a small Cézanne "he needed." At such a time a rare indulgence was an aesthetic necessity. Now the State was offering the equivalent of fifteen thousand dollars for the Cézanne, and Matisse could afford to donate the painting to the City of Paris without charge. "This work of Cézanne has upheld me morally in critical moments as an artist. From it I have drawn my faith and perseverance."

Picasso and Matisse first met warily in 1906 at the Stein salon on rue de Fleurus. The two painters, as Gertrude expressed it, "became friends but they were enemies. Now they are neither friends nor enemies. At that time they were both."

In the autumn of 1932, during an unusually dry and beautiful October, Gertrude was writing *The Autobiography of Alice B. Toklas,* a testament of personal and artistic nostalgia that settled not a few scores with her own friends and enemies. She and Leo had long parted company and divided the celebrated collection of modern art between them. They also in a sense divided painter friends between them, Picasso ever loyal to Gertrude. The formerly inseparable brother and sister were no longer speaking, and Gertrude had settled into a lifetime relationship with her companion, Alice Toklas.

Gertrude had also broken with her close friend Ernest Hemingway, and was thoroughly villifying him in *The Autobiography* as "fragile" and "yellow" and "ninety percent Rotarian." (Hemingway would brood on this for twenty years before taking his revenge on Gertrude in *A Moveable Feast.*) It was a time, at least Gertrude's time, of severing friendships. Her latest entourage of painters and writers, "the Young Men of 26" as she called them, were being blotted from her guest list and banned from her salon one by one. The flowers of friendship not only faded but were abruptly uprooted. Instead of a postcard stating that Gertrude Stein declined further acquaintance, the coup de grâce was now delivered by telephone.

Like Picasso and Matisse, success had caught up with their discoverer and patron as well. In 1933, following publication of *The Autobiography of Alice B. Toklas,* Gertrude Stein's enormous self-assurance was rewarded at last. With success she had become testy and unpredictable. She need no longer affirm, "I am I because my little dog knows me," for she was now known to *tout le monde.* After the long years of public neglect—the Stein persona and conversation were famous, but her book-length work went unpublished—the triumph of being a best-seller was a completely new distraction.

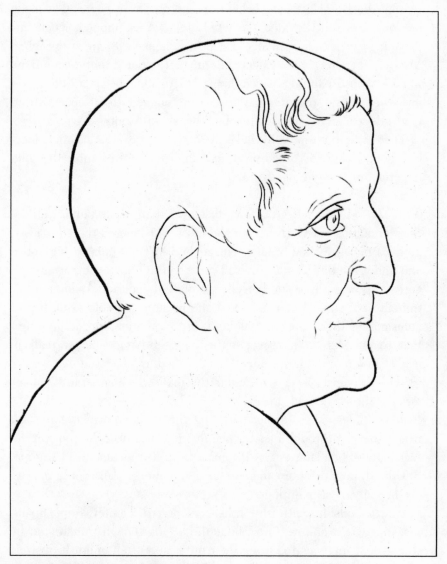

Portrait of Gertrude Stein by Louis Marcoussis.

Gertrude was finding less and less time for painters and painting. She did briefly take up the dadaist Francis Picabia, then Balthus for a season; the Russian Pavlik Tchelichev did a portrait of her that made her look, Gertrude decided, like a vulture, so Alice phoned Tchelichev declining further acquaintance. Pavlik Tchelichev was one of the Young Men of 26, along with Eugene Berman, Kristians Tonny, and Bébé Bérard, whose paintings, according to Gertrude, "began to disappear into the walls," and the painters were obliged to disappear from Gertrude's salon before they reached the age of twenty-seven.

There was nothing vulturelike about Gertrude Stein's appearance, but by now as Picasso had promised, she began to resemble the solid imperial presence he had painted.

SURREALISM HAD LASTED long, or longer than most such art affiliations endured, but Gertrude for the most part ignored the surrealists, perhaps because they became entrenched in Paris outside her scope and under the direction of André Breton in the role of the movement's guru. This was a role she herself had played alongside Apollinaire for the cubists; when Apollinaire died she became the sole explicator of cubism, and then altogether alone in the promotion and definition of Picasso and Matisse. However, in the theory and practice of surrealism, it was Breton's pronouncements that counted, not Gertrude's.

"The surrealists," she remarked tartly, "tak[e] the manner for the matter as is the way of vulgarizers."

Nevertheless she was intrigued by the manner of Salvador Dalí whom she met through Picasso: she thought his mustache (not yet the twin uptwists of later years) the most beautiful mustache in Europe. But she did not offer any memorable comment on Dalí's work, nor did she buy any of his paintings.

Her friendship with the other celebrated painter from Spain, Picasso, would endure throughout the 1930s though punctuated by stone-silent intervals following their bitter and often childish quarrels and impolitic behavior due to the volatile temperaments of each. One such diplomatic but perhaps mischievously deliberate blunder was Gertrude's reading aloud from *The Autobiography of Alice B. Toklas* with both Picasso and his wife, Olga, as audience. Rashly Gertrude read from the section dealing with Picasso's former mistress Fernande

Olivier: "Olga Picasso got up and said she would not listen she would go away she said. What's the matter, we said, I do not know that woman she said and left." Two years would pass before Picasso and Gertrude saw each other again, "but now he has left his wife and we have seen each other again."

Another Francis after Francis Picabia was the new young painter Francis Rose (anyone named Francis, Gertrude believed, was bound to be "elegant, unbalanced, and intelligent"), and perhaps in reaction against the surrealists, Gertrude purchased Rose's neo-Romantic canvas depicting a poet beside a waterfall. When Picasso asked her how much she paid for it, she told him three hundred francs, and Picasso said; "For that price you can get something quite good."

John Richardson wrote of Francis Rose (when Rose was a protégé of Jean Cocteau): "Nobody took his painting seriously then and no one takes it seriously now." The sponsorship of Francis Rose was symptomatic of Gertrude Stein's loss of judgment, lack of passion, and decline of influence in the world of pictorial arts.

When Gertrude learned that Picasso had stopped painting after the breakup with Olga and, according to the dealer Kahnweiler, was now writing poetry, it was her turn to exhibit disdain. To stop painting, especially in a season of domestic turmoil, was understandable—"Everybody is kind of stopping," said Gertrude, who was experiencing writer's block following the success of The Autobiography—but that painters should write poetry was foolish and unthinkable. Yes, Jean Cocteau did both, but neither Gertrude nor Picasso took Cocteau or his painting seriously.

Nevertheless Picasso was anxious to have Gertrude's opinion of his poems and soon subjected her, and novelist-playwright Thornton Wilder, to a reading of his recent verse. All Gertrude would say was, "It is interesting." This was not a comment Picasso could live with, having heard it expressed about his painting by those who knew nothing of art and had nothing else to say—so the banal invocation of "interesting" was a bitter frustration and provocation. He tried to get Thornton Wilder to tell him what Gertrude truly thought of his poetry but Wilder was too diplomatic to divulge Gertrude's forthright opinion.

Finally, in a confrontation at the Rosenberg gallery, where Braque was showing his paintings, Picasso brought up the subject of his poems once more, adding that André Breton thought his poems quite good.

The mention of Breton in conjunction with poetry only aroused Gertrude's further scorn, and when Braque joined in the discussion, pointing out that he too had written a poem (published in the magazine *transition*), Gertrude launched a tirade against both painters and their idea of poetry—including Salvador Dalí, who had also written a poem.

She shook Picasso by the lapels of his jacket and delivered a monologue that echoed the Molly Bloom soliloquy in James Joyce's (her detested rival in Paris) *Ulysses*: ". . . don't go on trying to make me tell you it is poetry and I shook him again, well he said supposing I do know it, what will I do, what will you do said I and kissed him, you will go on until you are more cheerful and less dismal and then you will, yes he said, and then you will paint a very beautiful picture and more of them, and I kissed him again, yes, said he."

IN SPITE OF Gertrude's assurances and without her knowledge of his unhappy circumstances, Picasso remained less cheerful and more dismal than at anytime of his life. The painter and his beautiful Russian wife, a former dancer with Diaghilev's *Ballet Russes,* had been living in the commercial center of the Right Bank at 23 rue La Boétie, a street of boutiques and art galleries, including Picasso's own gallery. The domestic arrangements of the mismatched couple had been fashioned to accommodate, in Brassaï's words, "[Olga's] desire for security, comfort and luxury." Picasso was indulging his wife's tastes, which inevitably became his own, until they were locked into this mode of bourgeois chic and pretense. Just as Pascin came to realize in 1930, and Gertrude Stein in 1933, success attained a worldly status of recognition and might also, in Picasso's case, attract upper-class patrons ready to bestow upon the artist their blessing, and a curse. It was Picasso's turn to enjoy superficially but secretly loathe the hollow pleasures of fame and fortune.

For two years Picasso virtually abandoned easel painting. This was the period when Gertrude Stein was withdrawing from the art scene; she considered painting a minor art, its excitement and importance passé. Independently, Picasso may have come to the same conclusion. Or simply that passion was lacking—or, if he did try to paint, he could inform his dealer Paul Rosenberg, when Rosenberg inquired about a canvas recently blotted out: "I am so rich that I just wiped out a hundred thousand francs."

As a place of escape from Parisian society—and from his wife, as their marriage deteriorated—Picasso purchased a château of the Louis XV period near Gisors, some seventy kilometers from Paris in the hamlet of Boisgeloup. He had converted the vast stables into a sculptor's studio, and by the time he met Brassaï he had completed over a hundred works of sculpture. Brassaï's collection of photographs, *Paris de Nuit*, had brought his work to the attention of the art world that same year, and Picasso was convinced this Hungarian nighthawk would be the ideal photographer to record on film the work accomplished at Boisgeloup.

"One winter morning in 1932," wrote Brassaï, "we climbed into a chauffeur-driven Hispano-Suiza with its mirrors, cut-glass bud vases and the uniformed chauffeur in his spotless white gloves shut the door behind us." Brassaï was more amused than impressed by the showy *mise-en-scène* so out of character, evidence in the self-conscious display that the monkey-suited "bootblack" had indeed come a long way from his humble beginnings on the rue Ravignan.

The stables at Boisgeloup contained the bulk of Picasso's recent work, and if his Hispano-Suiza failed to impress the photographer, the sculptures did. Brassaï attempted to photograph as many pieces—and one memorable portrait of the sculptor himself—before the light failed. There was a subtle mystery to the château Brassaï would unravel years later, but at the time he sensed, was almost aware of, a ghostly third presence at Boisgeloup. He had no more to go on than this vague impression, and the feminine curves to the stonework. This appeared to indicate the influence of a particular woman.

Brassaï took one more and final photograph by the flickering headlights of the Hispano-Suiza, that of the façade of the haunted château itself.

PICASSO WAS LOSING his affinity with friends and contact with cronies of his Bateau Lavoir days, for he had moved into what Max Jacob called his "duchess period." Braque merely shrugged off the distancing with the remark: "If we've grown apart, it's because we no longer need one another." The upward mobility into the ranks of high society had cost the painter a companionable relationship with his peers.

As Henry Miller had discovered, Brassaï was a congenial fellow artist with whom one shared a mutually rewarding sortie after dark. Picasso, not particularly rich in friends at that period, invited Brassaï to accompany him to the Cirque Médrano on boulevard Rochechouart. The Médrano and the Cirque d'Hiver, on place Pasdeloup, continued to inspire painters as it had since the time of Toulouse-Lautrec who had incorporated its performers in his canvasses. Newcomer to Paris, Alexander Calder, created an entire world of knockabout clowns, gymnasts, and trained dogs in an invented form called mobiles. (Even poets could find inspiration in the spectacle. Jean Cocteau rhapsodized over the beauty and grace of Barbette, prancing delicately across the high wire in pink tutu, and fell in love with the beautiful performer, never failing to respond with a delicious shiver at the startling finale when Barbette revealed her true gender as Vander Clyde, the cowboy from Round Rock, Texas.)

Texas cowboy Vander Clyde as himself and as Barbette.

Hercule pulling a car with his mouth in front of the Cirque Médrano, ca. 1930.

The panorama at the circus was a more natural element to Picasso than the fashionable salons of the Right Bank and nights beside Olga at the Opéra.

At the Médrano Brassaï photographed while Picasso made hasty preliminary sketches and studies for his series of lithographs, *Variations sur le cirque*. The Brassaï-Picasso partnership was much like the vagrant nightlife association Henry Miller enjoyed with Brassaï. While Picasso sketched, Brassaï noted the "fiery fixity of Picasso's gaze"—the same intensity that Leo Stein observed and remarked might burn the very words from a page Picasso read from.

(Just the other side of la Butte on the rue des Saules was another favorite attraction of the Montmartre district, a cabaret known as Le Lapin Agile—but of late Picasso would have avoided this *boîte de nuit* where Fernande Olivier, his former mistress whose very name so incensed Olga, recited poetry on the cabaret stage. After communal life at the Bateau Lavoir and the breakup with Picasso, Fernande had been reduced to a number of shifts to earn a living, fortune-telling among them, and was currently writing her memoirs, a book Picasso was desperate to suppress.)

Brassaï did recall one sour occasion when Olga joined her husband and the photographer at the Cirque Médrano, although this would not have been her choice for an evening's entertainment. Olga was ill-tempered throughout, and not at all drawn to the plebian spectacle, this sawdust ring instead of a ballet stage. Her contempt for Picasso was barely concealed, though Brassaï was unaware at the time of the state of the Picasso ménage—they were on the verge of separation.

Divorce was out of the question. Olga still clung to the privilege and prestige attached to her marriage with the artist-idol of *le tout Paris*. Picasso's name opened doors along the exclusive social circuit from salon to salon, from the literary company of Jean Cocteau to the world of chic created by Coco Chanel to gossipy exchange over luncheon with comte Etienne de Beaumont.

It may be said that Olga was not alone in her pursuit of the patrician class; Picasso himself was seeking society's limelight and delighted to receive its patronage and largesse. By cultivating the rich he had acquired an affluent clientele for his work. Olga was an advantage to all this; the graceful Russian dancer was an ornament he might display with the same pride of acquisition his château or the Hispano-Suiza represented. Olga had become another artifact of success and symbol of attainment by an artist having made his extraordinary way in the world.

BY 1932 THE domestic phase of Picasso's life had deteriorated from disappointment to bitterness, yet in the midst of that winter's discontent the painter produced two enigmatic oils of a model lying sensually asleep: *Le rêve* and *Nu endormi*. Who was she? Brassaï had sensed her effect and had drawn conclusions from the curving lines and gentle roundings of the sculptures at Boisgeloup—and Olga, beginning to be intrigued and surely troubled by the image of a sleeping beauty who had posed for these two quietly voluptuous works of art.

The model for the sleeping nude was a stranger to both Olga and Brassaï, unknown to anyone in Picasso's circle. Marie-Thérèse Walter was a charming, sweet-natured teenager Picasso had met while strolling past the Galeries Lafayette, a department store in his quarter. He had succeeded in engaging her interest with the incredibly transparent line: "Mademoiselle, I would like to paint your portrait." The young naif knew nothing of the name Picasso, yet she impulsively responded *"D'accord,"* to the crude approach of this importunate stranger.

Within hours of their meeting, Marie-Thérèse became Picasso's new model and latest conquest. For clandestine weekends she was transported to Boisgeloup in the Hispano-Suiza; and although she pretended to be living at home with her family, Picasso had installed his model-mistress in an apartment of her own at 44 rue La Boétie, across the street from where he lived with his wife, Olga.

Of all the women in Picasso's life, before and after, Marie-Thérèse was the most discreet, and exceedingly modest. From the beginning their affair remained an intimate and unbroken secret between the two lovers themselves, kept at silent remove from her family and his entourage. (The need for discretion was critical: the fifty-year-old painter was liable to prosecution for *détournement de mineur*: Marie-Thérèse was only seventeen at the time of their meeting.)

Picasso in his studio.

Picasso's model and mistress Marie-Thérèse Walter.

As Brassaï noted, Picasso's work had taken a new turn, inspired by his young lover-model, but public and critical response to the latest work was disappointing. A show at the Georges Petit gallery was badly received, and another show that same year in Zurich baffled or annoyed the Swiss. The psychoanalyst Carl Jung expressed the opinion that "Picasso's inspiration would appear to have been lifted from a classic case of schizophrenia."

Actually the inspiration was "lifted" from a pose by Marie-Thérèse standing before a mirror, for Jung no doubt referred to the convoluted design of *Jeune fille au miroir*, eventually considered a seminal work and important experimental breakthrough in the artist's middle career—if not the "very beautiful picture" Gertrude Stein predicted he would paint when he ceased being dismal and stopped writing poetry.

AS PART OF the divorce settlement Olga acquired the château de Boisgeloup. She had never visited the château and naturally loathed its associations, but she intended to deny possession of their love nest to her ex-husband and Marie-Thérèse, banishing the no-longer-secret lovers from their weekend Eden.

Picasso had by now disengaged from the bourgeois chic of rue La Boétie, as well as from his wife, and moved into the more aesthetically compatible dust and clutter of an ancient atelier on rue des Grands Augustins, a Left Bank street leading from St. André des Arts—the thoroughfare that "sang" to Henry Miller his first Sunday in Paris—to the quai on the banks of the Seine. Significantly he lived next door to the fictional setting of Balzac's *Chef-d'oeuvre inconnu*, *The Unknown Masterpiece*.

Before launching his own chef-d'oeuvre (far from *inconnu*) he pursued the theme of the mythological Minotaur in a series of engravings, the *Minotauromachie*, having derived that much inspiration for his contribution to Breton's journal *Minotaure*. He illustrated the journal's first cover, but except for a tentative friendship with André Breton and an even warmer relationship with Paul Eluard, Picasso's contact with the surrealists who hoped to enlist him into their ranks was marginal and wary.

Two works, again, were significant to a sea change in the painter, his latest persona in this new locale and altered circumstances: these were *Minotaure et femme* and *Faune dévoilant une femme*. The femme in these two paintings was not Marie-Thérèse Walter.

Picasso's mistress, the photographer Dora Maar.

The model for both works was photographer Dora Maar, a protégée of surrealist Man Ray. Dora was introduced to Picasso by Paul Eluard in a round-robin of changing partners: Eluard had lost his wife Gala to Salvador Dalí and was now with Nusch, who became the subject of a portrait by Picasso almost as a return favor for Eluard's having introduced Dora Maar to him. Dora was now sharing the atelier with Picasso and Marie-Thérèse in a seeming congenial ménage à trois. For longer than would appear possible, Picasso alternated models—and lovers—and sometimes painted the two women together until as far as could be discerned Dora Maar emerged at least in public the triumphant partner.

"It must be painful," Picasso remarked, "for a girl to see in a painting that she is on the way out."

The insensitive reference may not have applied particularly to Marie-Thérèse Walter, but certainly to the artist's distortion of Olga's visage as his marriage to her came apart. The disappearance of Marie-Thérèse from Picasso's life was actually a gradual process: the painter's great secret love of the 1930s lingered in the background until obscured by a procession of Picasso's not-so-secret loves.

During her tenure as Picasso's mistress Dora Maar conceived the theory that Picasso's changes of theme and style corresponded to shifting allegiances in his life: the model-lover of the moment, a poet (Apollinaire, Cocteau, Eluard), the location of his atelier, and finally the dog who was his devoted companion.

Picasso's dog at this time was an Afghan called Kazbec, and when he used Dora's face as a model he sometimes insinuated the long muzzle of Kazbec and his floppy ears onto the portrait, illustrating, as he declared, "the animal nature of women."

PICASSO'S ACQUAINTANCE WITH the Leftist band of surrealists was too superficial to arouse any revolutionary fervor in his essentially apolitical nature. In the precincts of art he was a revolutionist indeed, but only a civil war in his native Spain could arouse the political side to his volatile character. The Spanish Civil War also touched two other Spaniards in the Paris triumvirate of painters: Miró was obliged to return to Paris when hostilities erupted in Catalonia; and Dalí in his perverse way moved to the Right (in contrast to other surrealists) and embraced the fascism of General Franco.

Even Gertrude Stein, the least political of expatriates, was shaken by events in Spain: "All the time I am writing the Spanish revolution obtrudes itself. Not because it is a revolution, but because I know it all so well all the places they are mentioning and the things they are destroying."

Ernest Hemingway also "knew it all so well" (having been introduced to Spain by Gertrude Stein, background for his first novel *The Sun Also Rises*) and was drawn back to Europe because of the Spanish conflict. He used the Ritz Hotel in Paris as a staging area for sporadic forays into Spain to write for the wire service NANA and to collaborate with filmmaker Joris Ivens on a wartime documentary, *The Spanish Earth*.

Like Hemingway, Picasso's dormant political convictions were galvanized by events. At the beginning of 1937, six months after the fighting began in Spain, Picasso was commissioned by the Republic to paint a mural for the Spanish pavilion at the Universal Exposition of Paris. Naturally the government—under attack by rebel elements led by General Franco, allied with Nazi Germany and Fascist Italy—hoped Picasso's theme for the mural would illustrate a powerful prodemocratic statement and serve as a rallying cry useful to the struggling republic. The official announcement of the commission suggested that Picasso, like Goya before him, would exercise his genius in defense of "the people of Spain, who hold today in their hands the future of mankind."

Any propagandist theme was far from Picasso's conviction or intent. When he accepted the commission his subject in mind was the artist in his studio, with model (he had two to choose from), but he was slow to begin even this noncontroversial project. Distracted as he was by two simultaneous love affairs, and having just survived a galling divorce, Picasso at first chose to occupy himself with a less demanding subject, a series of illustrations for Buffon's *l'Histoire naturelle*.

On April 26, 1937, an act of chilling wartime barbarity affected the painter profoundly. A Nazi air squadron, the dread Condor Legion, attacked the Basque city of Guernica, an ancient center of Spanish culture of no strategic importance and populated by civilians only. *New York Times* correspondent Herbert Matthews (Hemingway's chief journalistic rival in Spain) wrote graphically of the three-hour German attack on the undefended city. For three hours Junker/Heinckel aircraft bombarded Guernica, blasting buildings to rubble, killing men, women,

Guernica, Picasso's masterpiece of political outrage, in its first state, as of May 11, 1937.

and children indiscriminately. Those who tried to flee to the open coun-tryside were machine-gunned in pass after pass of strafing aircraft.

Picasso learned of the horror from an account in *Ce Soir*, a Leftist journal edited by the poet Louis Aragon, and was touched with grief and smouldering rage he would transfer to a mural commemorating the dreadful slaughter of the innocents.

BEGINNING ON MAY Day 1937, and for two months of brooding anger and flashes of inspiration, Picasso completed over fifty ink and crayon sketches in preparation for the three-hundred-square-foot can-vas to be known as *Guernica*. In eight metamorphic stages, each pho-tographed by Dora Maar, the masterpiece of shock and outrage was completed in time for its installation in the Spanish pavilion at the International Exposition in Paris.

Reaction to the mural was mixed, rather more according to the polit-ical sentiments of the viewer than judgment on a work of art. There were those on the Right who had approved the shameless exercise in blitzkrieg and Leftists who feared the air attack was a strategic rehears-al for World War II. (Tellingly enough, Communists declared the mural "anti-social, ridiculous, and altogether foreign to the sane mentality of the proletariat.")

Picasso himself best expressed his intent in the first political state-ment of his life: "I am clearly explaining my horror of the military caste which plunges Spain in an ocean of sorrow and grief."

6

"UN BEAU CRIME, S.V.P."

—HEADLINE, PARIS SOIR

T THE END OF January 1933 Paris was muffled in the frigid gray of its usual long winter siege, and February promised more of the same cold and rain. The political climate was turbulent with crisis and Parisians in as foul a mood as the weather . . . a signal occasion, thought Henry Miller, to flee to some quaint provincial town and resolve his chronic indigence by accepting the offer of a paying job.

Before Miller's affair with Anaïs Nin erupted in full—and all signs indicated explicit sexual involvement on the horizon, if not already consummated—Hugo Guiler arranged for his wife's latest attraction to be hired as *précepteur,* teaching English at a private lycée in Dijon, and Henry accepted with enthusiasm. For Guiler's part, the removal of Miller from Paris spared the husband, at least for now, imminent cuckoldry; for Miller there was the opportunity for gainful employment for a change.

The gain proved ephemeral: no salary was attached to the job (Miller had failed to inquire about the financial stipulation)—only meals and lodging and a meager ration of coal for heating were provided in compensation for his labors.

How could Miller possibly have counted on the mustard capital of France to appeal to his wildly extravagant spirit—especially now that he considered himself "in love" and his love lived just outside Paris? The assignment to Dijon proved depressing beyond any episode in his expatriate experience so far, worse than his nightly confinement at the Cinéma Vanves . . . with considerably less comfort involved.

"[The citizens of Dijon] looked a little crazy, with the cold and loneliness. The whole town looked a bit crazy when the blue evening settled over it. You could walk up and down the main drive any Thursday in the week till doomsday and never meet an expansive soul. Sixty or seventy thousand people—perhaps more—wrapped in woolen underwear and nowhere to go and nothing to do."

Appalled by the sordid, narrow-minded provincial scene, Miller's heart cried out for Paris: "After a week it seemed as if I had been here all my life. It was like a bloody, fucking nightmare that you can't throw off."

Anaïs came to the rescue and bailed him out, with her husband's money, and supported him in Paris—by then they were passionately involved lovers—until Wambly Bald got Miller a job on his newspaper as night "financial editor" checking the day's stock market quotes, an ironic job for Henry Miller—but with an actual paycheck.

The Dijon experience did bear literary fruit for all its nightmare quality in the *précepteur* section of *Tropic of Cancer,* a chapter worthy of Miller's idol Louis Ferdinand Céline, especially the WC freeze that winter, and the comic-grotesque thawing of *merde* come spring.

During the several weeks Miller spent in Dijon, five competing government cabinets had shuffled in and out of power, unemployment reached crisis stage as the world Depression now included France, so the newspaper *Paris Soir* sarcastically declared that what the nation needed, to take its mind off politics, was a sensational crime.

The editorial writer at *Paris Soir* was no doubt thinking of a crime equal to the assassination of President Doumer the year before, a sensational enough act to provide scare headlines, since the assassin, Gorguloff, was a Russian, therefore believed by many to be a Bolshevik agent. (The fact that Gorguloff was a White Russian émigré, known to be deranged, was largely ignored by the newspapers.) The assassination of the president was a brief distraction from government scandals (many would say that Doumer got the bullet he deserved) and revelations of corruption in high places.

Not since the execution of mass murderer Landru in 1922 had the public been entertained by so long anticipated a spectacle as the beheading of the simpleminded Russian assassin . . . and so disorderly was the crowd at this event, it was the state's last public employment of the guillotine.

But even the execution of Gorguloff did not compare with the gruesome murders in Le Mans, exactly the crime *Paris Soir* was calling for.

BEFORE IT BECAME the auto-racing capital, Le Mans, only six hours from Paris, was a provincial bywater of complacent middle-class respectability and unexciting routine. M. Lancelin, a retired lawyer, had idled away the winter afternoon at his club until time to escort his wife and daughter to his brother-in-law's home for dinner. It was the custom of Mme. Lancelin and her unmarried daughter to enjoy a late afternoon stroll, but when Monsieur arrived at the house darkness had already descended; his womenfolk should have returned from their walk hours before. Yet no one answered his knocking, which became increasingly frantic (why was the front door bolted?). Even the window shutters were fastened, and no light appeared from the house except for a faint candle glow from the window of the servants' quarters in the attic. Despite his shouts and insistent banging against the door, no one opened to him, and even the feeble light from the attic was abruptly extinguished. Silence.

Could his wife and daughter have gone on to his brother-in-law's house without him? The servants had shown a light, but had not answered his knocking. M. Lancelin then hurried to his brother-in-law, M. Renard (also a lawyer), and the two summoned a trio of police agents to accompany them to the locked and darkened house.

By forcing open a window the police were able to penetrate the dwelling, followed closely by the distraught M. Lancelin and M. Renard. The electricity was off, and the group was led forward by an *agent de police* named Truth, who had a flashlight. M. Truth began to mount the staircase, stopped halfway up. He placed a restraining hand on M. Lancelin's shoulder.

"Proceed no farther, Monsieur."

Prudently M. Lancelin was led back downstairs by another policeman.

The infamous sisters Papin.

On the staircase a detached human eye was reflected in the flashlight beam, lying on a step. It was Mme. Lancelin's eye, and a few steps higher lay Mlle. Lancelin's eye. Near the upstairs landing the two bodies bathed in blood were sprawled at grotesque angles, their skirts drawn up, their skulls crushed horribly. In some bizarre sexual ritual the thighs of the two women had been notched and carved as if they were joints of beef prepared for the oven.

While M. Renard kept M. Lancelin apart, the troupe of investigators hurried to the attic where the two house servants, Christine and Léa, had retired to bed by candlelight, clinging one to the other (they were sisters, and lovers) after having washed themselves and their implements—butcher knife, hammer, pewter pitcher—of blood. They had even hammered out the dents in the pitcher, for they were scrupulous about their duties as housemaids, even beyond the call of their demanding mistress, Mme. Lancelin. In fact, the conscientious performance of their household duties had led to the drama.

As Christine, the elder sister, explained (Léa was virtually struck dumb from the moment of confession until the trial), the electric iron had short-circuited (for the second frustrating time!) and blew out the electricity in the house. When Madame returned from her walk she was furious, naturally. The feeble-minded Léa could only confirm her sister's grim account by nods and babbling.

The two sisters—Christine, twenty-eight, and Léa, twenty-two—looked so eerily alike; garbed in identical bedgowns of baby blue (yet hair in wild disarray from their exertions) that it was only by Christine's forthright admission of guilt and Léa's simpleminded reticence that the two sisters could be distinguished one from the other.

"Vous voyez, Messieurs," was Christine's polite form of address in response to any and all questions posed by the investigating party. Even in extremis she recited a banal sequence of events in the way of a humble and obedient servant.

The crime had taken place by candlelight, because of the loss of electricity. She explained how the electric iron had become "deranged" on a Wednesday, was repaired on a Thursday, and short-circuited again on a Friday—this time short-circuiting the house current. It was too much. When Madame returned with Mlle. Geneviève from their evening walk, finding the lights out, "She threatened to beat me. I tore out her eye."

In ritual obedience to her older sister, Léa gouged out the eye of Mlle. Geneviève, then followed in imitation of whatever orgiastic horror Christine perpetrated on Madame to do the same on the Lancelin daughter.

Not one of the investigators (including Truth) could make out a possible motive for the brutal massacre other than some pent-up sense of revenge lodged in Christine's sick mind.

Unable to pay for their legal defense, the sisters were represented by a distinguished Parisian attorney, Pierre Chautemps (cousin to Prime Minister Camille Chautemps)—not necessarily a *pro bono* gesture, since the publicity value of the trial would outweigh any financial consideration.

In view of the full confession consistently maintained by Christine, there was but one plea, that of insanity, to spare the two accused from the extreme penalty for their crime. This should have been easily enough established, especially in the case of the psychopathically mute Léa, but Maître Chautemps failed to take into consideration the narrowness and prejudices of a provincial jury and judge.

Simone de Beauvoir, twenty-five at the time of the trial, followed the events in *Detective* magazine, and deplored the photographs of the twelve members of the jury, all male: *"gros fermiers, des commerçants patentés,"* businessmen and fat farmers who were called upon to decide the fate of these two "enraged sheep." (Animal terminology, not always analogous, began when the newspapers got the name Papin incorrectly as Lapin, which means rabbit.)

Simone de Beauvoir may have seen the murders as a case of passive slavery revenged, however horribly and deranged. The jury was evidently more attentive to the prosecution's portrait of two disgruntled maidservants consciously seeking savage reprisal for injustices real or imagined on the part of their employer.

The sisters were never directly criticized by Madame; in fact, they had never been addressed personally by her in all of the six years of their service in the household. Reprimands were delivered by handwritten note from Madame via Léa to Christine. From their meager pay was deducted the price of a broken plate, and Madame once forced Léa to her knees to retrieve a scrap of paper she had neglected to sweep up. "One must not speak ill of the dead," was the unspoken note on which the trial proceeded. Madame Lancelin conformed to the typical bour-

geois employer of the day, and her maids may have been victims of
social circumstance, but she, after all, was the victim of a gruesome
murder at their hands.

There was good to be said of the Lancelin family: the maids were
allowed heat in their small mansard room, an uncommon privilege for
which they were grateful. In their dismally grim and limited lives, the
sisters never left the house on their day off but remained inexplicably
sequestered for the entire day, for whatever strange comfort this represented.

On the psychological issue, the jury preferred to accept the diagnosis of three "experts" from the local insane asylum than that of a *gros
légume* (big shot) from Paris, Professeur Logre. After no more than two
30-minute sessions with Christine and Léa, the three local doctors con-
curred in the conclusion that both sisters were indeed of sound mind
and "untainted background," perhaps untainted by the standards of Le
Mans. The alcoholic father had violated an elder sister, now in a convent; their mother suffered from hysteria; a cousin was confined to an
asylum; and an uncle "who took no joy from life" had hung himself.

Unfortunately for the defense, when he took the stand Professeur
Logre was obliged to admit that he had not interviewed the young
women at all, but had worked out his theoretical diagnosis in Paris from
written reports of the case. Maître Chautemps might have done better
to have engaged the esteemed psychoanalyst Dr. Jacques Lacan to
establish the mental state of the two accused. His essay on the murder,
Motifs du Crime Paranoiaque: ou le Crime des Soeurs Papin, appeared
(where else?) in the surrealist journal *Minotaure*. To Lacan, the entire
dreadful scenario had been brought on by a severe case of double (twin)
paranoia, though the jury, hostile to one more Parisian expert, would
surely have rejected Lacan's thesis out of hand.

Not that testimony or speculation for or against motive or manner or
mental responsibility mattered to either of the accused. They sat through
the entire trial as if in a trance. Christine was given to religious visions,
Léa to no visions whatsoever. The only reading found in their mansard
quarters were pious religious tracts, nothing of a revolutionary nature
that might have suggested that the dread communist virus had reached
and infected Le Mans, inciting two young women to criminal rebellion.

Awaiting trial, Christine in the throes of one of her hallucinations,
leapt to the topmost bar of a ten-foot-high window and remained hang-

ing apelike from the bar until she was brought down and strapped into a straightjacket. Confined apart from her beloved sister, she actually freed herself of the straightjacket, the only known occasion of a prisoner having escaped that medieval restraint.

Despite this manifestation—did the jury assume the sisters were playing at madness to receive a lighter sentence?—and Christine's statement about her love for Léa ("I sometimes believe in a former life I was my sister's husband"), plus the evidence of the murder's enactment, the Papin sisters were declared to be of sound mind and therefore fully cognizant and responsible for their crime.

The slavelike Léa was sentenced to ten years in prison to be followed by twenty years of "municipal exile," banishment from Le Mans. Christine, judged all the more "responsible" than her moronic younger sister, was sentenced to death. At the announcement that she was to die by the guillotine Christine fell to her knees, as if judgment had been rendered not by the judge and jury but by God. By law women could not be executed by guillotine (Christine was unaware of this) and the sentence was therefore commuted to life imprisonment.

TO THE AMERICAN colony, concerned more with their own pursuits among the French and among themselves, the gruesome crime in Le Mans received little comment and made no noticeable impact except by that astute witness to French manners and mores, Janet Flanner, the Genet of *The New Yorker's Letter from Paris*. The French found greater significance in the drama at Le Mans, from Simone de Beauvoir and Antonin Artaud (Theater of Cruelty) to Jean Genet, who wrote his most powerful play based on the Papin affair, *Les Bonnes*. Genet brooded over *The Maids* for fourteen years before writing his version for the stage—a far longer period of contemplation than that of the judicial proceedings in Le Mans, which took all of twenty-six hours to weigh the evidence and decide the fate of the two "enraged sheep."

7

THE CATALYST FROM CATALONIA

[Dalí] seems to have as good an outfit of perversions as anyone could wish for.

—George Orwell

*A*LONG WITH BRAQUE and Picasso, now it was Salvador Dalí (to Gertrude Stein's further exasperation and dismay) who also wrote poetry—particularly a verse-homage to Picasso. The Dalí-Picasso relationship was an odd one: at first a father-son attachment, but once the competitive spirit prevailed theirs became a frères-enemies rivalry.

Originally Dalí's obsequious cultivation of Picasso was sincere and would seem to have been an idolatry natural to a younger painter toward an acknowledged master and potential mentor. The friendship began on that understanding. Newly arrived in Paris (1929), Dalí immediately flattered the older painter by announcing he preferred paying his first visit to Picasso rather than touring the Louvre, to which Picasso replied, *"Vous avez bien fait!"* ("You have done well [to do so]!")

Soon enough, behind the pose of devoted protégé, appeared the less innocent intent to unseat his fellow Spaniard as foremost painter-celebrity of Paris. If not equal to Picasso in "genius," on Gertrude

Stein's terms, Dalí was nonetheless a gifted painter and superb drafts-
man, with a technical mastery Picasso was one of the first to recognize
and acknowledge.

Through Picasso, Brassaï met Salvador Dalí early on: "A thin almost
emaciated face and pale olive-hued skin, with a tiny mustache and jet-
black hair gleaming with brilliantine." The mustache that had so
impressed Gertrude Stein had not yet achieved the signature flourish of
a full-fledged exhibitionist, but other ostentations were already apparent. The hair glistened not with brilliantine but was plastered slickly
with painter's varnish for a heightened effect. (At one point, when his
father denounced him and barred him from the family home, Dalí
shaved his head bald.) Brassaï, forever concerned with the expression of
eyes, found Dalí's "hallucinatory"—all the more so for the lead shadow
the painter applied to the lids to imitate the American film star
Valentino's sexy gaze.

"The woman," as Brassaï described Dalí's wife, "was slender, small,
built like a boy."

This was "Gala," Elena Dimitrovna Diakanova, formerly married to
the surrealist poet Paul Eluard. Known as "the surrealists' muse" Gala
was the centerpiece in an uneasy ménage à trois with Eluard and
painter Max Ernst, until Dalí contrived a secret rendezvous with her
and overcame his lifelong impotency—according to his unreliable
account in *The Secret Life of Salvador Dalí*—at first sight.

For this initial tryst, or grotesque encounter, Dalí was wearing a silk
shirt with the sleeves cut away to reveal armpits painted blue. He sported a dog collar of pearls, a pair of bathing trunks donned backwards,
and a geranium behind his ear. Somehow this outlandish ensemble won
Gala's heart—or appealed to her Russian temperament, or overwhelmed her as a result of the scent Dalí had concocted from sheep
dung boiled in fish oil flavored with essence of aspic.

"I swear to you," Dalí swore to Gala, "that I am not 'coprophagic.'"
This was to account for the minutely detailed *merde* depicted in some
of his paintings. "I consciously loathe that type of abberration . . . but I
consider scatology as a terrorizing element, just as I do blood, or my
phobia for grasshoppers."

Gala confessed to an obsession of her own, a death wish brought on
by the instant, wanting suddenly to be slain by Dalí's hand . . . a desire
that strangely coincided with the very thought of killing Gala that Dalí

himself had entertained. However bizarre the telepathic exchange, this meeting of minds promised a love affair of constant surprise and continual menace.

Enthralled, Gala gave up her husband Eluard (and presumably discarded her then lover Max Ernst) for marriage to this exciting newcomer to the surrealist band.

In a sense Salvador Dalí had made a first strategic assimilation of the Picasso persona by acquiring, like his rival, a Russian wife. When Picasso, upon meeting Gala, discovered she had a mole on her ear identical to a mole on his ear, Dalí interpreted the coincidence as if some mythical liaison was made manifest.

Meanwhile Picasso and his Russian wife had separated. By 1935 Olga would finally agree to a divorce—the year Marie-Thérèse gave birth to Picasso's second child, a daughter named Maia after the goddess of fertility.

GEORGE ORWELL IN his attack-defense of Dalí's *The Secret Life of Salvador Dalí* (1942), wrote: "The important thing is not to denounce him as a cad, but to find out *why* he exhibits that set of aberrations."

Surely one reason was that Dalí seethed with the need to be in the spotlight center stage; Picasso as the reigning prince of Paris nudged Dalí to one side and cast a shadow across his light. Dalí cultivated the same celebrities and frequented the same salons as his rival Picasso, yet Dalí remained court jester to such socialites as Coco Chanel, Elsa Schiaparelli, Misia Sert, and Prince Mdivani. The collector most interested in buying and promoting Dalí's work was not the doyenne of the art scene, Gertrude Stein, who only admired Dalí's mustache, but the flamboyant heiress Peggy Guggenheim, who specialized in surrealist paintings and attracted the painters to her bed. (Peggy Guggenheim took up the work of Max Ernst after Gala parted from him, and later married the German-born painter when World War II began, because: "I didn't want to be sleeping with an enemy alien.")

Dalí was most notably successful in winning the favor and patronage of the vicomte Charles de Noailles, who took him seriously enough to sponsor the surreal films, directed by Bunuel, *Un Chien andalou* and *l'Age d'or*, which reinforced Dalí's reputation for *succès de scandale* but did nothing to dislodge his Spanish rival from preeminence. Dalí could and did outperform Picasso in showmanship and shock effect, for which Dalí had the greater talent and exhibitionist drive. No stunt was too outré if meant to bedazzle Dalí's calculated public.

Meanwhile Picasso attended the Cirque Médrano for such entertainment: he had left his own clowning behind at the Bateau-Lavoir.

AT THE TIME of Dalí's efforts to promote himself to Parisians, Gertrude Stein was enjoying the fruits of her uncommon celebrity during a sojourn in the United States, a first visit in 1935 to her native land since leaving for Paris at the turn of the century.

"The Mother Goose of Montparnasse," as she was called by journalists, created an enormous personal and professional success with her inimitable lectures and newspaper interviews. At last, at least in academic circles, she was being taken seriously after her first opera, *Four Saints in Three Acts*—music by Virgil Thomson, performed by an all-black company—was an unexpected hit. Audiences may have been baffled by its repetitions and non sequiturs set to music and sung with gusto, but charmed by so novel an experience calling itself opera. "Gertrude Stein makes sense," Thornton Wilder had insisted, though Americans, Gertrude discovered, responded as much to novelty and eccentricity as to sense (her famous ditty, "Pigeons on the grass alas," was first sung in this opera), and soon enough Dalí caught the drift, realized where instant popularity lay, and followed in Gertrude's wake across the Atlantic.

In 1936 Dalí eagerly accepted an invitation from Caresse Crosby, founder of the Black Sun Press in Paris, to be her guest in the United States; making an unaccustomed gesture of generosity, Picasso advanced the passage money.

The Dalís, Salvador and Gala, proved equal to Gertrude Stein in parading their individuality before the American public. In contrast to Gertrude Stein's verbal strategy (renewing the English language with fresh sentence compositions), Dalí (with no English) relied on pure visual effect, and such deliberate provocation as wearing an enormous loaf of bread strapped to his head when appearing onstage.

Dalí's photograph by fellow surrealist Man Ray appeared on the cover of *Time*, and Bonwit Teller invited the painter to design one of their department store windows in surrealist style. Dalí was more than equal to the challenge; traffic on Fifth Avenue was blocked by large crowds gathered to see his display: a setting of glass mannequins filled with water, goldfish swimming through the transparent nudes.

Although Dalí was finding it far easier to titillate Americans than to astonish the blasé French, he did misjudge the American character in one large respect: his final publicity salvo backfired. For Caresse Crosby's farewell surrealist ball, Gala came costumed as a nursemaid, and on her head Dalí had fastened "a very realistic doll representing a child devoured by ants, whose skull was caught between the claws of a phosphorescent lobster."

The effigy was said by reporters to represent the Lindbergh baby, only recently kidnapped and murdered. Public sensibilities were shocked by this mockery, but to Dalí's mind, and probably intent, bourgeois outrage only fed into a successful public-relations campaign. In any case, the Dalís were safely back in Paris when the storm broke in America, and Dalí's canvasses were selling for as high as fifteen thousand francs a painting, edging closer to the prices paid for a Picasso.

DALÍ WAS THE leading exemplar of a movement to which Picasso only marginally subscribed. (Cofounder of cubism with Braque, Picasso now abandoned the group theory of art and was content to remain a school of one.) Picasso did, however, share his poetry with Breton and designed the very first cover for Breton's surrealist journal, *Minotaure*. The mythical beast—a bull's head upon a lusty male torso—became an iconlike motif in Picasso's life and work, and immediately inspired a series of lithographs, drawing, and paintings. Evidently Picasso identified his own sexual nature with the man-beast symbol, a signature creature that appears repeatedly in his work.

Minotaure as a journal, was not as doctrinaire as its Marxist-inspired founder, André Breton, and not all contributors to its pages were hardline surrealists (or Communists), Picasso for one, and certainly not Matisse.

Surrealism evolved from the *épater-le-bourgeois* antics of Philippe Soupault, Tristan Tzara, and Francis Picabia, when dada was the rage in Paris and "anything goes" attitudes directed or misdirected the dadaists. André Breton refined that movement into a more disciplined philosophy of Marxist thought combined with Freudian dream theory applied to experimental verse, "automatic writing," and later to modern painting.

Café manifestos were drawn up; Breton was joined by poets Louis Aragon (whom Dalí referred to as "a nervous little Robespierre") and

Paul Eluard in defining the cult's doctrine. Considering the controversial natures and individualistic bent of painters and poets, it is surprising that the surrealist alignment remained unbroken for as long as it did. Throughout the 1930s the movement represented the predominant fashion in artistic and literary experiment. Even when the alliance dissolved, in the way of all such previous isms meant to define succeeding stages of modern art (fauvism, futurism, expressionism, cubism), a number of painters persisted in the surrealist mode. At least in France, dream imagery and sexual symbolism continued to appeal long after surrealism as a movement had faded from the Paris scene. Faithful to the Freudian influence ever after were Giorgio de Chirico, Yves Tanguy, André Masson, Max Ernst—and above all, Salvador Dalí.

In his *Mainfeste du Surréalisme*, André Breton described the surreal approach to art as purely psychic automatism—the absence of all control exercised by reason. But Breton's doctrinaire insistence was responsible for many of the defections and dismissals. One must write and paint as Breton prescribed. Alberto Giacometti innocently returned to the use of models for his sculptures: "When I did that the surrealists considered it a reactionary activity or whatever," and he was dismissed from the ranks because of a practice banned by Breton. The poets Aragon and Eluard broke with Breton on ideological grounds, refusing to adhere to Trotskyist principles Breton attached to surrealism—and the same shift in party line so disturbed René Crevel, author of *La mort dificile,* that he committed suicide.

Gertrude Stein pronounced the epitaph to surrealism: "They missed their moment of becoming civilized. . . . They wanted publicity, not civilization, and so really they never succeeded in being peaceful and exciting."

Miró abandoned the art scene in Paris to return to his native Spain, and Magritte quit the Paris group to return to Brussels where he founded the Belgian branch of the movement. Dalí, the young turk, outlasted the breakup of the fraternity to become surrealism personified. *"C'est moi,"* he declared, *"et moi seule,"* after being dismissed by Breton, who called him "Avida Dollars," a witty and pertinent anagram on the name Salvador Dalí.

8

A PAWNSHOP SCAM THAT
ROCKED THE NATION

*B*Y THE SUMMER of 1933 Wambly Bald—the name alone attracted a certain readership—had been writing his column *On the Left Bank* since 1929 and was growing skeptical of its relevance. For those four years he documented, in the Paris edition of the *Chicago Tribune* (the forerunner of the Paris-based *Herald Tribune*) with his informal gossipy account of the Parisian world of Arts and Letters, titillating tidbits about society's more colorful eccentrics along with feature items on the genuinely gifted and creative habitués of the Café du Dôme and environs, his headquarters. It would seem that Bald never ventured forth from his bohemian kingdom in Montparnasse except to cross the Seine and collect his paycheck at the newspaper offices on the Right Bank.

As a character in Henry Miller's *Tropic of Cancer*, Wambly Bald is given a more distinguished name, Van Norden, but a less than savory nature as a relentless womanizer without scruple. The fictional Van Norden in his obsessional fornications incorporated some of the more adolescent characteristics of Miller himself. Cronies and sometime roommates (*Quiet Days in Clichy*), Miller and Bald shared odd serial adventures and dropout philosophical attitudes when working on the newspaper together (Miller as "financial editor" but in fact a drudge proofreading the financial page). Ostensibly the Miller-Bald relationship came to an end when Anaïs Nin rescued the author from his expedient labors on the *Chicago Tribune* night shift (actually Miller was fired), and when Bald gave up writing his column *On the Left Bank*. For three years theirs had been a time of anarchic hijinks and comic hangover in the ribald spirit of the friendship, but 1933 was Year One of a sobering European malaise.

In France venal politicians were reacting passively, shamefully, or not at all to widespread unemployment and the threat of fiscal collapse. Adolf Hitler that year became chancellor of the German Reich, his foreboding treatise on Germany's manifest destiny, *Mein Kampf,* now available in French. The Great Depression was more than a term for financial crisis to the ordinary Frenchman; he was depressed and desperate. The man-in-the-street was "in the streets" to protest against the state in a series of strikes and marches, each more menacing than the last as the crisis continued.

In his soberer moments, Wambly Bald was not without perceptions of a larger order concerned with the world stage beyond the narrow confines of the Left Bank. Compared with outside events, Bald's newspaper notes on the activities and posturings of the personalities in his Bohemia had become an exercise in repetitious trivia, a shallow pursuit that led him, on July 25, 1933, to write a farewell column: "I've had a good time. I've seen them all: Derain and Braque and Chirico and Lillian Fisk and Foujita and Joe the barman . . . but this [list] could go on and on; I no longer wish it to go on and on."

OTHER JOURNALISTS WERE beginning to scrutinize the horizon and found indications of worse to come for the troubled nation faced with inner turmoil and fist-shaking dictators next door. Eric Sevareid was living at the Hôtel Sélect at 1 place de la Sorbonne (for fifty cents a night, including breakfast) and became alarmed early on about the Führer's militaristic posturing, but was assured in an interview with Gertrude Stein that Hitler was not "the dangerous one" but to beware of Mussolini. "[Hitler] wants the illusion of victory and power, the glory and glamour of it, but he could not stand the blood and fighting involved in getting it." Sevareid was not convinced, and William Shirer, just returned from Nazi Germany, even less so.

Anita Bryant, the widow of John Reed (whose *Ten Days that Shook the World* was a classic study and adoring account of the Russian revolution), shared Bald's carefree Montparnasse attitudes at first—and shared his bed for an interval before becoming the wife of William Bullitt, American ambassador in Paris. Bryant was capable of a perceptive article on the rise of Benito Mussolini despite being denied an interview with il Duce himself. "Women," Mussolini told her, "should write about blue skies."

The first to write an in-depth study of Adolf Hitler was Janet Flanner in her *Letter from Paris* for *The New Yorker*—also denied an interview. Wambly Bald was well aware that he was incapable of competing in the worldview league of journalism; his flair was for the local and small-scale. He was determined to bow out and leave the world scene, its beginning traumas and turmoil, to such inspired reporters as Walter Lippmann and Shirer. Bald's world, the Left Bank of Arts and Letters, was in stasis, holding its breath.

"I think art is a solace," wrote Bald, "but no solution. Montparnasse might wait a while, because the world now is interesting."

Not long after filing his final column, Wambly Bald met Ernest Hemingway in the Luxembourg Gardens. According to Bald, their dialogue went as follows:

HEMINGWAY: Where is everybody?
BALD: They've all gone back to the States.
HEMINGWAY: Don't you want to return?
BALD: I don't know.
HEMINGWAY: If you do I'll pay your way.
BALD: Why not?
HEMINGWAY: Here's the money.

Allowing Montparnasse to "wait a while," Wambly Bald quit the Paris scene altogether, just before a shady figure came onstage who would have felt at home in the colorful miscellany parading through the Dôme and appearing in Bald's *On the Left Bank*; but this remarkable character was more at home on the Right Bank, and in as showy a setting as possible: music hall, casino, racetrack.

To all appearances, Alexandre Stavisky personified the carefree boulevardier in the popular songs of Maurice Chevalier. Who would have believed this petty swindler of shifty charm, uninspired chicanery, and amazing persuasive power could, by controlling bonds issued in the name of two municipal pawnshops, bring France to the brink of revolution?

Both Janet Flanner and William Shirer had occasion to document the rise and fall of Alexandre Stavisky and to observe firsthand the catastrophic consequences. For French-speaking readers, the mystery writer Georges Simenon was engaged by *Paris Soir* to follow and attempt to untangle the convuluted and largely unsolved Stavisky Affair as if it were the latest in the fictional Maigret detective series.

Serge Alexandre (Sacha) Stavisky was born in Kiev in 1886, became a naturalized French citizen as a boy, then acquired convenient passports as a young man in the aliases of M. Alexandre and M. Niemens, documents mysteriously supplied and never explained by the French Sûreté. His respectable and hardworking father was a dentist whose first practice was in the ghettolike rue des Rosiers district, but Stavisky père soon prospered and opened an office in the rue de la Renaissance just off the Champs-Elysées, a move that may have inspired the young Sasha to imitate his father's upward mobility, but through a distorted variation on the bourgeois ethic and by a wayward path.

There were convenient shortcuts to financial reward open to an enterprising young man with a glib tongue and few scruples, so when Stavisky left the upper-class Lycée Concordet he did not, as his father proposed, continue on to medical school but chose instead to live off a woman *d'un certain age* and learn about life from the pimps and narcotic peddlers at Le Petit Pot, a disreputable hangout in the porte St. Denis district. He was attracted to the café-concert milieu as well, and even purchased a cabaret called the Cadet Rouselle on the rue Caumartin, a variety house catering to marginals more interested in cocaine than in vaudeville, with money provided by another woman "of a certain age."

The cabaret failed, but farther along the same rue Caumartin Stavisky opened a *bureau de contentieux,* a semilegal office for settling claims out of court, but a claim against Stavisky himself, a modest swindle of eight hundred francs in a theatrical investment, was settled out of court by his father, who simply reimbursed the disputed sum. Sacha's next fraud, however, in a phony corporation called the Cinema Trust, concerned two stockbrokers defrauded of 7.5 million francs, an amount worth the notice of newspapers, and Stavisky's arrest at a lavish dinner party in Marly-le-Roi made the front pages. The affair could not be bought off by a concerned father's intervention, and Stavisky faced jail. Unable to bear the public humiliation, Stavisky père committed suicide.

Awaiting trial, Stavisky spent eighteen months in La Santé prison, and during that grim incarceration he determined never again to spend time behind bars, not that he intended to follow the example set by his father (which only led to ignominy) but rather to profit from an essential lesson hard-earned and well-learned: one received the amount of justice one paid for. Evidently Stavisky reached the appropriate authorities with effective sums, for he was granted "provisional liberty" before trial, and the trial would be postponed nineteen times over the next sixteen years. For all its initial publicity, the sensational case was never to come before the courts.

From that time on Stavisky—or M. Alexandre, as he preferred to be known—cultivated the right people in high places to add a façade of legitimacy to his schemes as well as provide a *cordon sanitaire* against possible arrest. He was equally as adept at dispensing *pots de vin* (bribes) to politicians and police officials as spreading largesse among influential journalists and social arbiters. The judicial bribes were applied quietly, never traced to M. Alexandre.

Stavisky also eased insidiously into café society's limelight, if not into its brightest circles, for he enjoyed playing the man about town, especially in the show-business crowd. He took over the Empire Theatre and even mounted a successful theatrical production for popular Rita Georg. After each night's curtain he frequented the celebrated Zelli's cabaret—that is, until he swindled Joe Zelli by raising a two-thousand-franc check to sixty thousand francs. He was seen at Auteuil and Longchamps where his horses raced under bogus colors. Even the great Mistinguett wandered into the Stavisky entourage (innocently, she later insisted), photographed in the company of Jo-Jo le Terreur, Stavisky's formidable bodyguard.

He consolidated his position in society by marrying the beautiful Chanel model Arlette Simon, who had been awarded the Prix d'Élégance at a bathing-beauty contest in Cannes. If a shade lacking in elegance himself, the handsome Stavisky dressed handsomely. Perhaps a certain unsavory aura from his days at Le Petit Pot persisted, for it was said of him that *dans le milieu* (among the criminal class) he was considered a man of the world, but in the "world" he was considered *dans le milieu*.

At the time there flourished, or floundered, in Paris more than twenty daily newspapers of conflicting political hue and fluctuating circulation, each devoted to its avid readership, from the apparently neutral (and nationalist) pro-government *Le Petit Parisien* to the rabid *Action Française* representing the fascistic political movement of the same name. On the Left, *L'Humanité*, *L'Oeuvre*, and *L'Aube* each had differing political agendas, as did the Rightist journals *La Croix* (Catholic), *Le Figaro*, and *L'Echo de Paris* (the latter two owned by Coty, the perfume magnate), but by 1934 most newspapers of either camp were united editorially in opposition to the present parliamentary government.

The only other sentiment many of these newspapers shared was a pervasive anti-Semitism, of which Stavisky was aware; therefore, at the time he became a newspaper publisher he unobtrusively converted to Catholicism and preferred the more French-sounding name M. Alexandre.

The uses of the press was a factor of influence not lost upon Stavisky. The bribing of reviewers for favorable notices was common practice, even to the extent of insertion of brand names into news copy. The most immediate means of controlling the news was to found or purchase a newspaper, as Coty (perfume) and Taittinger (champagne) could afford to do. So Stavisky bought two newspapers himself, shrewdly counterbalancing the purchase of Leftist *Rampart* with pro-German *Volunté* on the Right. (Considering the odds—and Stavisky was above all a gambler—he might have subscribed to the Right only, since there were twice as many Rightist journals with eight times the circulation over newspapers of the Left.) In any case Stavisky, unlike Coty and Taittinger, had no political axe to grind, only personal advantage to consider.

But Stavisky's most successful purchase was the buying of officials wholesale to cover every contingency and accommodate every awkward circumstance. This scale of useful subscribers on the take was listed by the journal *Crapouillet,* in its postmortem summary of the Stavisky Affair: "two préfets de police, an ambassador, a general, financial journalists, lawyers, magistrates and the police of the Sûreté de la Préfecture."

Compared with the Aeropostale collapse in 1931 (also involving a corrupt and incompetent government), Stavisky's pawnshop sleight-of-hand was *"une scandale minime"* as far as newspapers were at first concerned. It was not until the extent of the scandal leaked out, and blatant stonewalling of the investigation began, that journalists could arouse the public to so high a pitch of outrage.

Unsecured bonds had been issued in the name of the municipal pawnshop of Orléans. When endorsed and promoted by a minister of state, M. Albert Dalimier, the impression was that the bonds were an official offering by the French government. Next, a further issue of pawnshop bonds came on the market from the city of Bayonne. (Pawnshops in France are municipal institutions operated by and for the profit of the city—and in 1933–34 would have represented stable and reliable bond offerings.) Insurance companies, including the state Social Insurance Fund, were the principal investors in the bonds, and these institutions eventually grew suspicious of such large offerings from two cities that would not likely have generated sufficient collateral to insure the bonds.

Management of the pawnshop bond offerings was by a series of interlocking companies; one such was S.A.P.I.E.N.S., an anagram meaning "Société Anonyme, etc." of intentional or unintentional irony—there is no other evidence of a sense of humor on the part of Stavisky, who directed the companies. In all seriousness he placed on deposit, at one point, "the crown jewels" of the German royal family, a collection of emeralds that even the most superficial evaluation would have shown to be green-tinted glass.

Stavisky had set up a typical pyramid scheme, using the Bayonne receipts to pay off interest on the Orléans securities. Presumably he intended to issue bonds on the municipal pawnshops throughout France ad infinitum. Even after the insurance companies sounded the alarm, newspapers remained silent. The one financial journalist who began to write unfavorably about the pawnshop bonds was beaten up (said to have been assaulted by Jo-Jo le Terreur) in a café on the Champs-Elysées.

By Christmas of 1933 the mayor of Bayonne was under arrest, along with the nominal director of the Stavisky enterprise, M. Tissier. Stavisky himself (or M. Alexandre) remained in the shadows until December 30, 1933, when his name first appeared in *L'Echo de Paris*: "A warrant for the arrest of Serge-Alexandre Stavisky has been issued by the Parquet of Bayonne. Age 47, of Russian origin, Stavisky has already been involved in suspect pawnshop operations in Orleans . . ."

From the time of the arrest of his director and of the mayor of Bayonne, Stavisky was (probably through his connections in the police department) "to disappear." When detectives and journalists appeared at the Hôtel Claridge to inquire after the delinquent financier, they were informed, *"Monsieur Alexandre n'est pas là."*

"Where has he gone?"

"Monsieur left no forwarding address."

At first he was believed to have fled to a private villa in the Atlantic seaside resort of Les Embruns, but that obscure locale would have proved unsafe when it was discovered that Leon Trotsky—another

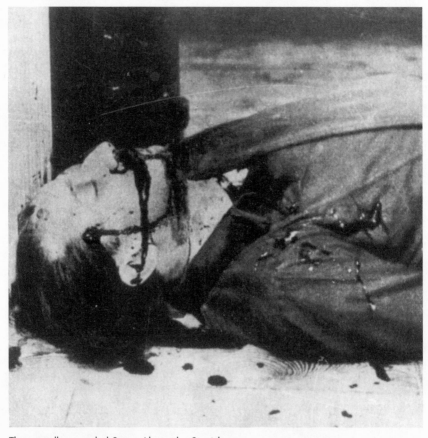

The mortally wounded Serge Alexandre Stavisky.

Russian, also in hiding and under an assumed name—was a near neigh-bor. Trotsky, in exile from Stalin's Russia, had been granted a temporary visa to reside in France, and two such celebrated fugitives in the same neighborhood would have been too much to expect the newspapers to ignore.

Stavisky next fled to the chic ski resort of Chamonix. The police were apparently in no hurry to follow him there, but the newspapers, notably *Action Française*, were on the scent; therefore the Sûreté Générale was at last obliged to "discover" the hiding place. The final word on Stavisky was issued by the Havas News Agency from Chamonix, January 8: "Officers in the service of the Sûreté Générale traced the *malfaiteur* Stavisky to a villa in Chamonix. When they received no reply from inside they were obliged to force the door, and at that moment Stavisky, alone in the villa, fired a bullet into his head. The doctor who was summoned found the wounded man in a state of coma, with no hope of recovery from the self-inflicted gunshot."

The public cried out for more.

On the following day, January 9, details were released that heightened the drama and at the same time obscured the facts. The villa had been rented in the name of a friend; a collection of Stavisky's cronies had arrived and departed the villa (with or without mistresses). One visiting couple, a masseur and his mistress, may or may not have been involved in the drama but had hastily departed Chamonix. The couple, by the name "Robiglia," were being "actively pursued" by the police, but were never found. The villa Le Vieux Logis was occupied by Stavisky alone under the curious alias of M. Danger.

The second report revealed that Commissaire Charpentier, before breaking down the door at Le Vieux Logis, placed an urgent call to headquarters of the Sûreté Générale in Paris—for instructions on how to proceed in the touchy affair. Also, it seems Stavisky did reply to the commissaire's demand that he open up, by asking, "Who is it?" Charpentier called out, "Open in the name of the law!" whereupon a shot was heard inside the villa. Or was the shot fired just as the door was being broken down—or immediately thereafter?

Whatever the preamble, Stavisky was discovered lying in a pool of blood at the front of his bed, dressed in ski garb (an ill-considered cos-tume for a would-be suicide), and as the police broke in Stavisky raised the pistol to fire into his temple once again but was in too weakened a

LE GRAND QUOTIDIEN ILLUSTRE

AUjOURD'HUI *

VINGT PAGES 25 CENTIMES

DEUXIÈME ANNÉE. - N° 259 — LE NUMÉRO : **0 fr. 25** — VENDREDI 5 JANVIER 1934

DIRECTION-ADMINISTRATION ET SERVICE DE PUBLICITÉ : 17, RUE D'ANJOU, PARIS (8°) — TÉLÉPHONE : ANJOU 13-50 A 13-53

LA COLOSSALE ESCROQUERIE DE STAVISKY

Au cours de la journée d'hier, le scandale Stavisky a pris des proportions imprévues. On sait maintenant que les sommes frauduleusement soustraites par le maître-escroc et ses complices seront probablement de l'ordre de cinq cents millions et de hautes personnalités sont nettement compromises.

De haut en bas et de gauche à droite : le siège des sociétés fondées par Stavisky, 28, place Saint-Georges; le dernier portrait de Stavisky; la plaque de l'une de ses affaires; la femme de Stavisky et ses deux enfants à la dernière fête des fleurs de Nice; le transport des dossiers à la suite de la perquisition, rue Saint-Georges; MM. Demay et Fontaine, juges d'instruction, quittant les bureaux de l'escroc. (Voir l'article page 5.)

INFORMATIONS

The Stavisky affair makes front page news: *Aujourd'hui*, January 5, 1934.

condition to fire a second time. Why the pistol was found not in the suicide's hand but on the bed was never explained.

Dr. Jamin, called upon to testify during an inquiry, declared, contrary to the original report, that the case was hopeless: "This man must be taken to a hospital where a trepanning operation might save his life." But Stavisky was left lying on the floor at Le Vieux Logis for nearly two hours, bleeding to death, before being transported to a local hospital to be pronounced dead officially.

HIGHLY SKEPTICAL NEWS reports and passionate editorials, particularly the one in *Action Française*, only increased public suspicion of police ineptitude and corruption, creating another wave of indignation and outrage. Parisians read of the criminal's *"suicide"* (placed in ironic quotes in *L'Echo de Paris*) when almost no one believed the official version issued by the Sûreté Générale. Even the pro-government *Le Petit Parisien* published an interview with Mme. Stavisky in which she stated inconsistencies in the police report (she found not just one but two shellcases in the room where her husband died), but the very next day she retracted what she had told *Le Petit Parisien*.

Why, after all, was Stavisky provided by the Sûreté a passport under an alias that would allow him to flee the country, thus safely removed from police pursuit, further newspaper inquiry, and embarrassing judicial inquiry? But Stavisky had chosen to hide out in Chamonix, perhaps with the understanding his bribed officials would protect him there. His choice was, in a sense, a way of suicide. He had left what was purported to be a suicide note, actually a farewell letter to his son from "your unhappy Papa," saying he might have to "disappear." *Disparaître* in French can mean either "to disappear" or "to die."

9

STREET SCENE

*T*HE PRÉFET DE Police de Paris, Jean Chiappe, was a short dapper Corsican who sported impeccably laundered white gloves—his blatant symbol of "clean hands"—whose investigation of Stavisky was constant ("I have had my eye on him for ten years")—but negligent at best. On three separate occasions beginning in 1931, criminal dossiers were drawn up by Inspector Cousin indicting Stavisky (or M. Alexandre), but when presented to Chiappe, the préfet took no action. Chiappe was known to have received Stavisky at police headquarters, but not even "preventative detention" was ever imposed. This was a sentence meted out frequently to Leftist demonstrators (three thousand Communists were detained one riotous May Day), for Chiappe was a hard-line conservative who once arrested Marlene Dietrich for wearing pants in public, and was dedicated to serve the purposes of the Right, as he saw them.

He broke up Royalist demonstrations as well, but handled the *Camelots du Roi* without breaking heads, *"avec tendresse,"* and released those arrested almost immediately.

The Communists did not protest his methods as much as commonly believed, declared Chiappe. "We treat them well. While in jail they are even given Gruyère."

The *préfet de police* enjoyed a certain popularity in the city for his tough if often brutal policing of "street crime," which to Chiappe's mind included Leftist agitation, though a laissez-faire attitude prevailed if Rightist groups like *Le Croix de Feu* and the *Camelots* took to the streets. Naturally this one-sided policy of favoritism made Chiappe a hero of the Right and the *bête noire* of the Left.

The *préfet de Police de Paris* Jean Chiappe, with his wife, at a police benefit concert, in February 1933.

Middle-class Parisians were inclined to respect Chiappe for his successes in reducing crime—or at least forcing the criminal element into the shadier enclaves, out of public view. Prostitutes were subject to arrest on the main boulevards, thus driven into the meaner side streets or into *maisons closes.* Chiappe invented the *passages cloués,* nails indicating crosspoints for pedestrians at busy intersections, which imposed discipline on drivers and pedestrians alike and reduced accidents by thirty percent. (Drivers joked that they were no longer permitted to run down pedestrians who walked *"entre les clous,"* between the nails.)

Certainly Chiappe was popular with the police force: he considered *agents de police* as an extended family, himself the benevolent father-figure. He saw to it that policemen's wives were favored for sought-after concierge positions, assuring tenants they were far safer when their

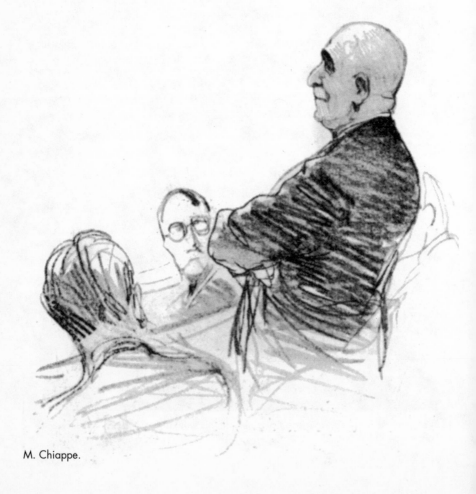

M. Chiappe.

concierge had a husband on the police force—though many tenants complained that the all-knowing concierges also served as spies for Chiappe's office.

One unsuccessful campaign sponsored by Chiappe "to raise the moral tone of the city" was to eliminate the *vespasiènnes,* the men's curbside urinals so dear to the eyes of Brassaï and Henry Miller. In this instance Chiappe had gone too far and completely misjudged the outcry (from men) that was to follow. The Art Déco comfort stations were allowed to stand—except during street demonstrations, when they were the first, along with kiosks, to be overturned.

Despite his popularity and power, in the Stavisky Affair Chiappe was an evident embarrassment to the government. A postmortem development was testimony by Madame Stavisky before a parliamentary committee of inquiry concerning certain assurances of "support" the *préfet* had made to her husband. The question for Premier Daladier was how to get rid of Chiappe without inciting demonstrations by his many supporters. His solution was to offer Chiappe the mainly honorary post of governor general of Morocco, a safe remove across the Mediterranean from Paris.

But Chiappe was outraged by the transparent maneuver and vehemently replied, *"Je refuse!"* His further remarks to the premier became a controversy of prepositions: if he was forced out of the *préfecture de Paris,* he would be *dans la rue.* But did he say *dans la rue,* meaning he would join in the street protests against the government, or *à la rue,* meaning he would be out of a job? The first was a serious threat, the second an appeal. (The satiric journal *Le Canard Enchainé* amused its readers with the idea that Chiappe had said neither, only that he would be *chez* LaRue, a famous restaurant.)

> *The rabble should have first unroof'd the city,*
> *Ere so prevail'd with me, it will in time*
> *Win upon power and throw forth greater themes*
> *For insurrection's arguing.*
>
> *Coriolanus,* William Shakespeare

Throughout the month of January 1934, following the death of Stavisky, sporadic demonstrations broke out in the streets of Paris, made all the more riotous by the dismissal of Chiappe. (He was replaced by the indecisive chain-smoking Bonnefoy-Sibour who had neither the confidence of the public nor the respect of the police.) In this atmosphere of social upheaval, a further incitement for "insurrection's arguing" was a production of William Shakespeare's *Coriolanus* at the Comédie Française. Added to l'Affaire Stavisky and l'Affaire Chiappe, l'Affaire Coriolanus would seem to be much ado about very little, but the choice of producing this particular play at such a troubled time took on ominous significance in the public mind and was the flashpoint to the most explosive rebellion Paris had known since the days of the 1871 Paris Commune.

Many had come to believe that Emile Fabre, director of the Comédie Française, had deliberately chosen the "antiparliamentarian" drama to illustrate general dissatisfaction with the Chamber of Deputies and Senate with Shakespeare's provocative and insulting references to "unwise patricians," "bald tribunes," and "reckless senators." The play was attended by members of both Leftist and Rightist cliques, who in turn cheered or jeered the lines that best expressed or appeared to condemn the political sentiments of their movement.

Impulsively and unwisely Daladier fired Emile Fabre, which prompted the newspapers to express agreement or outrage in the manner of rowdy audiences attending *Coriolanus*. Daladier then compounded his misjudgment by replacing Fabre with M. Thomé, head of the French Secret Service, the Sûreté, earning for himself exasperation and ridicule from both Left and Right: "A *policeman* running the House of Molière" was one sarcastic observation condemning the shift in directorship of France's revered classic theatre. A minor complaint at any other time, the incident became a final straw in the public opposition to elected authority.

Already members of the Chambre de Deputés had become so unpopular that certain restaurants and cafés posted notices saying, "We don't serve deputies here!" Outrage was general against the standing government, and the malaise was only increased by newspaper agitation from such incendiary editorials as those of Charles Maurras, writing for *l'Action Française*, listing deputies, including Premier Daladier and Socialist Léon Blum, "to be killed without mercy." (As to Blum, Maurras once declared: "He is a man who must be shot—but in the back.")

The riots of January took place on an escalating scale of violence culminating in a call to arms published in the newspapers of various *ligues* (political clans) announcing the date as February 6. Most clans of the Right, no matter what their allegiance to one another, planned to march at that time—and even the Left called for demonstrations, not, as was traditionally the case, to clash with Rightists, but this time to protest actions of the government in coincidental harmony with the Right. It was an explosive mix, and the target was the palais Bourbon, the Chamber of Deputies itself.

WILLIAM SHIRER WAS assigned by the Paris *Herald* to cover the scheduled demonstrations, but when he arrived at the place de la Concorde on the afternoon of February 6 there was only a beginning crowd, a scattering of pedestrian spectators, and the usual tangle of motor traffic spinning around the obelisk in the center of the place.

The place de la Concorde was directly across the Seine from the Chamber of Deputies, and the bridge leading to the palais Bourbon, the pont de la Concorde, was heavily guarded. A few hundred men were milling around the square and at the edge of the Tuileries; these were "shock troops" called out by *l'Action Française, Solidarité Française,* and *Jeunesses Patriotes,* not yet organized into any kind of threat. The demonstrators were effectively blocked by the police from crossing the bridge to the palais Bourbon, and on the Right Bank side of the bridge they were under surveillance by a large force of mounted police, the Garde Mobile, reinforced by gendarmes on foot. No leader had appeared to lead the attack on the Chamber of Deputies, no newsworthy incident had developed, so Shirer retired to the Hôtel Crillon on the north side of the square for a snack.

When he came back outside at 6:30 P.M. the scene had changed dramatically. A mob was attacking the Garde Mobile with paving stones, broken brick, garden chairs—any object at hand, including the grills ripped from around the trees in the Tuileries. The favored weapon against the mounted police was a cane or stick with razor blade attached to slash at the legs of the horses; some rioters tossed firecrackers or rolled marbles and ball bearings under the hooves of guardsmen's horses. A bus was on fire. The crowd was growing; the maimed and wounded among them were being carried across the *place* to the lobby of the Crillon where a first-aid station had been hastily set up.

To get a better view of the melee, Shirer went up to the third-floor balcony of the hotel to join some twenty French and foreign journalists gathered there. The balcony overlooked the place de la Concorde and across the Seine to the palais Bourbon where the Chamber of Deputies was in emergency session. The shouts of rioters and singing of demonstrators all across the *place*—nationalists singing the *"Marseillaise,"* communists the *"Internationale"*—carried to the Crillon balcony, and Shirer did not at first hear the sound of gunfire.

"Then [a] woman slumped to the floor. When we bent over her, the blood was flowing down her face from a bullet hole in the center of her forehead. She was dead, instantly." Later, the woman was identified as a thirty-three-year-old cleaning woman at the hotel.

Shirer's aerial view of the milling confusion across the vast battleground did not allow for the close-up testimony of another witness, the British correspondent Alexander Werth, caught up in the crowd below, near the burning bus: "The terrified passengers were driven out, all the windows were smashed, and the conductor was ordered to get off . . . with the help of a copy of *National,* the paper of *Jeunesses Patriotes,* they set fire to the stuffing of the conductor's seat." The mounted police were unable to disperse the predominantly youthful (and well-dressed, Werth observed, as if for a party) "Young Patriots," the most daring and ingenious of the rioters; when the fire brigade finally edged through the crowd, the Patriots cut the hoses trailing from the fire trucks. "For an hour or more the bus continued to blaze, filling the air with smoke."

From the upper level of the Jardins des Tuileries, demonstrators were ripping the benches from their cement supports and tossing them down to the mob below who then built up grillwork barricades between themselves and the *forces de l'ordre* and from behind which they hurled stones and broken pieces of macadam. Not only did the smoke from the burning bus obscure the battlefield, but the ornate Art Déco lamps around the square had been smashed, and only the flames from the bus and the floodlit obelisk cast a grim flickering illumination over the moiling scene of bloodshed and devastation.

IN HIS NIGHTLY tour of street carousing, Henry Miller was lost in thought and believed he heard the *"Marseillaise"* from one direction and *"l'Internationale"* from another. "I had not read a newspaper for a week or more, was engrossed in my [D. H.] Lawrence book . . ." and he wandered into the maelstrom quite by chance and unaware of what the singing and chanting was all about in the "sinisterly bare" vicinity of

Richelieu-Druout. Miller was thinking about his study of D. H. Lawrence as publication of *Tropic of Cancer* neared (the Lawrence study was a strategic effort to establish Miller as a legitimate author before Jack Kahane's pornographic Obelisk Press brought out his raucously erotic *Tropic*, which the public was certain to associate with Kahane's usual line of "d-b's" [dirty books]). That night a contingent of *l'Action Française* had chosen this very corner as a rallying post, while the mob streaming down the rue du Montmartre was probably a collection of communists from the working-class quarters around the porte de Clignancourt. (Baron Haussmann, when designing nineteenth-century Paris, had annihilated most of the popular neighborhoods, dispersing the *ouvriers* and the poor to quarters more manageable on the outskirts of the city.) ". . . And the very evening the crash came, I walked into the middle of it—instinctively."

Not quite the "middle," which was at the place de la Concorde, but in a danger zone of ostensibly opposing forces that frightened Miller into a cold sweat, as he first tried to dissolve into shadow, then scuttled out from the potential clash down the rue Notre Dame des Victoires . . . "Walked in and out again—in a hurry. Had the queer sensation (so true when you are in danger) that I was a target."

MEANWHILE, ALEXANDER WERTH was eager to know what was happening at the flashpoint, the Chamber of Deputies just across the Seine. He managed to cross to the Left Bank by the simple expedient of walking unchallenged across the pont de Solferino, the next bridge along the river from the Tuileries, which had been left unguarded and without barricades. He entered the palais Bourbon from the quai d'Orsay and, once inside, could witness the clamorous meeting of the deputies, almost as chaotic as the violence across the Seine at the place de la Concorde.

Somehow, despite catcalls and the screaming volume of insults hurled at one another (instead of paving stones), Premier Daladier managed to win a vote of confidence, 360 to 220, a *vote de combat* (one must not change the commanding general in the middle of battle) rather than an expression of support. In ominous counterpoint to their own turbulent session, the deputies could hear the rising volume of tumult from the bridge approaching the palais Bourbon, as if the invading forces had engaged the palace guards in the center of a medieval drawbridge and were marching on the besieged castle at the other end.

With cries of "*A bas* [down with] Daladier!" and "*Vive* Chiappe!" the battalion of rioters was forcing the security units to retreat. From the windows of the palais frightened deputies watched the Garde Mobile beaten back by the demonstrators who were gaining ground, meter by meter, across the pont de la Concorde.

Then came the sound of gunfire. There was a rush of deputies toward the exits—but only the rear door to the place du Palais had been left unbarred; all the other exits had been barricaded with the ornate gilded Louis XV furnishings.

The rioting in the place de la Concorde, February 6, 1934.

On the place du Palais, a troop of infantry stood in readiness as reinforcement to the police guard, for by now a massed contingent of *Jeunesses Patriotes*, who had gathered at the Hôtel de Ville on the Right Bank, were now marching along the boulevard St.-Germain in an assault formation from the east, chanting, "France for the French!" "Take your brooms and sweep out the rubbish!"—the rubbish being the deputies, and Premier Daladier.

The more disciplined ranks of *La Croix de Feu* ("The Cross of Fire," a union of ex-servicemen) had assembled at the militarily symbolic statue of Clemenceau, beside the Grand Palais on the Champs-Elysées. They were by now marching into the esplanade of the Invalides, having crossed the Seine by way of the pont Alexandre III chanting the *"Marseillaise"* along the way. The Invalides, where they reassembled in military ranks, was adjacent to the palais Bourbon; now the ranks of the *Croix de Feu* were the most immediately threatening to the Chamber's vulnerable southwestern flank. Strangely, these troops of military veterans chose not to assault the Chamber, but only to make their numbers, and potent opposition, known.

Their commander, Colonel de la Roque, was an inspiring figure at political rallies calling for an end to the Third Republic by force, considered France's "man on a white horse," but in the present circumstances was unready to present himself as dictator of the nation, or even to place himself at the head of his assembled followers.

IF THE REVOLUTIONARY mob was essentially leaderless, the defenders of the State were equally deprived of a commander.

Alexander Werth noted: "A pale-looking man with a fur collar and bowler hat was walking up and down the [secured section of the] bridge in a state of terrible anguish. It was Bonnefoy-Sibour." Chiappe's chain-smoking, nerve-wracked replacement as chief of police paced helplessly and hopelessly, a woebegone sentry on the few meters of the pont de la Concorde left to him.

By this time the panicked deputies had discovered the unlocked rear door and were fleeing the palais en masse. Few newsmen lingered in the press room—the news was now outside, raging through the streets of Paris—but a wag had placed a notice on the door: *"Avis à MM Les Manifestants—ici il n'y a pas des Deputés."* (Notice, to the Messieurs/Mesdames demonstrators—there are no deputies in here.")

An emergency aid station had been set up inside the palais Bourbon where wounded defenders from the bridge were being treated, some for ghastly injuries, especially those of the Garde Mobile who had been crushed beneath their toppled horses. Three of the mounted guardsmen were never found, assumed to have been thrown from the bridge into the Seine. Janet Flanner witnessed one horse guard knocked from his mount, the pride of the Garde Mobile: "detrousered . . . being paddled bloody by his own saber."

IN THE AFTERMATH an official estimate of deaths was from twenty to seventy, a figure judged suspect by Janet Flanner who insisted the total number of deaths and injuries was bound to be higher than the published report, considering the extent of rounds fired: some twenty thousand.

One ironic complaint to the government was that the Garde Mobile, before firing into the crowd, failed to sound the regulation three trumpet calls, therefore resulting in deaths and wounds "illegal." Furthermore, since all factions had obtained valid parade permits, the shooting of demonstrators was forbidden by law.

The Great Riot had ended without the deputies (or Daladier) being massacred, or the palais Bourbon being invaded, but the Duc de Guise believed his hour had come round at last, that Paris was crying out for the return to an imperial France. The next day's papers published his pathetic appeal:

> Frenchmen!
> From foreign soil where I am cruelly banished [exile in Brussels] I bow with deep emotion before the dead and wounded who, at the risk or loss of their lives, have defied an unworthy and impotent government.
> To maintain itself in power . . . [the government] has not hesitated on the frightful night of Tuesday to fire upon war veterans, on the mutilated of the Great War, and on our youth, the hope and saving of the country.
> Blood has run in the streets of Paris which can only have been shed in a sacred cause!
>
> In exile, February 7, 1934
Jean, duc de Guise

The duke believed the "sacred cause" for which the demonstrators had fought and died was to restore the Orleans monarchy by crowning his nephew, comte de Paris (pretender to the Throne), as emperor of France. The monarchist league known as *Les Camelots du Roi*, Partisans of the King (although *camelot* in French means "street peddler of cheap goods"), may have espoused the sacred cause of monarchy but not necessarily to sponsor the royal return of the present Pretender.

Other *ligues*, factions, and parties had diverse motives for bringing down the Third Republic besides working out their frustrations with government in anarchy and rampage.

Janet Flanner summarized various reasons for revolution by comparing disparate headlines on the day following the riots. ". . . *l'Humanité* informed [its readers] that the fight the night before had been against Fascism and that the Working Man of Paris Had Answered. *L'Action Française*, Royalist gazette accused of Fascism, said that the noble riot had been against Communists, Socialists, Radicals, Republicans, Jews and Freemasons. *La République* (Left-Wing Young Radical) said that the Republicans Had Quelled the Uprising. Léon Blum's Socialist *Populaire* said that dictatorship had been attempted by War Veterans and the Right . . ." and so on through the list of Paris newspapers expressing their radically opposed interpretations of cause and consequence. "Only *Le Matin*, sole among twenty-seven dailies, simply had significantly called the sixth 'A Day of Civil War.'"

Flanner failed to add that the Battle of Paris '34 was as much provoked by rival newspaper instigation as by bloody confrontation in the streets. The newspapers published inflammatory manifestos and declarations of war signed by the owners of the papers themselves. Heroic leaders to implement the provocative editorials were as scarce as the white horses to carry them forward.

Of course Daladier was obliged to resign in disgrace, replaced by aging Gaston Doumergue (characterized by Colonel de la Roque as "a poultice on a gangrenous leg"), recalled to power from retirement to his beloved rose garden in the suburbs. Doumergue was the only political figure deemed worthy of the premiership, since he alone had long been out of office and therefore had fewer enemies capable of forming opposition.

Former *préfet de Police* Jean Chiappe might have rallied sufficient public support as a short-term dictator, but did not have the staying power or widespread popularity of his hero and fellow Corsican, Bonaparte. De la Roque, of the military contingent *Le Croix de Feu,* did not intend to bear their standard, "the cross of fire," before his troops; and Maurice Pujo, leader of the royalist *Les Camelots du Roi,* disappeared as soon as the riots began and for two days could not be found by either friends or the police.

In this misbegotten revolution there arose no dauntless leaders like Danton, Marat, or Robespierre to sweep into power—perhaps no figure of current influence wanted to suffer their fate. Men like Pierre Taittinger, of the House of Champagne, remained on the sidelines convinced that words alone would suffice to stir his *Jeunesses Patriotes* into seizing power in his illustrious name. Of the House of Perfume, François Coty, leader of the storm troopers of *Solidarité Française,* proved to be no "friend of the People" as his newpaper *L'Ami du Peuple* proclaimed, but altogether *hors du combat,* barricaded in his château outside Paris.

THE MOST OUTSPOKEN revolutionist and foremost rabble-rouser, Charles Maurras of *l'Action Française,* had remained sequestered at home throughout the night of crisis he had so passionately called for, writing poems in Provençal dialect dedicated to "Pampille," Léon Daudet's wife. When his followers came to him on the morning of February 7 seeking further orders, asking "What next?" Maurras irritably sent them away with the comment, "Why do you disturb me at this hour? I have not yet had time to read the morning papers."

10

THE SCENT OF PRINCESSES

Monsieur is very much afraid of the scent of princesses.

—PROUST'S HOUSEKEEPER BARRING
ARISTOCRATIC VISITORS TO HIS BEDSIDE

*I*N THE PERFUME trade it was advantageous, if not essential, for one considered to be *un nez*—the blunt citation of A Nose accorded to those gifted with superior olfactory discrimination—and to be born on the flowering isle of Corsica. Thus the honorific of A Nose was bestowed on François Coty from an early age when he was discovered to be hypersensitive to the scent of flowers.

Born François Joseph Marie Sportuno, he learned little about his shadowy orphaned origins except for his mother's maiden surname, spelled Coti. In later life he invented a lineage extending to the Bonapartes, a further advantage to a man seeking political power as well as business success was an association by bloodline to the island's most celebrated native son. The kinship to Napoléon was a spurious claim, but a rumor Coty encouraged (and originated) for its political leverage as well as for his own self-regard.

In Paris, Sportuno discovered that his meridional name plus the comic accent that went with it, his diminutive stature, and his blazing red hair made him something of a joke to Parisians. He exchanged Sportuno for his mother's maiden name, Coti, or Coty as he spelled it, when he embarked on a quixotic political career in that snobbish city.

He soon realized that his nose was a bankable asset in a country already known for its exquisite perfumes, and his talent for discerning the subtlest gradations of scent was verifiable. In Corsica Coty was recognized as an inventive, enterprising genius of A Nose. The provincial island (said to be Shakespeare's model for the magic isle in *The Tempest*) was an idyllic setting for an apprenticeship, but no center of commerce equal to Coty's aspirations—what would have become of Napoléon, he might have asked himself, if the future emperor of France had remained in Ajaccio? Coty knew that to become the leading *parfumier* in France he must somehow establish himself in the very heart of Parisian elegance, power, and display: the place Vendôme.

In the center of the *place* rose a monument dear to Coty's ambition, the imposing Vendôme column supporting at its pinnacle the earlier swashbuckling buccaneer from Corsica, Bonaparte.

COMPARED WITH HIS rumored forbear, Coty was a leader well out of public sight except as a brand name on his vials of perfume and as proprietor of his newspapers, but a leader he was, a shadowy figure as obscure as his origins but whose influence was as pervasive as his perfumes, if nowhere seen. His very reticence made him a public figure of mystery and speculation. Understandably a need for secrecy was essential to the blending of his "magic" formulae, his methods vulnerable to imitation by competitors. But this reclusiveness was more of an eccentricity in a man who hoped to wield power at the head of an extreme Right political cadre: *Solidarité Française* or antigovernment influence by way of his two daily newspapers.

Coty was the proprietor of *Le Figaro,* decidedly Rightist but a lukewarm promoter of racism compared with *L'Ami du Peuple* (The People's Friend), propaganda sheet for *Solidarité Française. L'Ami du Peuple* was distributed at a mere ten centimes a copy, effectively undercutting the twenty-five centime price of the Big Five newspapers—of which, ironically, Coty's *Le Figaro* was one—to the outrage of other publishers when the sales tactic gained for *L'Ami du Peuple* a subscription of a million readers and an estimated circulation of over three million, the largest in France.

A leading journalist with *Paris Soir,* Pierre Lazareff described *L'Ami du Peuple* as "a strange sort of newspaper—drab, boring, full of interminable articles in which Coty tirelessly proclaimed that what France needed was a Bonapartist Republic—amounting, in fact, to some vague sort of Fascism."

Any attack against the propaganda sheet and its subsidy by the proprietor failed. When the Hachette Agency, which had a monopoly on newspaper kiosk distribution, refused to sell a newspaper at ten centimes a copy, Coty defiantly declared: "I'm rich enough to take care of the distribution myself."

(Before the advent of *L'Ami du Peuple,* another wealthy proprietor with political motives, Hennessy of the Three-Star cognac firm, attempted similar tactics with his daily *Le Quotidien,* but, according to Lazareff, Hennessy "began to dream of the laurels of Hitler and Mussolini" with his mouthpiece newspaper, misjudged his readership (or journalistic gifts), and failed. At least his political ambitions were rewarded with a ministerial post and an ambassadorship.

Meanwhile Coty, publisher and editor (though his signed editorials were actually written by the professional anti-Semite Urbain Gohier), was seldom seen outside his Paris apartment or his château at Louveciennes, its walls reinforced with concrete, the wine cellars stocked with as many firearms and munitions as with vintage wines, ostensibly in defense against his "enemies" but more like a private armory for the storm troopers of his *Solidarité Française* in readiness for the open insurrection he predicted. (That uprising did break out on February 6 but Coty believed the revolution would come from the hated Communist Left he intended his troops to oppose with arms; instead, the riots were instigated by the extreme Right, of which he was a dedicated proponent and partisan.)

Coty brooded on the insurrection in solitude, hiding as much from his litigious ex-wife who threatened his empire more than any armed assault.

WHEN NOT CONFINED to his château in Louveciennes, Coty secreted himself at his Paris laboratory on the quai Javel. There, in paranoiac solitude, the master blender of exotic aromas operated alone or with a single trusted assistant at his side. His aide could be designated as a sorcerer's apprentice in the fabled mystique of perfume blending, a process that conjured association with witchcraft, an alchemy of subtle suggestiveness and irresistible allure in the creation of an aphrodisiac.

The origins of perfumery contributed to his legend. Ingredients necessary to the amalgam were ambergris, taken from the inner ear of the sperm whale, and musk, from the abdominal sac of the male musk deer of Lapland or the rare fatty substance extracted from a sac behind the testicles of the wild civet cat of Southeast Asia (after the captured beast was fed on bananas and slightly rotten fish entrails to flavor the secretion).

Coty, and most modern of *parfumiers,* relied on compounds of crushed and liquefied flower petals, or their chemically blended resemblances, to accomplish the sorcery of aroma.

Behind locked doors and sequestered with his collection of odoriferous plants from his native Corsica and from the flower fields of the Midi region of Grasse—rose petals, *genêt*, lavender, mimosa—reduced to elixir, to be combined with nutmeg or vanilla, citronelle or ginger, and in the ultimate stage submitted to a fixative of alcohol to prevent decay . . . Coty conjured his commodity of sensual essences. Seventy-five workers had toiled under the southern sun harvesting a ton of flowers petal by petal, distilled into a mere kilo of attar of rose or jasmine, at an equivalent of $240 per kilo. It was a tedious and intricate process, critical at every stage in the creation of a successful scent and the eventual *voila!*

The first work Coty found in Paris was as *un nez* for the prestigious Guerlain firm, freelancing his own formulas on the side. Pioneers in the industry were the Guerlains, Jacques and Aimé, who in their day blended each bottle of perfume to satisfy individual client preference in the manner of a fashion salon draping a garment to measure (or rather like a pharmacist preparing drugs to individual prescription). Guerlain changed all that at the turn of the century by successfully promoting a "universal" perfume under the trade name Jicky.

The ambitious Coty was said to have achieved an initial success by dropping a mason jar of his private blend on the floor of the department store Printemps, an aromatic spill that so excited women shoppers that they demanded the store stock Coty's concoction. In any case the name Coty became known apart from his connection to Guerlain, which led to his dramatic move from Guerlain at 23 place Vendôme to his own establishment directly across the square at 2 place Vendôme.

Following the trend of Guerlain's success with Jicky, Coty marketed his own universal scent under the name La Rose Jacqueminot, "rose" for the cabbage rose that anchored his formula, "Jacqueminot" for a French general Coty happened to admire.

To enhance the value of his expensive elixir, Coty presented each bottle of perfume in its own silk-lined casket like some precious gem, the bottle itself an Art Nouveau design by the famous glazier Lalique—but mindful of the middle-class market for his expensive essences, the flask's interior was reduced by thickening the glass, to make certain perfumes deceptively affordable.

Having fulfilled his commercial ambitions (bolstered by founding his own banks to finance his expanding empire), Coty embarked on the acquisition of Parisian journals to attack his enemies on the Left and disseminate his turgid philosophy of the Right. His private army, *Solidarité Française,* was modeled on Mussolini's Blackshirts—seldom paraded in public but prepared to "defend" the cause when called upon. Coty's rabble-rousing editorials were ghost-written, and the arts page reflected his retrograde tastes with the employment of fellow xenophobe Camille Muclair as art critic for *L'Ami du Peuple.* Muclair wielded a vitriolic pen against "invaders" from outside the borders of France who had come to dominate Parisian art galleries; he railed against the mostly Eastern European and Russian expatriate painters and sculptors of l'École Juive: Pascin, Kisling, Soutine, Chagall, Lipchitz, and, in mistaken vehemence, against "half-Jews like Picasso[!]"

In a social climate where political ambitions could be fostered and fed by salon life—the typical Parisian salon having shifted from the original dynamic (or subterfuge) of promoting art and culture to a much more evident political stance—and although many upper-class Parisians were in accord with his Rightest perspectives, François Coty was too reclusive and distrustful to engage in political nourishment by way of a salon. He had run for office on only one occasion, and been elected Senator from Corsica, then was shown to have paid for the majority of votes cast in his favor (which was a time-honored custom among Corsicans, who were known to count even the dead as voters), and was removed from office. Coty possessed a mistress (more than one over the years), but not a mistress powerful enough to establish an entourage for his support, in the manner of the marquise de Crussol, whose salon promoted the policies and politics of her lover Edouard Daladier; or more notably that of Madame de Portes, whose lover Paul Reynaud was the centerpiece of attraction *chez elle,* though Reynaud was also a starring member of the Countess Montgomery salon, she of the Noilly-Prat aperitif fortune.

(One salon, that of Countess Marthe de Fels, brought together both literary and political prestige in the person of Alexis Léger, Secretary General of Foreign Affairs, who wrote poetry under the pseudonym Saint-Jean Perse—a salon exceptional in its comparatively liberal and progressive tone.)

Thus via their salons and the political figures each represented, women were gaining a modicum of power in the male enclave of government, secondhand and behind Aubusson drapery of a palatial residence in Neuilly or Auteil.

Coty understood women by their preferences for his aromatic commodities—his only notable, or remembered, remark: "Perfume is a woman's love affair with herself"—but the master blender of luxury fragrances misunderstood or gravely underestimated (in the personal instance of his wife Yvonne) the independent-minded modern Frenchwoman. He might well have considered the example set by the two formidable female entrepreneurs with whom he shared the fashionable commercial quarter of the place Vendôme, "Coco" Chanel and Elsa Schiaparelli. Women were beginning to emerge in power and prestige apart from the privilege and reflected image bestowed upon them by a male partner.

In order to marry his much younger mistress, Coty instigated divorce proceedings, for a Frenchman an uncharacteristic tactic when the custom was that a husband maintain both wife and mistress, the twin ménage kept acceptably separate and discreet, but understood by both women, either of whom might voice recriminations but muted and in private; this compromise meant to represent a certain domestic stability and harmony. (Political figures and celebrities were particularly subject to this unwritten law.)

The *written* law rendered unto the husband every conceivable advantage, and therefore François could assume the Code Napoléon to favor and defend himself in divorcing Yvonne, just as it had when Bonaparte set Josephine aside. Under the code, the wife is subject to extreme financial disadvantage. (Equally unhappy and unfair strictures apply to the advent of marriage: the wife cannot seek employment, open a separate bank account, or travel outside the borders of France with their children—without notarized permission granted by her husband.)

Coty's vast holdings and swollen fortune would, presumably, remain in his exclusive possession at the conclusion of his marriage to Yvonne. François had not taken into consideration an escape clause to this statute, which his wife Yvonne took implacable advantage of.

A modification in the articles of the civil code allowed for a prenuptial agreement known as *Séparation de Biens,* or right of entitlement to wealth and property shared equally by the married partners. François Coty had either forgotten he had signed such an agreement or assumed that its articles did not apply or would not be invoked against him in divorce court.

Yvonne Coty thought otherwise. She succeeded through persistent litigation in winning her share of the estate, a cash award of 268 million francs, plus half the Coty holdings in such enterprises as his newspaper empire. As in the case of so many multimillionaire financiers, Coty's cash was in *placements* (investments); in court he protested that he lacked the liquid assets to pay the full amount imposed. Yvonne insisted on full and immediate payment; her demand was upheld by the court, and so she gained controlling interest in Coty's treasured newspaper, *Le Figaro,* the one journal he intended making into a prestigious mouthpiece of café society. Instead, he discovered one morning that his name had been removed from the paper's masthead. In the sole gazette left to him, the shameful but widely circulated *L'Ami du Peuple,* he spewed out (or it was spewed out for him) his most vituperative editorial to date, but even that tawdry rag would be denied him when *L'Ami du Peuple* went into receivership.

Yvonne Coty became Yvonne Cotnaréanu when she married the Franco-Romanian banker who would join with her in directing the fortunes of *Le Figaro* on its rise to one of the powerful daily newspapers of France. (Yvonne had no doubt signed a *Séparation de Biens* agreement at the time of her marriage to Léon Cotnaréanu.)

Having met his personal Waterloo on the domestic battlefront, the tame Napoléon was nowhere evident at the place de la Concorde for the insurrection of February 1934. If *Solidarité Française* participated on that chaotic battlefront, the troops did so under another banner than that of the Friend of the People. A decline in health coincided with Coty's decline in fortune, and not many months after the great predominantly Rightist uprising the Bonaparte of bottled scent succumbed to pneumonia behind the fortress walls of his château in Louveciennes.

11

PLACE VENDÔME — I

There is even a Place Vendôme style, a style recognized in dresses and jewelry as well as in admirable façades with their pure symmetrical columns. But what constitutes this style? An inimitable mélange of order and fantasy.

— ANDRÉ MAUROIS

FROM THE ORIGINAL garden plot surrounding a cloister of Capuchin nuns, the architect Jules Hardouin-Mansart had been commissioned by the Sun King, Louis XIV, to create a stately ensemble of town houses, *petits palais*, and *maisons particuliers* to reflect the glory and magnificence of *le Roi Soleil* himself. Mansart accomplished the project with exactly the rich substance and harmonious design the king had in mind, and from the first the place Vendôme represented an urban centerpiece of both speculative and substantive wealth.

The roving rioters of February 6, 1934, made no mutinous incursion into this sacrosanct enclave, an unforgettably lovely square at the epicenter of the commercial Right Bank, a mere three blocks behind the Jardins des Tuileries where surging mobs engaged in fierce confrontation with mounted police on the place de la Concorde. The aristocratic octagon symbolizing fashion and wealth was this time ignored as a *champs de bataille*. Since the 1934 riots were more clearly a manifestation of the Right, primarily orchestrated by fascistic *ligues* versus the Third Republic, the place Vendôme was spared. The Left did marginally participate in the uprising, but the Leftist agenda of grievances would not come due until May of 1936 when the "Popular Front" arose from a makeshift alliance of socialists and communists.

THE INCONGRUOUS CENTERPOST, with proud Napoléon surveying the nearby rampage from its summit, standing defiant and aloof atop the Vendôme column—although in 1871 when it was known as the Austerlitz column, it became the target of rioting Communards and was toppled. The original effigy of Napoléon Premier had been cast of melted-down cannon from his victory at Austerlitz, a symbolic structure of empire hateful to the Communards. The column was attached by cable to teams of horses and pulled down to crack apart upon a prepared cushion of horse manure.

The destruction of the Austerlitz column had been devised not by some rabid anarchist but by Gustave Courbet, painter of the Barbizon school, elected Councilor of Beaux Arts by the self-governing Paris Commune. This was not the first desecration of the place Vendôme's central trophy: during the French Revolution the original monument, an equestrian statue of Louis XIV, was pulled down and decapitated—as was, soon after, the Sun King himself.

After the Commune was bloodily suppressed by loyalist troops garrisoned at nearby Versailles, Courbet was arrested and briefly imprisoned—but in prison he continued to paint, with brushes and colors smuggled to him by admirers—and fined the cost of restoring the monument, which he never paid, having escaped to Switzerland on his release.

THEREAFTER THE PLACE Vendôme became a tranquil enclosure dedicated to wealth, grand style, and decorum where demonstrators feared to tread (until the *grève générale* of 1934, when placards were the only threatening weapons), perhaps inhibited by the somber façade of the Ministry of Justice located there, next door to the Ritz Hotel.

How the *place* became the fashion center of France, and the world, may have first come about through the genius for design of a snobbish Englishman.

Frederick Worth had received royal imprimatur of a sort when the Empress Eugénie broke with tradition allowing for the first time a foreigner (Worth was born in England) and a *man* to drape her majesty's

Place Vendôme in the 1930s.

form and flesh. This was a daring novelty at a time when women personally chose their fabrics, then engaged a trusted seamstress to fashion a garment à la mode. Thus Worth became the first true couturier in Paris.

There was no question of impropriety of male dressmaker draping female client: Worth kept an inventory of dressmakers' dummies like a waxworks museum, the mannequins modeled on the forms of each individual patron of the establishment, convenient to the infinite number of fittings required. By Worth's employ of inanimate mannequins, his fashionable clientele of stage and court—the comtesse Greffulhe, the actress Lillie Langtry, the empress herself—were spared the tediousness of pins and hems and last-minute stitches. The final execution was supervised by maître Frederick himself, accompanied by his beautiful wife, Marie, in the manner of a society physician who discreetly includes his nurse in the examination room for that ultimate and intimate inspection.

Inspired by Frederick Worth (actually an apprentice at the house of Worth for several seasons), Paul Poiret was the next male fashion designer to dominate the market for upscale adornment. Something of a fantasist and sensual eccentric, Poiret was convinced that he had been a Persian prince in another life and therefore he designed, and lived, according to his theory of reincarnation, with princely sumptuousness and abandon. He did, however release women from the hourglass cages of Madame Gringoire (corsetière to royalty and the rich), whose whalebone straightjackets were de rigueur until Poiret appeared on the fashion scene. He emphasized the vivid fauve shades Matisse favored, and he dressed women in loose-fitting, free-flowing garments modeled on the ballet costumes of Léon Bakst for the Diaghilev ballet production of *Mille et une nuits*. Poiret's wife was said to be endowed with wealth, but evidently not rich enough to sustain the fashion designer's reckless extravagances; he went through her fortune, and several others, before ending alone in an attic (but an attic on the fashionable faubourg Saint-Honoré) with a list of names pinned to the wall, entitled: "Friends Who Have Not Helped Paul Poiret."

ONE WHOSE NAME would have been on the list of neglectful friends, or rather on a list of implacable rivals, was Gabrielle Chanel, who eventually usurped the designer's sovereignity.

After the Great War, when women were women no longer confined to the household or grandes dames paraded in high fashion through the Jardins des Tuileries, an ornament to male pride, Chanel was one of the first to see that these women in the audience at the Comédie Française were as artificially costumed as the actresses onstage in *Le Bourgeois Gentilhomme*. Indeed, Poiret had freed society women from the restriction imposed by their corsetière, then burdened them in fanciful excessive overdress—worse, his ankle-length dresses included the hobble-skirt, exotic and feminine, yes, but in the way of an inmate of a seraglio or a mincing foot-bound geisha.

"*That* can't last," she declared to her companion at the theatre. "I'm going to dress them simply, and in black." With Arthur "Boy" Capel's help, she did.

Boy Capel was nothing like the arriviste "*bourgeois gentilhomme*" of the play they watched, but a genuine English nobleman of considerable wealth. At the time he shared Mademoiselle Chanel with another lover, Count Etienne Balsan, who typically thought of his mistress as the light-minded lovely cocotte her nickname "Coco" suggested. Unlike the Frenchman, Capel recognized the business potential of his beautiful mistress and saw fit to realize her dream of a millinery boutique near enough to the Hôtel Ritz to assure a well-to-do clientele for the modiste Chanel.

The choice of the Ritz Hotel as an identifying landmark and location guaranteeing success brought her free and clear of her peasant background as an unwanted illegitimate daughter in the backwater Cévennes. The place Vendôme was a powerful symbol obliterating Chanel's tawdry climb from bed to bed as the "*grande horizontale*" her early poverty and desperate determination had condemned her to.

"She lies," Capel told one and all, "and when she is found out she lies again." Chanel was a natural mythomane who denied her sordid and ignoble past with facile substitution. Artifice was a component part of Chanel's creative nature: she would, for example, be the first to design jewelry of such unlikely substances as rhodoid, galalithe, and nacrologue instead of genuine precious stones. This costume jewelry was the ultimate subterfuge, an adaptable fantasy and gemlike accessory that could be discarded and reinvented with each new season's demands.

The embroidered fictions of Chanel were often transparent to everyone but Coco herself, for she was in the constant process of designing

Coco Chanel, ca. 1937.

Arthur "Boy" Capel.

a Coco Chanel that required change and shift in her personal history. In the style of Proust's *prisonnière* Albertine, Chanel could charm and amuse in her reinvention. Also like Albertine she had a fixation on the Ritz Hôtel (as did Proust himself), and may, like Albertine, have had proclivities toward bisexual passion, sexual adventures with Colette at one time, then with her closest companion Misia Sert. When Albertine craves an ice cream from the Ritz, the narrator evokes for her: "Vendôme columns of ice [cream] . . . votive pillars erected along an avenue devoted to the glory of Coolness."

The avenue of coolness Chanel would choose to establish her house of fashion was the rue Cambon, directly behind the Ritz and offering discreet access to that palatial hostelry by its rear entrance. She would take a permanent suite there on the Vendôme side, for convenience, while she received and entertained in a lavishly furnished apartment filled with coromandel screens against beige walls above the Chanel salon.

Boy Capel and Coco Chanel on the beach at St. Jeau-de-Luz.

Chanel's romance with Boy Capel waned as her success rose. She assumed they would marry, but Capel became engaged to an Englishwoman of Capel's own class and background. Chanel was spared the social humiliation of her lover's marriage to another, though she would suffer a greater shock, the ultimate tragedy of Boy Capel's death in a driving accident near St. Raphael on the Riviera.

The loss of the one great love of her life was at first unendurable and for a time Chanel lapsed into a state of grief and lethargy. Her bedroom at the Ritz was draped in black, the very color she had sworn to Capel she would make fashionable, and did.

Friends rallied to her side. In her period of mourning, Jean Cocteau consoled her, returning solicitude for Coco's financial support during his opium cures, for the poet was a confirmed addict and Chanel had twice paid for his disintoxication. Also, Misia Sert, Chanel's lifelong friend and most intimate companion—Misia had been the toast of the Banquet Years, now married to society's pet decorator and painter, José-Maria Sert—offered constant comfort to the bereaved dressmaker-to-society. Spiritual counseling was provided by Max Jacob, poet and mystic, companion to Picasso during the early Bateau Lavoir studio days, more recently "superstitions consultant" to Paul Poiret, advising which colors were likely to engender *bonheur* (or *malheur*) to individual clients.

Jacob, a Jew who had converted to Christianity, suggested that Chanel, as she rose from her slough of bereavement, trim her hair in the manner of Jesus Christ then and, in her inimitably shrewd and persuasive way, launch the coiffure to nest the new diadem style of jeweled headdress. Chanel was the first fashion designer to promote precious stones in garland settings as part of a modish ensemble effect. (The *beau monde* again responded to the Chanel style; those affected financially by the Depression in France could always resort to Chanel's plastic baubles, the costume jewelry that nevertheless denoted a modicum of chic as long as the brand name read "Chanel.")

Gabrielle Chanel possessed too much creative energy and natural joie de vivre to lament forever her deceased Boy Capel. Misia Sert convinced Coco to change her bedroom color scheme to pink—which she did, and then made pink the fashionable color for a season. Another friend in Chanel's entourage—for Chanel had now arrived in society as

The writer Colette, who may have been one of Chanel's lovers.

well as in fashion design—was Marthe Davelli who, at one of her high-season parties, introduced Chanel to Grand Duke Dimitri Pavlovich.

Exiled Russians in Paris had been rendered penniless by the Bolshevik revolution, and now obliged to make their way as best they

138

An illustration from Coco Chanel's "Russian Period."

could. Russian princesses became governesses; generals of the defeated White Army now devised battle strategy as taxi drivers in combat with traffic on the thoroughfares of Paris. Chanel employed the regime's disinherited princesses as seamstresses. Several of the most distinguished and least scrupulous of the exiled royalty used their titles to insinuate themselves into the heart of faubourg St.-Germain society or into the hearts of expatriate American heiresses. The tsarist title no longer served as a valid certificate of aristocracy, but enjoyed a certain nostalgic currency among competing arrivistes yearning to be known as *comtesse* or *princesse*.

At twenty-nine, the Grand Duke was eleven years younger than the grande dame of fashion, but at their initial encounter, Dimitri made evident his interest in the older woman of means. Chanel had inherited forty thousand pounds from Boy Capel, and was further financially advantaged by her successful fashion enterprises, now including a wildly successful perfume (originally offered Coty, but the Corsican saw no future for it), Chanel #5.

The scenario that followed their meeting might have been conceived by Chanel's friend and companion, Colette.

The Grand Duke Dimitri was also the current lover of the party's hostess, Marthe Davelli. Dimitri's Russian extravagances were exceeding Marthe Davelli's means, and she could no longer afford him. The introduction of Dimitri to Coco was ostensibly to help end Chanel's mourning for Boy Capel, but in the hope—she admitted later—that Coco would be amenable to "adopting" Dimitri next.

A spark had been ignited between the two, and Chanel was agreeable to the installation of the Grand Duke into her nest at the Ritz. Chanel was not only a woman of the world by now (Davelli's plot was clear to her from the outset), but a woman of *that* world.

The Franco-Russian liaison did not long endure—Dimitri's title and attentions were openly on the market—but the romance did serve to ease Chanel over a sad and depressing interval. If she was unduly wounded by the Grand Duke's mercenary change of heart (as she truly had been by Boy Capel's announcement of his engagement), Chanel outwardly displayed no chagrin. Her enterprises flourished, her bedroom remained pink.

BESIDES THE DISTRACTION of work—and Chanel took personal responsibility for the details of millinery, jewelry, dress design, and perfume that

flaunted the Chanel label—there was the comfort of friends, old and new, to compensate for her misadventures with men. She was closer than ever to Misia Sert; the whisper went through café society that they had become lovers when José-Maria Sert left Misia for a twenty-year-old art student, Roussadana Mdivani, he had "adopted." Coco was invited to California to design costumes for cinema stars but found no acceptable challenge in vapid Hollywood; she returned to Paris to design the costumes for Cocteau's *succès de scandale, Les Parents Terribles*—while continuing to pay for the poet's drug disintoxication cures.

Of new friends, the Spanish fantasist Salvador Dalí was the most intriguing and exasperating. Dalí could offer a surrealist touch to the Chanel line, and contributed his flair and capricious whimsy to the more staid of Chanel designs, as long as Coco kept him in check. Because of his tiresome monologues, Dalí in person was too egotistical a dinner guest to endure. When they dined together *chez elle* at her rue Cambon apartment, Chanel set an alarm clock for ten minutes, the time she allowed the loquacious painter his nonstop soliloquies.

Fashion, its accessories and by-products, had come to represent France as the ultimate in commercial creativity, a lucrative export—not even the advance of a world depression seriously diminished the demand for expensive dresswear, for the rich (as Poiret noted early on) are always with us. The nerve center and acknowledged capital of this sumptuous bazaar of luxury goods was of course the place Vendôme, over which, until 1935, Coco Chanel reigned supreme.

OTHER HOUSES EMINENT in French dressmaking shared the prestige and occupied the same general Right Bank vicinity—Lanvin, Vionnet, Molyneux—vying for the premier reputation in transcendent chic. These establishments enjoyed voguish successes in turn, or created the "look" that was in for a season or more, but no lasting challenge appeared to Chanel's predominance in the field until "l'Italienne" (in Chanel's acid designation) opened her House of Schiaparelli at 21 place Vendôme, the salon diagonally across the square in full flaunting view (only the Vendôme column intervening) of Chanel's stately mansard windows at the Ritz.

When Schiaparelli began to make herself known in fashion, Chanel could still declare with pride and conviction, *"L'élégance, c'est moi!"*—

Chanel with Salvador Dalí, 1932.

and she was right, as she would continue to be throughout a lifetime of designing. Elsa Schiaparelli revealed a gift of a different sort, a fanciful flair for the outré in design that women in society (and those who wished they were) had been waiting for. She achieved not only elegance in dress but a playfully individual display that made one *noticed*.

The two couturieres could not have come from more dissimilar origins, with contrasting natures and a sense of style at variance one from the other. In personal appearance, Schiaparelli could never equal Chanel's acquired grace and innate beauty—Schiap (as she was called by intimates) was of the type known as *"jolie-laide,"* homely but in a striking, almost pretty, way. In one respect the two women were alike: both possessed indefatigable creative energy and a competitive drive to succeed.

ELSA SCHIAPARELLI WAS born in Rome of a distinguished Italian family who would watch with dismay their daughter's rebellion against a heritage of culture and privilege, first by a careless marriage, then as a "seamstress" in Paris.

In London, sheltered from World War I, the young Elsa met and married, on impulse it would seem, the eccentric comte William de Wendt de Kerlor. The couple went to America where Kerlor was engaged to lecture on theosophy and where their tempestuous alliance lasted long enough to produce a child, after an accommodation to Kerlor's wild fling with dancer Isadora Duncan.

Left penniless in America when Kerlor deserted her, Elsa Schiaparelli did find the means to make her way back to Europe—with help, no doubt, from her family, who expected their daughter to return to Rome chastened and prepared to take up her proper social role there. The single mother, with no prospects in sight, entertained no intention of returning to Mussolini's Rome—and anyway preferred the life and prospects Paris offered.

Elsa was devoted to her daughter, Yvonne, whom she called Gogo, and who was a sustaining consolation for the failed marriage—Schiap henceforth would view male-female alliances with a cynical eye, but maintained an enduring maternal-filial amitié with Gogo.

Chanel had many lovers but never married, and was known to her staff by the vaguely demeaning but formally correct title, "Mademoiselle,"

while Schiaparelli, despite her acquired antipathy toward men, was entitled to be called "Madame."

A CHANCE ENCOUNTER with the couturier Paul Poiret, before Poiret's
downward slide and destitution, led to Schiaparelli's entry into the profession of fashion design. Schiaparelli had wandered into his salon and
tried on an evening jacket she had no intention or means to purchase.
When Poiret himself stepped forward to compliment the woman so perfectly suited to this particular creation, she confessed, "I can't afford it."

"Nevertheless, the jacket is yours."

Poiret was in the habit of dressing certain women gratis. He supplied
a complete wardrobe for the entertainer Josephine Baker for the publicity value of the gesture, though Baker was better known for the G-
string of bananas she wore onstage than for Poiret's "robe Josephine"
she wore on the street. But in Schiaparelli, who was unknown at the
time, no advertising advantage was intended or implied. Poiret could be
extravagantly generous with his stock in trade as with compliments,
which was perhaps one of the reasons he went bankrupt.

"I have no place to wear it."

"You, Madame, could wear this jacket anywhere."

Through some instinctive and indefinable rapport the two became
friends: Poiret was the first mentor in the field of fashion to this fascinating "Italienne."

Another defining instance, an epiphany of the sort Chanel had experienced in the audience of the overdressed at the Comédie Française,
occurred when Schiaparelli wandered onto a nudist beach on the Île
de Porquerolle. Shrinking from the blatant display of flesh, she came
to the conclusion that "The human body is truly ugly—until properly
and stylishly clothed." The demands of a future career evolved from
this insight.

Schiaparelli plunged into the profession of dress at the very top,
skipping the normal stages of couture, from *arpette* (apprentice) to
première main (supervisor) to become immediate *directrice;* for one
thing, Schiaparelli, despite her convent upbringing, had never learned
to sew. Unlike Chanel, the obsessive perfectionist in detail work,
Schiaparelli was content to innovate assemblage on paper, then
orchestrate the finished garment with the help of those who could
perform brilliantly where she could not function at all.

■ ■ ■

THE FIRST SCHIAPARELLI salon was at 4 rue de la Paix, one of the feed-er streets leading to the place Vendôme, on the edge of Chanel territo-ry but not yet an incursion worthy of her rival's notice. What Chanel could not fail to notice was that the boutique was called Pour le Sport, in imitation of Chanel's own introduction of sportswear for women ten years before. Schiaparelli carried the sports theme past Chanel's origi-nal and simpler designs by displaying such novelties as swimsuits in fish motif, leather unisex flying suits (aviation as a female pursuit came into vogue when Anne Morrow Lindbergh and other women were included in the cockpit), even golfing togs for women.

From sportswear Schiaparelli moved deeper into Chanel territory with dresses "Pour la Ville," then to evening wear "Pour le Soir," with one notable gown that Chanel herself might have designed, a thrifty, timesaving linear model, *"la robe sirène,"* convertible by redraping from an afternoon tea to formal soirée or an evening on the town with no change called for.

What must surely have sounded an alarm for Chanel was Schiaparelli's first important breakthrough with peasant sweaters in Art Deco patterns. The rage for designer sweaters would renew an earlier coup scored by Chanel herself, in women's jerseys (inspired by her "British period" with Boy Capel) of imported Scottish woolens. The demand was so great for Schiaparelli's *"pulls* [pull-overs] *paysans"* that she hired forty peasants to hand knit the sweaters to order.

BY 1935 SURREALISM was definitely the latest artistic thrust in the merger of the arts and the art of dress design. Cubism as an influence had waned by the end of the twenties when Picasso dropped out, and Art Déco was dépassé except when resurrected by Poiret, and in Schiap's peasant sweaters. Schiaparelli recognized the rise of surrealism from the first, when she met and made friends with Francis Picabia and Marcel Duchamp in New York, the dadaists who pioneered the surreal-ist wave to come.

As a major trend-spotter of the decade, Schiaparelli could discern the possibilities the dream merchants with their colorful fantasies might contribute to haute couture. In Paris she soon came to know Cocteau, part-time surrealist filmmaker (with Bunuel) and full-time

JEAN · COCTEAU

Schiaparelli
A grey linen dress embroidered
with Cocteau's design—hair golden,
lips pink, eyes peacock blue,
and a blue Cellophane hand-
kerchief.

Chanel
White marocain tumbling with
black paillettes, a black ribbon
belt and a mad coiffure concocted of ribbon, feathers and
a pailletted veil.

Jean Cocteau : toilette du soir de Schiaparelli, 1937 : © Harper's Bazaar, Londres.
Surrealism in fashion: Jean Cocteau's designs for Schiaparelli and Chanel.

poet and painter, as well as Proustian butterfly of society, flitting from Coco's indulgent patronage into Schiap's occasional employ without unduly ruffling the feathers of either. "[Schiaparelli's] establishment in the place Vendôme is a devil's laboratory," declared Cocteau. "Women who go there fall into a trap, and come out masked."

Or a little mad. Art Déco sweaters were perhaps a season's caprice, but even more capricious was Schiaparelli's "Mad Cap," a stocking cap that could be flattened into a beret, shaped as a sausage-skin of a chignon, become a surreal elfin bonnet, or what you will. Ridiculous, thought Chanel, but it was also cause for competitive concern because the Mad Cap was taken up by socialites Daisy Fellowes (French, despite her English name, daughter of the duc Decazes) and by Nancy

Cocteau at his sketchpad.

Elsa Schiaparelli in 1936.

Cunard (of the British steamship line dynasty), clients Chanel herself catered to. Taste in millinery was as ephemeral as any other, but this latest *folie* as part of the contest for clientele drew attention away from Chanel's traditional sober tone and indicated a change of direction toward the whimsical Schiap.

It was inevitable that Salvador Dalí would be drawn to Schiaparelli, a defection from Chanel, to feed and elaborate on Schiap's innovative ideas. In fashion design the clown prince of surrealism found an outlet for his piquant playfulness (and money, always a consideration with Dalí) plus the occasion to *"épater les bourgeois,"* another essential consideration.

Not even André Breton, dictatorial high priest of surrealism, could dissuade Dalí from his irrepressible hijinks in the fashion world: he was beyond the discipline of hard-line surrealist orthodoxy, but his eye-catching monkeyshines appealed to Schiap in her more mischievous seasonal collections.

When film star Mae West made a brief visit to Paris, Schiap, with Dalí's collaboration, adapted the sex symbol's bosomy curves to the perfume bottle for a Schiaparelli scent she called *Shocking. Schocking,* in fact, became the leitmotif of the Schiaparelli establishment from that time on. To promote her "Shocking Pink" Dalí created a stuffed bear as a display mannequin, its fur pink, its abdomen implanted with drawers. The mannequin inspired a dress with trompe l'oeil drawers for pockets, complete with bone handles attached.

By the mid-1930s the telephone had become a commonplace convenience, but phone service was erratic and the instrument a possible danger. One subscriber picked up the receiver during a thunderstorm and was shocked insensible, then sued the PTT with considerable fanfare. Schiaparelli took advantage of the ensuing publicity to launch a "shocking" handbag Dalí designed in the shape of a telephone.

RUNNING A FASHION SALON took the skill of a military general; securing the assurance of a faithful following demanded the diplomacy of a minister of state. Aristocrats, arrivistes, and celebrities were the true walking-mannequins of any salon, as both rival couturières were well aware, and needed to be subtly cultivated less for their trade than their publicity value. Trailing behind the gown on display was the prestige of name recognition for model and modiste alike.

Advertisement for the Schiaparelli scent *Shocking*.

The socialite of the moment was Mrs. Wallis Simpson, of Baltimore (and China, where her first marriage took place), now of London and Paris, cast in the public spotlight because of a romance with his royal highness the Prince of Wales. The prince was destined to become king on the death of his father, so the courtship of Wallis and Edward

IMAGES DE CHAQUE HEURE

MADAME J.-M. SERT : tailleur flanelle grise, sweater et feutre marine, manteau de vison.
Pour la ville : tailleur lainage noir, sweater et calotte noir, collier hindou du soir.
Pour le cocktail : tailleur en satin ciré, blouse lingerie, calotte parsemée d'étoiles.
Pour le dîner : robe de crêpe noir ornée d'une fleur-bijou et d'un bracelet en corail.
Pour le soir : robe en paillettes bleu électrique sur tulle noir. Le tout de Chanel.
MADAME R. ESNAULT-PELTERIE : tailleur en tweed noir, Schiaparelli. Feutre de Talbot.
Robe de Lanvin en crêpe noir, collerette gaufrée en chevreau argent. Breton de Talbot.
Pour la ville, manteau en lainage noir de Lanvin, large col en renards argentés.
Pour le soir, paletot de Lanvin fait de bandes de renards argentés, têtes appliquées.
Robe du soir de Lanvin, en crêpe violet, ceinture en crêpe blanc, dos entièrement nu.

proceeded from castle to castle in England and France (more openly in Paris, at Bricktop's and other *boîtes de nuit* where stylish Wallis loved to dance and display her latest garment) and took on the aura of fairy tale. Evidently the prince was greatly smitten by his American mistress, and the glass slipper appeared to fit her slender foot.

The villains of the story would not permit a happy ending to the affair. When it seemed Mrs. Simpson might indeed be destined to become Edward's wife, the Archbishop of Canterbury (supported by the prime minister and his cabinet) resisted the nightmare of this parvenu "clothes-horse" American (and twice divorced) seated on the throne beside their king.

Meanwhile, in Paris if not in London, Wallis Simpson, ever conscious of appearance, set all the fashion designers into competition for her custom. It would seem that Schiaparelli had the edge when Dalí created the most outré garment of the season for her salon: an evening gown of orange-parboiled lobsters crawling along its length. Only fashion-plate Wallis could wear the gown, and she did.

The next move on the part of a Chanel or Schiaparelli would be the final triumph, to design the future queen's wedding trousseau.

Designs by Coco Chanel featured in *Vogue*, December 1936.

Schiaparelli's beach robe, on the cover of *Vogue*, July 1938.

12

THE WOMAN WHO WOULD BE QUEEN

*O*N THAT FOG-shrouded evening in December 1936 outside the wrought-iron gate to Fort Belvedere, the troubled king kissed his mistress farewell. She must, he insisted, wait for him; he would follow her "to the ends of the earth"—though he need but travel to the French Riviera, her destination. Her escort, the baron Peregrine "Perry" Brownlow, helped his distraught and tearful passenger into the backseat of the king's Buick where she crouched on the floor and Brownlow covered her with a sable car rug to disguise the woman as an inanimate mound of luggage. Her actual luggage, sixteen trunks and thirty-six suitcases, was already en route for Cannes in the charge of her personal maid. The king then withdrew into the mist surrounding Fort Belvedere while "Mrs. Harris" sped away from the love nest. The king disappeared behind the wrought-iron gate that offered only symbolic privacy to the affair—all of England, though newspaper silence prevailed, was party to the romance of the century. It was "the greatest news story since the Resurrection" according to Henry L. Mencken, the American journalist who need not abide by the gag order imposed on the British press.

"Mrs. Harris" was Wallis Warfield Simpson, the king's mistress, an American divorcée blatantly displayed in public—albeit in Paris, and on the French Riviera—to the dismay of the royal family. That the king should take a mistress was a monarch's prerogative, a traditionally acceptable *droit de seigneur,* and as Prince of Wales Edward had enjoyed the favors of more than one, practically a requisite exercise in evidence of the virility of an heir apparent. Even so, Edward's comportment as a lover had been belittled by two preceding mistresses, though their reports may have shown an expected bitterness at having been thrown over for an American commoner. As a mistress, yes—but that he intended to *marry* the "quite unlovely" parvenu (a woman who was seeking a *second* divorce) was unprecedented scandal.

Fort Belvedere, the English residence of the Duke of Windsor in 1936.

At the recent death of his father, George V, Edward VIII ascended to the throne by proclamation. His wife, should he marry (and marriage was expected of him), would then become queen. The formal coronation ceremony had yet to be enacted, and the monarch was adamant that he would not be crowned king without his beloved at his side, his wife to be, Wallis Simpson, whom he could not marry until her divorce became final six months hence.

The couple could not be married in the Church. The state and Church of England were inextricably one, and adamant if he should marry Mrs. Simpson he must renounce the throne. At this stage of impasse, the loving couple (though Wallis appeared to be less in love with the king than with the crown) had taken on two powerful enemies: the Archbishop of Canterbury and the prime minister, Stanley Baldwin.

The woman who would be queen had to be hustled out of England for more cause than her embarrassment to church and state—her life was believed to be in danger. The two press lords, Beaverbrook and Rothemere, had agreed to suppress news of the royal scandal out of loyalty to the crown, but the American and French press were not party to this agreement and were naturally eager for every scrap of tantalizing news.

Beaverbrook joined a government conspiracy to lure Wallis out of the country by assigning one of his reporters to leak news of a plan "out of Amsterdam" to assassinate Mrs. Simpson—or to throw vitriol into her face so that she would be scarred for life. The king took the report seriously, as did Wallis: both believed she would be safer in France. The French police had been alerted, and to insure her safety, the king had assigned Inspector Evans of Scotland Yard to accompany "Mr. and Mrs. Harris" across the channel and then to Paris.

IN THE FOUL weather on the French side of the channel the car windows were rolled up against windblown sleet and snow, but Brownlow's broken hip flask leaked scotch whiskey fumes into the car, sickening Wallis, who was trying to breathe from beneath her ermine rug. The windows had to be opened for ventilation, snow blowing into the car, but Wallis was still gagging on the fumes. In a small coastal town they spent the night at a Hôtel de la Poste. According to Brownlow, Wallis was tearful to the point of hysteria and asked him to sleep on the extra bed in her room, though neither Wallis nor her escort was able to sleep.

By the time the fugitives took breakfast at the Hôtel de Paris in Moulins, they decided to abandon the plan to spend time in Paris, Wallis to be cosseted by octogenarian friend Lady Mendl (Elsie de Wolfe) of the English-speaking social set of Paris, famous for her "scintillating" soirées at Versailles, along with her stunt at eighty years of age of standing on her head. Chez Lady Mendl, Wallis Simpson was modishly garbed and lavishly bejeweled in love tokens given her by the king—*not* the Alexandra emeralds, rumored to have been expropriated by Edward for Wallis's adornment (they were baubles from the national trust and were not the king's to give). She would stay at the Meurice on the rue de Rivoli, Wallis's favorite hotel in Paris, where the putative queen was catered to as Her Royal Highness she seemed destined to become.

Alas, the Buick had been spotted at the ferry slip (its British license plate inadvertently spelled out an obscenity in French) and now newshounds were on the scent, baying in pursuit not far behind. The Meurice would surely be besieged, so Paris was ruled out. The wary fugitives bypassed the capital and headed south to Lyon through more wretched weather, Wallis miserable in the backseat enshrouded in her folds of sable, tearful again; whether from separation from her lover or having abandoned a triumphant return to Paris, Brownlow could not say. (There was the persistent question of whether Wallis was merely using Edward as an ingenious means of acquiring the highest social position to which she could aspire.)

Not just the Meurice, and the Lady Mendl set, were bitterly cancelled but also clothes-conscious Wallis would miss the occasion to replenish her wardrobe in the place Vendôme. Hard-faced and unattractive, Wallis was blessed with that social attribute so valued in a woman who craved notice: she knew how to dress, giving the appearance, if not the substance, of wealth. She was endowed with a slender if angular figure that adapted admirably to modish apparel. Instinctively she donned what most flattered her figure and perfectly conformed to the occasion. To ameliorate her somewhat horsy features, there were the latest Helena Rubinstein cosmetics (one "secret" formula: a hare's foot dipped in terracotta powder as an antidote to the overpopular rice powder that cast so many socialites into bland phantom presences) and a red and mauve shading at the corners of the nostrils that effectively redefined a too-large nose. Lady Mendl had coached her in certain social graces such as lowering the tone of her naturally strident voice to a soothing drawl of her Baltimore background. Allow men to talk about themselves was one of a woman's ten social commandments. Wallis possessed the chic and drive to make herself almost beautiful—and to compensate for superficial deficiencies with a calculated southern charm.

En route Wallis learned of the general strike that had closed down the Paris fashion houses as well as every other enterprise in the city, so that her scheduled shopping spree would have given scarce satisfaction and she could adopt a fox-and-grapes attitude toward the canceled opportunity to linger in Paris. (The general strike took place during the Léon Blum administration, a time of the Popular Front, which had brought about large social change advantageous to the French working class, but the alliance of political parties Blum had so skillfully brought together fell apart following the *grève générale*.)

Wallis would have discovered an unfamiliar Paris where workers danced in the streets, a reprehensible spectacle to her friend Coco Chanel, appalled that the House of Chanel would have pickets pacing in front of her shop windows on the rue Cambon. Chanel was particularly galled that her rival Schiaparelli's establishment had been spared. "L'Italienne" was known to be on warm and friendly terms with her staff, while "Mademoiselle" Chanel had the reputation of making high-handed demands. Chanel was no less demanding on herself in the course of that frenetic business, but this quality scored no appreciation from seamstresses, models, and *premières mains* (first assistants) determined to strike.

In England the Right was in power, but Edward VIII attempted a show of liberal concern to parallel events taking place in France. The Depression was widespread in England, no area more desperately affected than the mining villages of Wales where the king made an inspection tour. The tour was perhaps a sincere expression of concern, but the result of this gesture was a feckless and ineffectual statement by the king: "Something," he said, "must be done."

IN THE RISE of the extreme Right in England, a highlight was the legion of Blackshirts led by fascist Sir Oswald Mosley (close friend to both the king and Wallis Simpson), suggesting the same sharp confrontation between Left and Right so destabilizing to Britain's Republican ally across the channel.

Another reason for her enemies to want Wallis Simpson out of England during this decade of political threat from within and without the kingdom was Wallis's flagrant cultivation of both Italian and German sympathizers (who may have been enemy agents) and her suspect relationship with Joachim von Ribbontrop, Hitler's devious and manipulative foreign minister. From the time of the king's first sign of interest in the American divorcée, the British foreign office had placed her under surveillance and directed SIS (Secret Intelligence Service) to investigate her background and associates. It was feared his mistress wielded a pernicious political influence over the king.

As the British constitution stipulated, the monarch had (in principle) little power to effect foreign policy, but in public posture the monarch represented symbolic potential that might prove damaging to the state. Already his rightist sentiments were known to the British Union of Fascists, and his friendship with their leader, Mosley, earned for the king a salute whenever his Buick passed a group of uniformed Fascists. The king's ardent relationship with a woman who was a friend to fascism was welcomed and supported by the empire's most dangerous element.

Wallis's influence was overestimated in respect to the king's tilt to the Right. As the foreign office was surely aware, Edward VIII had been pro-German all along, loyal to his Hohenzollern royal bloodline (and just as fiercely hostile to the Bolsheviks who had murdered his father's cousin Tsar Nicolas, of the same royal line), his esteemed German antecedents. He approved Hitler's regime altogether, naively believing the Führer wished for a rapprochement of the two royal houses and an alliance of the two peoples in the face of their common enemy, Soviet Russia.

Routinely, important foreign office documents were passed to the king for his scrutiny and review; several of these secret documents escaped the king's "black box" and turned up, according to British Intelligence, at the German foreign office in Berlin. With her "access" to Edward, Wallis Simpson was believed to be the source of the leak. There was no proof of this, nor any likelihood that Wallis would be involved in so serious a security breach or in outright espionage; still the surveillance of the king's mistress was intensified and investigation of suspect associates extended to include her Baltimore background and especially her sojourn in China where she lived with her first husband, naval officer Win Spencer.

Her "file" would have had to reveal her illegitimate birth in Baltimore in the cavalier fashion such invasions of privacy take. Word passed around the anti-Wallis crowd was that "her disgraced mother took in boarders." The most damaging revelations came out of the China residency. Since Hong Kong, where the Spencers Win and Wallis lived before their divorce, was a Crown Colony, records and rumors were handily available to SIS and any other inquiries in the incestuous club atmosphere of a colonial enclave. Indeed, Wallis did have an affair with the Italian vice consul, which took an unfortunate turn when Wallis became pregnant and to avoid the scandal of an illegitimate birth was obliged to abort. The operation rendered her sterile, so that if the king's mistress should be crowned queen there could be no royal progeny, thus no heir to the throne.

What was of more importance to SIS was that Wallis Spencer's partner in the adultery was Count Galeazzo Ciano, notorious fascist leader and suspected assassin of Matteotti. Ciano was now the Italian foreign minister and Mussolini's son-in-law.

THE UNCERTAIN TELEPHONE service in France, especially in the small villages the fleeing car passed through, was a nagging frustration to the distraught Wallis until Brownlow badgered one village PTT, after hours (*"pas possible!"*), to put through a call to the king's residence, Fort Belvedere, so that the lovers could exchange endearments, and Wallis assure the king she was safe (if miserable without her "little man"), and apparently to have outdistanced the newsmen in pursuit. She then placed an unwise call to Madame Point, patronne of the celebrated Restaurant de la Pyramide in Vienne. She should have known (and perhaps did know) that her stopover at that famous gourmet establishment would draw reporters, sure to be tipped off by Madame or one of her employees.

But Wallis was not to be deprived of a three-star restorative repast en route. Madame admitted the fugitive band by the back door and escorted them to a private room on the first floor. She then made herself available to the reporters beginning to assemble downstairs.

In the course of this sojourn at la Pyramide, Wallis did agree to an interview with Jean Bouvard of *Paris Soir*. In her school French she complained of mind-numbing fatigue, saying, "*Je ne rien à dire*—I have nothing to say . . . except that I wish to be left *tranquille*."

While Wallis and her escorts devoured their meal in private, Madame Point took the reporters aside and over apéritives announced excitedly her news in lieu of the scoop *les anglais* upstairs had failed to provide: the patronne of la Pyramide had decided to change the name of her famous restaurant to the even more famous "Mrs. Simpson's."

PLAYING THE HONEST broker back in London, Winston Churchill attempted to mediate between Edward VIII and Prime Minister Baldwin. By his loyal support of the king (and friendly backing of Wallis Simpson, whom he knew socially) Churchill delayed his own election as prime minister for many months. But Churchill's friend Edward was determined to end the crisis by renouncing the throne "for the woman I love." The policy of wait-and-see was no longer at issue. Baldwin was prepared for the desperate measure of abdication as the only solution. Churchill proposed a morganatic marriage. But the Archbishop of Canterbury opposed any compromise liaison between the king (Defender of the Faith) and a divorced woman.

During an emergency cabinet meeting, crowds gathered outside 10 Downing Street, despite the heavy December downpour, shouting, "Edward's right! Baldwin's wrong!—We want Edward!" Another crowd outside Buckingham Palace was singing "For he's a jolly good fellow" and shouting: "We want Eddie and we want his Missus!" Mosley's Blackshirts were out in force in support of the king, opposed by riot squads of London police.

When next she was able to get through by phone to Fort Belvedere Wallis spoke in code so as not to be overheard: "On no account is Mr. James to step down." "Mr. James," of course, was Edward VIII. Wallis then bravely offered to give him up, renounce their love, and disappear from his life.

Again, Edward swore to track her down "to the ends of the earth" to be with her. In any case, the abdication order was in hand:

"I, Edward VIII, of Great Britain, Ireland, and the British Dominions beyond the Seas, King, Emperor of India, do hereby declare My irrevocable determination to renounce the Throne for Myself and for My descendants, and My desire that effect should be given to this Instrument of Abdication immediately."

The Windsors being greeted by Adolph Hitler.

Only the matter of future financial arrangements had yet to be concluded. And the king, after abdication must never (Baldwin's stipulation) return to England unless granted permission by the government.

162 MONSIEUR POINT LED Wallis and her English escorts through la
Pyramide's kitchen under a panoply of copper-bottomed casseroles to a
scullery at the rear of the restaurant. The single window was just large
enough for Wallis to squeeze through and escape unnoticed, which evasion she performed with the help of Brownlow who hoisted her to the
edge of a deep sink below the window, Monsieur Point and Inspector
Evans waiting to catch her as she squirmed through the window and
leapt into their arms. Madame Point poured another round of apéritives
to hold the company of news reporters at bay.

The driving snow had turned to sleet as the royal Buick plowed south-
ward, Wallis pale and stoic seated upright in the backseat. By the time
they reached Cannes the weather had cleared completely to make way
for the fabled azure sky over the Mediterranean, and Wallis's spirits took
an upward and hopeful shift, a cerulean mood to match the setting. She
had reached the tranquil sanctuary offered by her most considerate and
supportive of old friends from the China days, Herman and Katherine
Rogers, at their luxurious estate Lou Viei ("The Old Place" in Provençal).

At Lou Viei the car had to inch its way through the crowds gathered
in front of the gate in the exclusive hillside suburb of la Californie.
Wallis had landed in her element of the rich and famous (Picasso had
a house and studio nearby) far from the ongoing melodrama taking
place in London—though the crowd of reporters and sightseers had
come for a chapter in that very fascinating serial now set in France, the
crowd a reminder that she was the celebrated, or notorious, heroine of
the world's foremost saga of the moment.

Well, there *had* been talk of a morganatic marriage. As a commoner
she could not be included on the Civil List for personal income; any
children (and Wallis knew there could be none) were excluded from
royal privilege, nor could they inherit the throne itself. She could
assume the title of duchess, but the honorific Royal Majesty was denied
her . . . though Edward would see to that, or she would see to Edward
to see to that.

A morganatic marriage would represent at the least a partial triumph
over her odious oppressors.

What Wallis did not know was that the haggling over the king's income had been resolved—a yearly stipend of twenty-five thousand pounds sterling worth closer to half a million current dollars—and the draconian stipulation of permanent exile agreed to. Edward's haunted aspect dissolved at the very moment of signing, his eyes (the saddest eyes in the world) verily sparkled. The burden of constant crisis had been lifted with his signature; he said that he felt like "a swimmer surfacing from a great depth."

The former king (his brother, the Duke of York, replaced him) then met with Winston Churchill for last-minute editing of the abdication speech. The speech was a noble and generous expression of regret and undiminished love of country. Churchill was near tears.

Before the dénouement of the crisis could be broadcast, some five hundred uniformed Blackshirts clamored outside Buckingham Palace: "Sack Baldwin! Long Live the King! Long Live Bessie Warfield!"

UNDER SIEGE AT Lou Viei, Wallis listened—"quietly," she said, "grief-stricken"—to the moving address to his nation her "little man" made in farewell. It was the most attended radio broadcast of the decade. "Yet while I think I did the right thing, the only thing, I was to realize all too soon the minute I put my foot inside France, I had ceased to exist . . ."

Sojourning in one smart set or the next had come to an end. She would perfect her French, find a house in Paris (and another on the Riviera) for Lady Mendl to decorate; she would be the leading socialite of an international salon, a tragic figure with her chin thrust forward, Wallis Simpson intended to shed no tears (in public). When Edward gave up the throne for her, Wallis came to love him a little, and at last.

WHILE WALLIS SIMPSON may have "ceased to exist" in England, and as Duchess of Windsor forbidden to touch its shores ever again without permission of the state, in Paris she was still the heroine of the era's foremost romance and the sought-after celebrity who would cast her favored couturière into a shared spotlight with her wedding in France. Both Chanel and Schiaparelli had cultivated her as client in turn—but so had Vionnet and Molyneux received her custom. Who then among the prestigious designers was to create the duchess's trousseau? Paris society held its collective breath.

The choice went neither to Chanel nor to Schiaparelli, but to a couturier from the American Midwest who had suddenly stirred excitement among the knowing of French haute couture. Mainbocher had combined his first name, which meant "hand" in French, with his Germanic surname, and it was Mainbocher who received the nod from the woman who would be queen.

13

PLACE VENDÔME—II

*I*T HAD BEGUN as a nun's cloister given over to the devotions if not the prayers of womankind. Patrons attracted to the place Vendôme as a bazaar of opulent acquisition were predominantly women, accompanied or not by escorts willing to pay for these expensive splendors and wanting to calculate the measure of expenditure in dress, scent, and feminine adornment, to calculate the depth of affection his *placement* had purchased. This was especially true of transactions with Chaumet, Cartier, Van Cleef, and Arpels in the selection of precious stones and their settings. (The place Vendôme itself was like an octagonal gem set between its two strands, the access streets of the rue de la Paix and equally chic rue de Castiglione.) There was a degree of male pride involved in such investment, and a reflection of social status according to the hierarchy of the day.

Placements in the place Vendôme went beyond the purchase of dress and accessories for women; behind the austere façades by Hardouin-Mansart there did exist a man's world as well (and not just the male boutique, Charvet, for men's tailored shirts and silk cravats). One discreet retreat was the tastefully palatial salon at 8 place Vendôme where Joseph Duveen had seemingly collected a miniature Louvre of classic artwork. Here he received his "squillionaires" to show his Renaissance masterworks with the apparent pride of ownership. Actually he represented the original owners, and the paintings were "on offer," as was the antique Venetian loveseat the squillionaire sat in.

On one casual visit by J. P. Morgan, Duveen earned a commission of $750,000 on bibelots alone. When the banker James Stillman visited Duveen he came in the company of Mary Cassatt, the painter. If he hesitated before a purchase Mary Cassatt would insist: "Buy it! It's shameful to be rich like you." (Stillman was the most hated financier on Wall Street.) "Such a purchase will redeem you."

Duveen attempted to "redeem" another shamefully rich entrepreneur (and neighbor, on the *place*) in collecting the paintings he had for sale, but Ivar Kreuger took no interest in trophy art, only in collecting companies and old wines, and respectfully declined.

AT A *SOCIÉTÉ ANONYME* over digestifs of Armanac and Courvoisier, the air perfumed with the aroma of prime Havanas rather than misted by atomized Coty or Guerlain, men spoke in lowered yet confident modulation of French, Swiss, and Belgian francs, of English pounds and German marks, and most assuredly of dollars. Yes, the stock market debacle of '29 was a black memory for some, but Old Money had survived and important lessons learned. Despite the onset of the European Depression, slowly taking a stranglehold on the economy, there were still golden opportunities in the 1930s to be exploited—hadn't this Swedish investor shown it to be so?

The names of these private *sociétés* for banking and investment might appear on the polished brass plaques beside the formidable eighteenth-century portals, or announced circumspectly against a stone lintel beneath the establishment's canopy: the name, followed by the code letters "Ltd" and "Inc," or their French equivalents "NA" and "SA." Public recognition of legitimacy was thus accommodated in the announcement that the Rothschilds, Morgan-Hartjes, Westminster

Foreign Bank, and the Société Foncière (de la place Vendôme) were resident business at these ornate premises.

The general public might be invited to enter the marble lobbies of the larger establishments, and to pass legal tender through the bars of cashiers' cages, but formal admission to inner chambers where common banknotes were nowhere present was by invitation only, dependent on reputation and assurance of *gros revenus* beyond the fiscal means of everyday depositors. (A financier like Stavisky could not have got past the lobby, his oily confidence-man's countenance alone proof of questionable credentials. The name Stavisky eventually trailed such malodorous fumes that President Lebrun refused to bestow the *Légion d'Honneur* on composer Igor Stravinsky for fear the public would confuse the names and believe he was honoring slain Stavisky.) Stavisky's only entrée into the *beau quartier* of the place Vendôme was by way of marriage to one of Chanel's loveliest models, Arlette Simon.

One exceptional investor who penetrated the secretive financial circles of the place Vendôme was a Swedish entrepreneur named Ivar Kreuger who had the foresight to purchase a town house on the *place* where he would be in close contact with the Parisian financiers who operated essentially out of sight. Kreuger had built a formidable edifice of investment virtually of matchsticks, having begun with two small match factories in Sweden, then by shrewd licensing and contractual guarantee created monopolies approved by heads of state for the control of match sales worldwide. Kreuger's speculations were many and soon escaped the rectangular confines of a matchbox, every investment lucrative to the extreme. He seemed to have built an investment empire impervious to cyclical downturn, steady in every stock market upheaval, barely nicked by a financial cut during such catastrophes as the Wall Street Crash of 1929.

The house of Kreuger was primarily concerned with the humble kitchen match—which may have been the centerpiece in his success. The intrepid Swede had veritably cornered the market in that most unglamorous but vital household product. He was called the Match King and took no offense at that derisive title.

WITH FRANK BLUE-EYED candor, exquisite manners, and soft-spoken charm, Ivar Kreuger was a convincing mogul. He had taken into account the truth that most civilized virtues tended to be polish and veneer only, covering what was most essential in "society": the acquisition of wealth and, eventually, the achievement of power. He had done so, by respecting and abiding by the manners and rituals of the monied set.

His International Match Company (IMCO) was underwritten by the investment banking firm of Lee, Higginson, Inc., prestigious Wall Street underwriters of such monoliths as AT&T, General Motors, and General Electric.

During the frenzy of stock speculation in New York of the late 1920s, Wall Street and Ivar Kreuger enjoyed mutual opportunity to form alliances that would evolve into a construct of nearly four hundred interlocking enterprises directed by Kreuger, though the wily Swede might hold no more than one percent of controlling stock, and others— the Dutch company Garanta, or the Spanish match monopoly he was said to have signed with Primo de Rivera—existed merely in the Match King's imagination but could be exploited as genuine collateral for further pyramiding of IMCO.

What convinced bankers to underwrite Kreuger enterprises and heads of state to accept massive loans in return for granting monopolies to his match-making was the understated style and personality of Kreuger himself, his extraordinary financial intelligence, his poise and polish. The successful march of Kreuger's "little wooden soldiers" was too tempting an example to be ignored—such success, bankers and brokers believed, must beget success. Even after the Crash of 1929 when gloom descended on Wall Street, Kreuger's holdings and securities remained stable, and the loans he was capable of making were at rates lower than his competitors could believe profitable. As the Depression spread to Europe by 1932, draining liquidity in a desert of despair, Kreuger appeared to conjure cash out of the very air. The brilliant Swedish entrepreneur was considered a genius ("maybe") by the leading economist John Maynard Keynes, and Jean Monnet, father of the European Common Market, would cautiously concur.

While Kreuger thrived on the dynamics of Wall Street, he felt at home in Paris (as much as any city where he was heavily invested could be considered "home"), most clearly for his having fallen for the charms and allure of Frenchwomen. His mistresses in Paris were many, and in *la ronde* of ever-changing partners he never entered into a contract of marriage, preferring, as he explained with a pun, "a Swedish match."

To enhance his prospects for financial advantage and feminine conquests in Paris, Kreuger purchased the *maison particulier* at 7 place Vendôme, with headquarters for IMCO at street level; high above he renovated a twenty-room *garconnière* (bachelor's quarters). Forever fascinated by the character and daring of Napoléon Bonaparte—another overreacher like himself—Kreuger had a balcony constructed on the top floor overlooking the place Vendôme at the same lofty eminence as his hero atop the Vendôme column. Alternating mistresses had the advantage of the deluxe shopping center their openhanded lover had chosen as sanctuary (Kreuger was princely in his disbursement of largesse), along with discreet access by the cagelike hydraulic lift to transport them to after-hours rendezvous.

Would his women have been dismayed or amused to know of the notebook Kreuger kept with dossiers on each of them, their physical attributes and performance, graded A, B, or C?

Actually the little black book of sexual memoranda was the only written record-keeping Kreuger permitted himself. His memory for figures was legendary, though he sometimes toyed with a souvenir abacus for the amusement of a colleague or current girlfriend, pretending "to calculate my millions on it," though he needed no such device to calculate the millions in assets, real and phantom, or their disposition filed away in the vault of his brain. There he kept a running inventory of comparative rates of interest, shifting dividends due, and future earnings anticipated, locked in that same vault.

Secretive to the point of obsession concerning the jigsaw puzzle of merger and monopoly in an early system of arbitrage, Kreuger was careful to drink moderately (though he had a weakness for fine wine, and bought out the whole of Paillard's wine cellar to stock his own *cave* at 7 place Vendôme) since he feared to be talkative and indiscreet from the effect of drink. Voluble he could be, and was known to recite an infinite list of statistics over lunch at Maxim's, and who could resist joining a consortium directed by a man who could quote French tax receipts, German reparations payments, the Hungarian national debt, the Italian gross national product to the last lira from 1919 to 1930? (One of his favorite tactics was to memorize these statistics prior to a business luncheon, then adroitly stage-manage the conversation to include his subject of present expertise.)

The bankers and financiers of the place Vendôme were a breed far more conservative than their Wall Street counterparts, ready to turn bearish at the first scent of weakness, quick to sell short at an initial crack in the façade. But even these fiscal conservatives with endemic French suspicion of foreigners, subscribed—with Keynes's cautious "maybe" in mind—to the soft-spoken proposals of the man they called *l'Oiseleur*, the bird charmer.

One important holdout in the universal admiration society was Kreuger's American rival, J. Pierpont Morgan, who declined to come aboard the overloaded Kreuger investment vessel, which could well have been called the SS *Opportunity*. Morgan was immune to the persuasiveness of mere words. Acquisitive in other ways than the accumulation of wealth, he was an avid collector of objets d'art while Kreuger collected nothing but monopolies (and women for his transient pleasure rather than possession). When approached by art dealers on the place Vendôme, Kreuger protested that he already had two passions, his "little wooden soldiers" and wine—a third would be devastating. Meanwhile Morgan sought out such substantive offerings as the Titian on Duveen's wall, priced and authenticated by Bernard Berenson, in preference to Kreuger debentures backed by "poetic" balance sheets of a warbling bird charmer.

Morgan's personal antipathy to the Match King was due more to competitive pique than innate distrust. Along with the majority of the investment banking clique and international dons of economics, Morgan was convinced that Kreuger was indeed a financial titan of superior trading instinct and an adversary to beware of, but worthy of respect. What galled Morgan was that Kreuger had direct and private access to Premier Poincaré and had tendered a massive loan to France at five percent interest, effectively canceling Morgan's own prior state loan at eight percent since the government could now repay Morgan and associates from the seventy-five million dollars Kreuger offered, denying the Morgan combine millions in anticipated interest payments.

And Kreuger had accomplished this *coup de main* alone.

Since the loan included the usual proviso of a state match monopoly granted to IMCO—which Poincaré, in his eagerness for the dollars, agreed to—the proposition was opposed by the Socialist and Communist parties and was finally defeated in the House, a startling setback for one of the world's foremost capitalists. The Leftist opposition leader could declare a victory: "The Napoléon of Matches has met his Waterloo in our finance committee [of the Chambre des Deputés]."

Waterloo, not at all. It was a defeat that set the French bears, the most conservative and suspicious of Kreuger investors, to sell short, increasing IMCO's liquidity crisis. But the Napoléon of Matches was as daring and resilient as his namesake atop the Vendôme column, and Kreuger subsequently launched an even greater campaign. In 1931, despite worldwide cash flow having slowed to a trickle (or because of this), Kreuger audaciously proposed a merger of his Swedish telephone company, L. M. Ericsson, with the American Goliath I.T.T. in the first maneuver to create a transatlantic communications monopoly. Actually Kreuger was in desperate need of the eleven million dollars tendered by I.T.T. as part of the stock transfer. Interest payments would come due on July 1 for bonds issued by IMCO and other Kreuger enterprises, and the Match King had to dispel the growing cloud of suspicion with a dramatic show of solvency.

But the French bears continued to sell short, and even Kreuger's own accountants began to question the director's persistent secrecy concerning accounts, heretofore considered an essential modus operandi of his investment strategy.

The Ericsson-I.T.T. merger involved Kreuger's reliable underwriters, Lee, Higginson, Inc., who were fast losing faith in their most favored client; issues connected to IMCO and subsidiaries continued their fall on the stock exchange, a rare reversal for Kreuger securities. Lee, Higginson was calling in the auditing firm of Price, Waterhouse to examine IMCO's books.

The rumors rocketing down the Wall Street canyon did of course come to the attention of J. P. Morgan, who sat on the board of I.T.T. and now expressed doubts about the merger with Ericsson without an immediate show of cards. In the poker game of high finance, Kreuger was effectively being "called." Did the Match King hold high cards this time or not?

The essential tactic was to bluff; Kreuger had played that game before, and won. It was the only way to forestall an audit, for actually Kreuger was holding a hand of marked cards. His position was unassailable, he declared, offering low-keyed assurances of an ace in the hole in the way of operational funds and extraordinary collateral. He bore himself with habitual dignity and calm, but when challenged by his own accountants he became uncharacteristically testy and insistent. Within his own family of funds no one dared question Kreuger's financial wizardry.

In his private vault, Kreuger had tucked away sufficient proof of capital backing in the form of Italian state bonds, acquired through personal arrangement with Mussolini himself. To satisfy his own staff, the bonds were made available in a brief display of the actual certificates. This was an impressive "hand of cards" and appeared to answer the most immediate of pressing questions.

Dated: Rome, August 15, 1930, these were forty-two certificates bearing a face value of half a million pounds sterling each, plus promissory notes worth a million and a half each, five in all, representing a total in assets of 142 million [dollars] worth of bonds and notes. This was in addition to a scheduled interest payment due from Spain from the Spanish match monopoly, 4.7 million dollars, delayed because of the current political crisis.

Spain's political crisis was real, but the Spanish match monopoly was a complete fiction. As were the Italian state bonds. The certificates from "Rome" had been lithographed by Kreuger's own firm, at his direction and following his design. The signatures of the general director of the Italian monopoly administration, Giovanni Boselli, as well as that of the minister of finance, Antonio Mosconi, were as impressive as having been signed by Mussolini himself—except that both names had been forged by Ivar Kreuger. Alone, after flashing the certificates before the eyes of his accountants to satisfy any question of solvency, Kreuger examined the bonds and notes in private. Damn. He had spelled the director general's name three different ways: Bosselli, Bosseli, and Boselli. Not that the bonds made any great difference in the final stage of Kreuger's fiscal crisis; they were only a means to stall, a last tactic before he would be obliged to show his hand.

A delegation of bankers and investors from New York were to meet with Kreuger on March 12, 1932, for a confrontation over lunch at the Hôtel du Rhin on the place Vendôme.

"I HAVE BUILT my enterprise," he once confessed to a woman he had known for two years, "on the firmest ground that can be found, the foolishness of people." Two years was quite a lengthy interval for Kreuger to have known any one woman, but he had surely taken too much wine that night or he would never have allowed that casual admission to escape his lips.

An indifferent sybarite, and certainly a careless and forgetful Don Juan, Kreuger did have an abiding need of sexual relief from an unbearable solitude of mind, especially at this time when he felt "the firmest ground" shaking and heaving beneath his feet, an inner fear he had never experienced before.

Late on the night of March 11, 1932, he telephoned the obliging (and perhaps devoted) Finnish beauty he had known since 1930—who, having lasted so long in his favor, surely rated the highest citation in his notebook of sexual mementos and deserved the seignorial summons on this night of nights. She came to him within the hour. Her dress and form-fitting bolero jacket no doubt escaped his distracted notice, and he did not likely discern which of her favorite perfumes she wore—though he had paid for both the bolero jacket and the perfume; the perfume he inhaled was the woman-scent that signaled fulfillment of tonight's needs. He greeted her with his impeccable politesse and sad uncertain smile, nothing out of the ordinary in his usual wintry demeanor. As he led her from the hydraulic cage he lightly kissed her on the wrist—because of a morbid fear of germs he never kissed a woman's hand (though his concern did not extend to sexual contact)—and escorted her into his vast bachelor's lair.

Kreuger's Finnish lover, as reported by the concierge, departed his apartment on the morning of the twelfth at 8:30. This was the chill and mournful morning set aside for the *pompes funèbres* of several times French premier Aristide Briand, Nobel Prize winner for his work at international understanding (especially French rapprochment with Germany, a noble but vain effort at healing old wounds between the two perennial enemies). Kreuger would have had to cross the procession along the rue de Rivoli and at the assembly point at the place de la Concorde as mourners gathered in a cluster of black umbrellas to file along the route to Notre Dame cathedral. The gray day and sobering chill of a funeral cortège under way was a setting appropriate to Kreuger's grim errand.

At 39 avenue Victor Emmanuel III he stepped into the shop of gunsmith Gastinne-Renette where he calmly examined a small Browning automatic as if toying with his abacus while calculating sums in his head.

"Trop petit," he told the salesman, who then showed him the next larger model, which Kreuger also found to be too small. Finally he settled on a 9mm automatic along with four boxes of cartridges, one hundred shells in all. The 330-franc transaction was Kreuger's last known speculative gesture.

Due at the critical luncheon engagement at the Hôtel du Rhin on the place Vendôme, Kreuger returned instead to his own quarters. He was known for his punctilious observance of business protocol. Therefore when he failed to appear at the designated hour, his luncheon guests were at first uneasy, but perhaps, they reasoned, he had been delayed by the funeral procession for Aristide Briand. When much later that excuse seemed unlikely, uneasiness turned to alarm; they phoned Kreuger's residence. Yes, replied the concierge who answered, Monsieur had gone out briefly, but was now at home. She thought he might have taken an afternoon's *sieste* for he appeared to her unusually fatigued.

Perhaps Monsieur Kreuger had forgotten an important appointment for lunch at the Hôtel du Rhin—would she please check?

The concierge shortly returned to the phone in panic and extreme distress: Monsieur was not asleep, but dead.

Having achieved the respite of orgasm the French call *la petite mort,* the "little death," the night before, Ivar Kreuger had by noon accomplished the larger death by a single bullet from among the hundred cartridges he possessed, fired into his heart.

14

WIDENING CIRCLES

*T*HEY GOT OUT of the cab at the rue St. Denis on the edge of les Halles, the central marketplace of Paris, where they would excite no particular notice—even dressed as they were, in striking contrast to the blue *salopettes* worn by the denizens of this hive of nighttime activity. Parisians in evening attire, on slumming expeditions after the theatre or opéra, often ventured into this animated concourse Zola called "the belly of Paris" to satisfy late appetites, particularly to dine on the reputed onion soup ladled out in bistros known for this simple, hearty fare (the onions fresh perhaps from that very barrow wheeling past, the Gruyère from the giant wheel of cheese in the stall nearby).

The Guilers, Hugo and Anaïs, intended a different adventure than the gastronomic tour of les Halles, to satisfy other appetites than the *soupe à l'oignon*. Anaïs had obtained an address from Henry Miller who was a regular of les Halles at night and well knew where the Guilers might escape their haute-bourgeois scene at home "to breathe the charged and holy air of Paris." This was typical Miller territory, and of Brassaï who had scavanged for photos in these same precincts.

This was the time of night when the vast central Halles took on a hustling frenzy under the arc lights of the ancient Baltard ironwork sheds, a graceful ensemble of hangars commissioned at the turn of the century by Emperor Louis Napoléon: "What we need [for les Halles] are parasols." In the allées between stalls of fruit and vegetables were bonfires of cratewood whose flames were reflected in the red sweating visages of *les forts* who paused in their exertions only to break for a coup of marc or calvados to restore energy. Through the smell of smoke from the bonfires was an earthy scent of produce trucked up from the southern gardens of the Midi: pyramids of stacked tubers and tomatoes, garnished at intervals by crates of pale winter greens. The bonfires somewhat tempered the night chill but cast sinister shadows across their path, and Anaïs trembled slightly.

"Do you have an intuition?" she asked her husband.

"About what?" he returned in all innocence.

Ahead of them ambled what appeared to be an entire treeload of bananas, two burlesque legs showing beneath the stalks; then swiftly an aged but agile crone snatched a banana from the ambulant tree. She peeled it and was eating the phallic fruit with a toothless salacious grin as if to illustrate the suggestive question Anaïs had put to Hugo.

Her husband must surely be aware of her wild and hopeless entanglement with Henry, an affair not easily hidden (and still, the *fort* staggering on with his bananas, was deceived, quite ignorant of the theft by the aged scavenger) . . . but Hugo would *have* to have divined the very flare-up affair he himself predicted that night in Louveciennes when he warned her, "Beware of being trapped in your own imaginings."

Because of Hugo's slow perceptions—and faith in Anaïs, or devotion (or his unwillingness to believe that his own prophecy had come to pass)— he had concluded that his wife's fascination with Henry Miller was nothing more than "intellectual stimulation." However, the details of the affair, in Anaïs's graphic-romantic flair for overwrought analysis, appeared in her diary. Hugo was free to read the obsessional confession whenever he cared to (and may have done so, for surely he *knew*); he kept a journal of his own, twin to hers if far less forthright, so that in some psychological sense of equal time he might emulate the artistic narcissism of his wife.

Hugo would have joined, if he could—staid Sinclair Lewis banker that he was, three-piece business suit and conservative tie—her cabal of litterateurs living in agitated communal exchange and bohemian disorder in the rue villa Seurat. In spirit and soul Hugo Guiler was addicted to banking and aspirant to a successful and secure workaday career. The money he earned made the liberated literary life of Anaïs (and largely the parasitic existence of Henry Miller) possible. Hugo was deeply in love with his wife and her literary pursuits, believed in her profoundly, though he was (Miller believed) "a man without ecstasy . . . a boy, a boy!" Therefore Anaïs was a child too (critic Edmund Wilson called her a child-woman), and Henry, despite his gangster-author reputation, was an arrested adolescent who, for all his "experience," might never advance sexually past puberty.

In his sophomoric shy fear of rejection by Anaïs, Henry wrote her a passionate note overflowing with love for her; then, at the entrance to his hotel, he told her to read the note silently. If what he had expressed and suggested was too crude or in any way displeased her, she should turn and walk away.

"But I follow him. His room, I do not see. When he takes me in his arms my body melts. The tenderness of his hands, the unexpected penetration, to the core of me but without violence."

If Hugo believed his wife was in love with Henry's self-portrayal in *Tropic*, and Henry had fallen in love with the portrait of Anaïs in her diaries, he had guessed correctly but could not extend that insight to the lovers' discovery of each other in sexual harmony at Henry's hotel. They were no longer in love with each other's writing, but what "are we in love with now?"

Significantly, the face of June, Miller's absent wife, stared at them from a framed photograph on the mantel. Anaïs had read of Mona in *Tropic of Cancer* and heard so much about Henry's great love living in New York, she now included June as a component in the mystery of this new attachment.

IT BECAME NECESSARY, Anaïs believed, to introduce Hugo to the "ecstasy" he lacked and she could not completely inspire in him. Miller suggested to Anaïs, who suggested to Hugo (appalled), that they venture beyond the conventional boundaries of their—his, rather—middle-class sexual strictures, that they swim out past the shallows and routine strokes into an area she defined as "widening circles." Hugo took this to mean taking multiple sexual partners and was naturally repelled by the suggestion. But he would deny his wife nothing: thus the address Miller had given them and they were headed toward.

"I need two lives," Anaïs wrote in her diary. (She needed more than two, having instigated, then aborted, an affair with her homosexual cousin Eduardo.) "By giving myself [to Henry? to Eduardo?] I learn to love Hugo more."

They were now out from under the emperor's "parasols," moving away from the arc lights and frantic agitation into a darker, quieter region removed from the central market, wary of the slippery vegetable discard underfoot, traveling the meaner streets ribbed outward from the spine of rue St. Denis. Here was a shadowed hinterland to the market, where one edged through narrow wheelbarrow passages, walked between the tightly parked and tilted produce camions jammed fender to fender against the curb.

Oddly, it had been Miller who wallowed in guilt over their affair, willing enough but unhappily so, when Hugo was away on business and Anaïs proposed: "Come and be my husband for a few days." (Perhaps Miller felt more keenly the deception because he had been the victim of June's infidelities and knew the same ignoble despair the cuckold Hugo suffered.)

When either of the lovers spoke of Hugo it was invariably to recite his virtues, the large capacity for kindness, his unbounded affection for his wife, an innate sense of decency. He was generous to a fault, Henry could add, being principal beneficiary of Hugo's largesse. But where did generosity and kindness come into play in the misfire of sexual delight and absence of rapture?

Henry offered the only gift he had to give in return for Hugo's benevolence, meant as a solution of sorts to overcome dysfunction in physical ardor, a way to widen circles . . . an address.

The address had been given Miller by Brassaï, where Henry might find outré material for *Tropic of Cancer,* and was now offered to the Guilers where they might find a resolution to a dilemma in sexual intimacy.

THE WOMEN ALONG the street curbs were variations on the prostitute *Mademoiselle Claude* (Miller's first sustained and successful piece

Les Halles.

of writing), many unexpectedly attractive, some perhaps fresh-faced and fair beneath the mask of garish cosmetic, all showing an ample expanse of bosom that reminded Anaïs of her own sensation when striding through the streets of Paris destined for a rendezvous with Henry, "breasts taut and tingling." The women moved out of shadow at their approach, to display themselves as enticingly calculated as the stalls at les Halles offering a succulent assortment of fruit, but there was scarce room to solicit the sidewalks, barely space to patrol near the curb where market trucks were double-parked or commandeered the narrow ill-lit concourse.

Anaïs was reminded also (and felt strangely about the recall) of June's photograph in Henry's hotel room, and his evocation of her as Mona in *Tropic*—there was always the hint of the prostitute in Henry's references to June. But why should Anaïs's breasts, thinking of June, be "taut and tingling" now?

At the address 32 rue Blondel, Anaïs chose to enter first and negotiate *le tarif*, as she had done at the Hôtel Anjou to Miller's amazement at her brazenness, naming her own price for the room (twenty-five francs after the concierge asked thirty) and taking the key number 3 off the board herself.

To the Guilers' surprise one entered directly into a room full of nude or half-dressed women, women only, as in a *maison close*: there was no stage for the *expo cochon* they expected, with no vestibule or concierge booth as a transitional intervention. Patrons sat at ordinary bistro tables while the women circulated restlessly like moths flitting from table to table; one ordered a drink, then chose partners for one's private performance from the nude ambulant assortment.

The patronne informed the Guilers there would be no man available for the private show: they were to choose two women from the ensemble, one of whom would perform as a man. Anaïs swiftly made the choice: a Spanish type, and a small feminine "almost timid" one. "The two girls will amuse you," the patronne assured them. "You will see everything."

Without a heterosexual combination, it was not to be Hugo's night. Anaïs wanted to see lesbian poses, and the two women were prepared to oblige. In an upstairs room "softly lighted and the bed low and ample" the women chirped together with birdlike cheer and each washed the other in turn at the bidet. The big woman, the Spaniard, strapped an artificial penis around her pelvis, a rose-colored apparatus, and with the caricature penis performed sexual variations on the "timid one." The woman with the artificial penis announced each variation as she performed: standing up when one hasn't the price of a hotel room; making love in the back of a taxi, love when one partner is too drowsy to respond.

But Anaïs asks for lesbian demonstrations (Henry's June has been known to engage in such acts . . . June is often in Anaïs's thoughts this night).

The smaller woman has responded only half-heartedly to the mock heterosexual entwinings, but now shows a genuine passion in response to her partner's probing tongue, and Anaïs is aroused to an essential sensual revelation: "a secret place in the woman's body, a source of new joy, which I had sometimes sensed but never definitely—that small core at the opening of the woman's lips, just what the man passes by."

The smaller woman moaned in ecstasy, and it was evident her trembling orgasm was genuine. Hugo was in turmoil, Anaïs excited beyond all reason: "I am no longer woman," she confesses, "I am man," and then oddly recalls June again: "I am touching the core of June's being."

Anaïs became aware of Hugo's reaction, aroused although there had been no male participant in the exhibition to illustrate by proxy the banker's erotic imaginings.

Since Hugo remained tumescent, Anaïs proposed he take the small feminine woman to relieve his desire, and insisted she would not mind. Not only would she not mind, but it seemed she urgently needed to see Hugo copulate with another woman. But the room suddenly appeared "dirty" to them both, and the Guilers returned to Louveciennes to become the child-woman and the boy again, sinking into "sensuality together with new realizations"—though not resolutions. "All that we know is that the evening was beautifully carried off."

But Anaïs continued to be haunted by the photograph on Henry's mantel. June was the missing element to the night's new stirrings and widening circle.

MILLER'S FRIEND BRASSAÏ had his first glimpse of the legendary June when he saw a man and woman in violent confrontation, a clash of verbal abuse in gutter English on both sides, beneath a street lamp. It might have been a prostitute and her pimp, and Brassaï would have the advantage of their distracted combat to take one of his underground photographs. But he then recognized Miller's bald dome in the lamplight. The woman, an American, was unknown to him.

"What I saw was a neck as long as a swan's emerging from a tight black velour dress, a neck out of a Modigliani painting, supporting a wide and striking face with prominent cheekbones. Beneath green makeup, [her] eyes sparkled, and her full lips, which were very red, stood out against her pale face. I had never seen a face that pale. It was the color of coconut milk and rice powder."

15

LIAISONS DANGEREUSES

THE 1930S HAD begun the dark years for James Joyce, grown darker by the evidence of his daughter Lucia's mental decline and his own deteriorating health and eyesight. His chronic stomach pains were attributed to "nerves" by Joyce's "crazy woman doctor" (as Samuel Beckett called Dr. Fontaine, who failed to diagnose a duodenal ulcer). No doubt the intestinal complaints took second place to the more apparent and immediate concern of recurrent crisis, the eye operations performed at intervals to forestall total blindness—which they did, but barely. After one such operation, blood was discovered to have penetrated the anterior chamber of the eyeball; leeches were applied to drain the blood, but "the creatures," as Nora called them, kept falling off, so that she and an attending nurse were obliged to pluck the creatures from the floor and attach them again.

Under this cloud of general gloom Joyce's father, John Joyce, died during the Christmas season of 1931 in Dublin. The crusty old fellow had begged his favorite son to come see him one last time, but that deathbed farewell was not to be: Joyce's bitter aversion to Ireland was unforgiving; he intended never to return to the land of his birth.

John Joyce's last words were, "Tell Jim he was born at six in the morning." This cryptic message was a reply to Joyce's inquiry about the exact time of his birth, needed for working out his horoscope. His father's death further dimmed Joyce's somber outlook and placed new weight on his conscience.

Joyce had crossed the Channel earlier that year, not to honor his father's dying wish but to put his domestic affairs in order. His son Giorgio had married a wealthy American divorcée, Helen Fleischman, of the New York circle of German Jews known as "Our Crowd," and was now pregnant. (Helen was ten years older than Giorgio, and her affluence meant that Giorgio had even less necessity to pursue a career.) The prospect of a grandchild prompted Joyce to regularize his conjugal position vis-à-vis Nora.

James Joyce and Nora had lived together since fleeing Dublin in 1904; they were married, Joyce insisted, in Trieste that same year, but Nora was said to have married under the name Gretta Greene. This was not widely believed or readily proven, and in any case not legal under British law "for testamentary reasons." (Once when Nora lost her temper and flung the word "bastard" at Lucia, her daughter screamed back at her, "If I am a bastard, who made me one?" This outburst gave Joyce all the more reason to satisfy the social demand of a legally recognized matrimony.)

The Joyces hoped to complete the residence requirement and resolve the marriage question quietly in London, and to spare Lucia and Giorgio, and themselves, any publicity. (Unknown to the British press at the time, their regent Prince Edward VIII had met and was fascinated with an American woman presented at court, Wallis Simpson.) The wedding of the author, whose book *Ulysses* was banned for obscenity in England, became the story of the moment. When James and Nora Joyce emerged from the Kensington registry office, married at last, the photographers and news reporters awaited them in force.

"All London knows you're here," the bride informed her husband.

Joyce continued to insist that he had merely married his wife.

FOR LUCIA THE embarrassment of the marriage was almost as unhappy as the revelation that she was illegitimate, following as it did on the marriage of her beloved brother to an American heiress. It was she who wanted—and needed, she believed (as did her parents)—to be married. She initiated a campaign of promiscuity that began with Alfred Hubbell, an art student whose estranged wife turned up in Paris and reclaimed her husband. Another artist, Alexander Calder—originator of mobile-sculpture—was attracted to Lucia, and she to his studio at 7 villa Brune, where no doubt the childlike Lucia was fascinated by Calder's wire-sculpted circus figurines and perhaps by his ingenious system of strings and pulleys; from his bed he could open the door to her, and extinguish the light, without getting up. But in 1931 Calder met Louisa James on board ship bound for New York, returned with her to Paris where she became his assistant performing the miniature circus of wire figurines, and they married.

In her distraught innocence, Lucia became receptive to almost any amorous approach, or imagined attraction, with the desperation of the "sex starved," as she described herself.

Lucia nourished a long-term love of the Irish writer Samuel Beckett, a one-sided affection Beckett did nothing to encourage except to haunt the Joycean household on the boulevard Raspail. (Actually Beckett was one of the several young men who looked to Joyce as the centerpiece of their Parisian world, the equivalent of Gertrude Stein's entourage of Young Men, Joyce in addition being father of an attractive, if somewhat unsettling, young daughter.) Lucia would be at the door to greet Beckett, and again—after his session with her father, helping with the typescript of *Work in Progress* or taking dictation from the near-blind master—to see him out.

The romance was getting nowhere when Lucia decided to invite Beckett to a restaurant in the quarter, an intimate candlelit bistro where she was certain the shy Irishman would declare himself. Beckett was embarrassed by the invitation, knowing its purpose, but could see no way to refuse; however, he invited along a friend as a buffer companion to thwart Lucia's evident intention. Lucia retired from the café in tearful frustration. At last Sam Beckett decided to end the farce of unrequited love, and when next he appeared at the apartment door, he announced bluntly that he came to the premises only to see her father.

This rejection brought on one of Lucia's violent episodes, and so upset James Joyce and Nora that Beckett was forbidden the house, and their friendship with him was canceled as abruptly as Beckett's cruel end to (as they believed) his courtship of their daughter.

Lucia continued to succumb to any infatuation that occurred or took form in her imagination. She confessed to her father that she had been seduced by these young men (no doubt including Samuel Beckett) who came to the Joyce apartment; her father, ready to believe any fanciful tale told by his daughter, dismissed any of the young admirers Lucia accused of having seduced her.

Both parents were baffled and frustrated by circumstances: how to handle Lucia, how to help her. Often they took opposite positions on how to deal with Lucia's desperate need to acquire a man, and were driven to encourage the most unlikely liaisons, like the one with Robert McAlmon who had married the Ellerman heiress, Bryher, in a *marriage blanc* to secure Bryher's inheritance of a trust fund, followed by divorce—which subterfuge brought McAlmon a tidy income and earned for him, among Left Bank cronies, the name McAlimony. McAlmon volunteered to marry her, if it would resolve Lucia's obsession. McAlmon was homosexual, and when Nora got wind of his proposal of marriage she had the good sense to cancel the scheme forthwith.

A more serious attachment was contrived when Paul Léon (Joyce's replacement for Sylvia Beach as his "representative") convinced his young brother-in-law Alexander Ponisovsky "to do the right thing" by Lucia, after engaging in a superficial flirtation with her. Lucia would turn twenty-five in July of 1932 and was desperate to marry by that date, convinced that if she did not marry in July she would never marry.

Alexander Ponisovsky proposed on a Tuesday and was (of course) accepted. He may have regretted the prospect, but in any case Lucia broke off the engagement the following Saturday. Ponisovsky was a Jew, and Lucia now declared she hated all Jews, probably in reaction to her brother's marriage to a Jew, thus "depriving" her of Giorgio.

Joyce held nothing against Ponisovsky as a Jew, but as a Russian. This was a random prejudice that did not prevent Joyce from enlisting the Russian Paul Léon (actually Leopoldovich) as his substitute "seeing eye" assistant and devoted messenger, to replace the long-suffering Sylvia Beach in that role. Still Joyce gave his paternal blessing to the engagement, as soon as Lucia accepted Ponisovsky once again, the following Sunday.

Nora was less sanguine about the engagement, but she too went along with the arrangement since Alexander Ponisovsky was so much more acceptable than any of the young men who had previously presented themselves (or been pursued by Lucia). At this point it was Giorgio who showed the only semblance of balance in the family. He was shocked by the plot to marry off his sister, and raged: "You can't talk about engagement with a girl in Lucia's condition."

To celebrate the engagement in style, Joyce gave a party for the couple at Drouand's, the ultra-fashionable restaurant near l'Opéra. Before the festivities got under way, Lucia stretched out on a sofa at the Léons' apartment to relax, but when summoned to the waiting taxi she went rigid as if struck by some mysterious paralysis and could not be roused from where she lay, her eyes staring open in a catatonic state.

Giorgio's warning was confirmed. By now even her misguided father had to admit that what Lucia needed was hospitalization, not marriage.

THE DIARIES OF Anaïs Nin, the collection of journals Lawrence Durrell called The Monster, by now had reached some forty volumes. Anaïs referred to these confessions and daily memoir as "my kief, hashish, and opium pipe . . . my drug and vice" and as the affair with Miller caught fire, she wanted to spare Hugo the shame of her infidelity if he should read the present volume. So she now kept two diaries, the false one bound in green, the true volume in red—but was confused herself about which diary was which, since the red contained many falsehoods, as did the green, until finally neither was the "true" diary.

Henry Miller served as much as literary mentor as lover, and tried to convince Anaïs to translate her memoirs into fiction, as he did, but she was addicted to her drug and vice of diary writing. However, at about the time Henry found a publisher, Jack Kahane, for his Tropic of Cancer, Anaïs Nin was to be published by Edward Titus at The Black Mannikin Press, out of his bookshop on the rue Delambre. Titus was estranged from his wealthy successful wife, Helena Rubinstein, who was supporting the literary pursuits of Titus without being aware of how of her money was being put to use. Titus was enthusiastic about Anaïs Nin's unprofessional study of D. H. Lawrence, and even more enthusiastic about the beautiful author herself, and made an approach, calling her his "honey girl." Titus failed to seduce Anaïs, but his assistant editor, Lawrence Drake, in the course of preparing D. H. Lawrence for publication, succeeded.

Though the affair with Henry Miller was inevitable—Hugo Guiler predicted the event that first night when he said to Anaïs, "I'm going to lose you to Henry"—Hugo did not in fact lose out to him, nor Henry to Hugo, for Anaïs remained steadfastly in love with her husband during the long and labyrinthine involvement with Miller, with emotional space to spare for other lovers and alliances in passionate and soul-searching excess. Henry Miller came along as the timely personification of Nin's long-dreamed-of "Shadow" so often cited in her diaries. This Unknown, an imagined demon-prince, would someday appear on her doorstep and release her from "under a glass bell" the constricted life at Louveciennes had become. The Shadow was destined to free an Albertine from her plush confinement, save a Madame Bovary from boredom in suburban limbo.

Miller performed as Shadow exactly as preconceived by Nin, but was one Shadow enough for her? Could the Shadow appear in the form of a woman?

Nin's affair with Miller had begun as an exchange of literary confidences and critical readings of each other's manuscripts, finding themselves on the same emotional plane—"Miller is flamboyant, virile, animal, magnificent. He's a man whom life makes drunk. He is like me"—if not always in agreement on literary style. (Anaïs was capable of confessing to her diary: "Henry, save me from beautification, the horrors of static perfection . . . precipitate me into the inferno.")

On the practical plane (and Miller could be eminently pragmatic when his stomach growled), he had acquired not only a lover but a patroness: Anaïs generously contributed half the household allowance of four hundred dollars monthly to Henry . . . she wanted him closer than hotel rooms in Paris allowed for: the apartment over the garage might be made over into a working-living studio where Henry could live and write. But for all his free-ranging libertinism, Miller was governed by some compunctions: he would never flaunt his affair with Anaïs under her husband's very nose.

Before the subject of the garage-apartment came up again, Miller suddenly announced, having only recently digested the advent himself, that June was in Paris.

"I'm living the life of a full-blooded schizerino again."

WITH NO ADVANCE notice given to her husband, June arrived at the gare Saint-Lazare, set forth on her own, and found a hotel for herself on the rue Princesse. For two days she explored the city alone, involved in whatever adventures, and with whom, Henry could only imagine. When pressed to pay her hotel bill, she sent Henry a *pneumatique* to inform him that she was in Paris. Miller, in an agitated state, went immediately to the Hôtel Princesse where he found his wife sharply annoyed to be awakened late at night. As part of her snappish greeting, she gave Miller ten days to come up with the room rent. Money remained the eternal motif in the Miller ménage.

They began the quarrelsome routine Miller thought he had said good-bye to in New York, but he discovered he still had amorous feelings for his wife, was attached to her by a stronger bond than ever. June recognized this, and thought to dangle Henry from her puppet strings anew.

What most intrigued June about Henry's life in Paris was the friendship she had heard of with the banker and his wife. She was anxious to meet Anaïs Nin, and when Anaïs heard of the arrival, she was just as eager to meet June. The Millers were invited to dinner at the Guilers' house. June pretended indifference to the vine-covered manse, and arrived determined to impress by shock effect, wearing a stained red velvet dress and a dirty fedora perched cockily on her head. In contrast, her hostess met the raffish guests under the Persian lamp at the gate dressed in a hand-designed *robe de soir*—large eyes aglow and avid for a first glimpse of the legendary June—a studied pose of her own.

Dinner was a self-conscious affair, an overelaborate display of tortured cuisine served beneath the vast astrological charts on the walls, June's careless chatter across the candlelit table (she was the center of interest to Anaïs), Henry and Hugo agonizing through banal man-to-man talk (brandy and cigars after dinner) while aware of the fascinated gaze Anaïs fixed on June.

Anaïs Nin's calculated campaign to woo Henry's wife into a semblance, at least, of intimacy amused June, who accepted the challenge by allowing for a schoolgirl crush of hand-holding and stolen kisses. The two women did meet in Paris for an adolescent flirtation that went unrecorded in Nin's diaries, but served June primarily as a way to try to make Henry jealous. When June showed Henry a love letter penned by Anaïs, Miller was only too aware of the Anaïs Nin style, full of sound and fury, signifying very little. June was annoyed at Henry's tepid reaction to what she intended as a challenge, and said to him, dismissing the entire drama: "They [the Guilers] just took us up because they're bored."

Meanwhile June began running up bills in Paris, knowing Henry would provide the wherewithal out of money he could coax from Anaïs. By now all parties to the four-way connection were exasperated with June Miller and she with them.

June's Paris visit came to a near hysterical dénouement when she sneaked a preview of herself as model for Mona in *Tropic of Cancer*. Henry had deliberately kept the book from her, but when he got back to the hotel one afternoon he saw the manuscript pages scattered across the bed and June, a stricken look on her face, holding a page to the light. Miller had written about what he called June's "mysteries" and left her, she thought, denuded of magic and charm.

"You," said June acidly, "are the greatest enemy I have in the world!"

She then wept and moaned, reminding him of all she had done for him: he would never have come to Paris, or been a writer, without her. Now *this,* this vituperative portrait. Anaïs Nin must be the reason behind the portrait. "You think you love her, but she's just another little lesbian—you only love her because you're a homo yourself."

With that, Miller ceased to try to reason with her, and June flung herself out of the room screaming, "You can find our marriage license and my wedding ring at the bottom of the Seine, if you care to look."

June had threatened to tear the manuscript to pieces, and might have done so if Miller had not come back in time. He gathered the scattered pages together, half demented himself, despondent in his love-hate of his wife.

The drama was still to be concluded with help from Alfred Perlès, Miller's crony in Clichy, and Anaïs, who would put up the money for June's return steamship ticket to New York. Perlès accompanied June to the boat-train, less an escort than a witness to make sure she did depart. To keep Miller away, Anaïs sent him to London, since June knew Henry detested England and would not look for him there—but Miller's messy exit was thwarted by British Immigration: he was sent back to France because he couldn't show sufficient funds for a sojourn in England. He hid out at Louveciennes instead.

Perlès reported June's last words on boarding the train: "I feel like Alice in Wonderland."

Her last words to Henry were scribbled on the only scrap of paper she could find. He found a sheet of toilet paper where she wrote: "Get a divorce, and right away."

IN HER DIARY of that time, Anaïs wrote: "Henry interests me but not physically. Is it possible I might at last be satisfied with Hugo?"

16

PORTENTS AND ALARMS

Europe is not big enough for a war anymore, for a war countries should be bigger.

—GERTRUDE STEIN

They've got too many guns and now nobody can think what to do with them but shoot them off.

—CLARE BOOTHE LUCE

TEN YEARS AFTER his amazing New York—Paris solo flight in a primitive monoplane *The Spirit of St. Louis,* the Lone Eagle was back in France, this time to flee the United States, effectively driven from America by the intrusive and abusive press coverage of the 1932 kidnapping and murder of his child. Lindbergh's sensational exploit a decade ago had been the headline news of the century; the twenty-five-year-old pilot became the most celebrated hero of all time, an unfortunate fame that the modest young man accepted with diffidence and grace at the time but would so bedevil his life thereafter until notoriety led fatefully to the murder of his baby son.

News coverage of the crime had been nothing less than hysterical. So outrageous were reporters after the body was discovered that one news photographer invaded the Trenton mortuary and pried open the infant's coffin to take a sensational photograph.

To escape the aggressive newshounds of the American variety, the Lindberghs sought sanctuary abroad, first in England where a traditional respect for privacy still prevailed. But Lindy found the British lacking in "vigor" and sadly unprepared to face the challenges and dangers he perceived for the modern world.

His close friend in France, Dr. Alexis Carrel—whose eugenic theory of racially pure bloodlines in a "disciplined society" were close to certain of Lindbergh's own elitist beliefs—introduced Charles and Anne Lindbergh to the scattering of islands off the coast of Brittany, one of which, Illiec, proved an idyllic hermitage for the press-besieged exiles. They would be sole occupants of an unheated but handsome manor house, no other inhabitants on the isle except for servants housed in separate quarters. It was the paradise they had been looking for, rugged but remote from newsmen and photographers.

But Lindbergh was restlessly concerned with the critical state of the Western world, too concerned to remain apart from events. The excuse was that the Lindbergh children would be deprived of companions of their own age for any extended sojourn on the island, so the family moved to Paris, ostensibly for access to schools, but actually a convenient takeoff point for Lindbergh to monitor and assess preparations for the growing threat of another European war.

The American hero and French celebrity Charles Lindbergh inspecting German air force base.

Paris, the scene of Lindy's heart-swelling reception in 1927, now appeared to him as demoralized and static as he had found London. "There is an air of discouragement and neglect on every hand, and people seem to be waiting almost from day to day for something to happen . . . [one] finds such a fear of military invasion, such depression and such instability."

In Germany, by contrast to England and France, Lindbergh discovered a revitalized and forward-looking nation. With his lasting celebrity as the world's foremost pilot, Lindbergh was made enthusiastically welcome by the Nazi hierarchy, especially by Hermann Goering, head of the German Luftwaffe. German airfields and factories were made open to aviation's minister-without-portfolio, and Lindbergh was greatly impressed, perhaps overimpressed, by the German aircraft industry, its present power and future potential. (Critics of Lindbergh's shuttle-inspection tours and glowing reports of the strength of the Luftwaffe repeated the rumor that the Germans, to exaggerate their predominance in air power, kept moving aircraft from hangar to hangar, from one airfield to another along Lindbergh's state-sponsored itinerary.)

At a celebration in Lindy's honor, he was surprised to be presented by Goering the Service Cross of the German Eagle, "by order of der Führer," an honor Lindbergh accepted as he had other medals at similar ceremonies—but this, in the light of Germany's recent Nuremberg Laws stripping Jews of civil rights, played against Lindbergh's own acknowledged "racial purity" views, would prove to be less an honor than, as his wife, Anne, expressed it, "an albatross."

Back in France Lindbergh was also given access to recent production in warplanes, but discovered that the French were producing fifty aircraft a month, to Germany's five hundred.

CHARLES DE GAULLE, another colonel, tall and slim as Lindbergh (called *la grande asperge,* the big asparagus, at the French equivalent of West Point, St. Cyr), was voicing the same concerns expressed by the American. France was criminally negligent about national defense in the face of the armaments buildup just across the border. De Gaulle had served as secretariat of Defense Nationale from 1932 to 1937 under the discredited and corrupt policies of fourteen different (or the same, reinstated) ministries. He had written a book, *Vers l'armée de metier,* documenting the need for a modern, mechanized army, but the book sold a mere four hundred copies (nothing to compare to the sales of *Kiki's Memoirs*) and was completely ignored by the French military. De Gaulle carried his argument to the most celebrated general in France, Marshal Pétain, begging for more tanks and planes.

"Mais nous en avons," protested Pétain. "We have them."

Not only did France not have them, but there were not the trained personnel to man the tanks and planes in production or in reserve. World War I had decimated the male population of France, and the declining birth rate had led Clemenceau to remark of France's far more fecund neighbor: "There are thirty million Germans too many." (France offered medallions and monetary reward to mothers of *famille nombreux* but the birth rate continued to decline.)

What de Gaulle had to contend with was the frozen and aged attitudes of the French military mind, the belief that if war should erupt on the eastern front any attempt by the Germans for a breakthrough at the border was an impossibility. This was because of a brilliant engineering feat known as the Maginot Line, named for engineer and minor politician André Maginot (who died in 1932 before he could oversee his defense masterpiece to completion). The labyrinth of reinforced concrete bunkers stretched for eighty-seven miles connected by underground tunnels and punctuated at intervals by gun turrets shaped like the cloche hats popular at the end of the 1920s.

An ominous provocation was staged by Hitler in 1936, testing the resolve of "the French hydra" (Hitler's term for his neighbor-enemy, but judiciously deleted from the French translation of *Mein Kampf*) by sending troops into the demilitarized zone adjacent to the Maginot Line on the Franco-German border, the Rhineland, a flagrant violation of the Versailles Treaty. Hitler was prepared to withdraw the troops if challenged by the French—the German military buildup was not yet at a level to insure overwhelming blitzkrieg in case of engagement—but the French, whose policy was by then *"pas des histoires, pas des provocations, pas de bruit"* (no fuss, no provocations, no noise), did not respond. The Germans proceeded to build their own series of defensework bunkers at the Westwall, known as the Siegfried Line.

The Maginot Line was referred to by generals in their dotage as impregnable. (Pétain: *"Ils ne passeront pas!"* was an echo of la Pasionara's defiant "They shall not pass!" in Spain where at that very moment Franco's forces continued to pass in triumph through the Republic.)

In speech after speech Lindbergh advanced the salient argument that modern warfare would be fought primarily from the air; concentrated lines of defense on the ground were folly when modern aircraft could fly at heights well above the bunkers and beyond the range of the outdated 75mm cannon protruding from their concrete cloche hats.

One further and even ridiculous flaw in the Maginot Line theory was that the "impregnable" defenseworks did not extend to France's most vulnerable front, the border with Belgium, the corridor to the northeast the Germans had breached twice before, first in the Franco-Prussian War in 1870, and again as recently at 1914 during World War I. It was as if the house of France took the precaution of being locked and barred to intrusion but left its front door open wide. (Political figures explained the short-sighted lapse as a necessary diplomatic gesture to assure the Belgians, with whom France had a mutual-defense treaty, that they would not be militarily sealed off from their powerful ally and left exposed to be overrun once again.)

But the warnings of Lindbergh (who believed, in any case, France stood no chance against a re-armed Germany) and the entreaties of de Gaulle went unsatisfied. The French general staff was committed to its retrograde *château-fort* mentality, reliance on a "castle-keep" strategy or "castling," the most passive defense-move in chess.

Politicians in and out of power in the Third Republic agreed with the general staff. "Entrenchment and hold," Premier Daladier intoned when de Gaulle came to him with his plea for a modern army of tanks and planes. "The rest is just words."

FOR CIVILIANS IT was the heyday of soothsayers and *voyants*. A condensed edition of the prophecies of Nostradamus was selling well at the bookstalls along both banks of the Seine at two francs a copy. Michel de Nostredame was a sixteenth-century astrologer and seer who compiled a massive volume of prophecies based on the configuration of the stars and planets, then rendered his conclusions in quaint Old French quatrains. Like the Book of Revelation, also referred to in uncertain times, the predictions of Nostradamus could be interpreted in infinite variation. The couplet referring to "the destruction of Paris by birds from the east" could well be a warning of German warplanes (Nostradamus had foretold of submarines as armored fish), but the dénouement in the next couplet of an eventual triumph in a French victory was more obscure, and the most essential element to a sigh of relief was left unsaid—*when?*

In certain stressful circumstances the French are distracted from an essential pragmatism and Cartesian reasoning to seek solace from a fortune-teller or ecclesiastical magic. Clear-thinking Marcel Proust turned often to his palmist Madame de Thebes for answers not apparent in social discourse or the news of the day. In the Great Flood of 1176 the Bishop of Paris was called upon by the populace to hold aloft a nail from the true Cross at water's edge and intone: "That thy dread waters return to their banks and spare these unhappy people further misery." According to legend the rains ceased, the sky cleared, and the floodwaters of the Seine began to recede.

AS TO IMAGE and totem reflecting prophetic catastrophe, the surrealists took the lead (Picasso's tragic *Guernica* was a painted reaction after the fact). The normally placid-natured Miró was painting a series of canvasses shifting from the theme of psychosexual dream life to outright nightmare—surely affected and influenced by the grim news, as Picasso had been, from their native Spain. The monsters, female, painted by Picasso were related to his wife Olga during their vicious divorce proceedings, but where did the inspiration derive for happily married Miró's monsters?

The most eerily prescient painting was created by Max Ernst (German born, but assimilated into the French surrealist brigade under the command of André Breton). Ernst's *Europe After the Rain I* showed a beleagured surface indistinctly recognizable as Europe, a wasteland devastated not so much by flood, as the title suggested, but scarred and fire-scorched with borderlines between nations indefinably blurred.

THE SEINE DID not flood this time as in the twelfth century (or as in 1910, taken by some as an augury of the Great War that followed); but another flood was taking place as ominous a foreboding as the Seine's implacable spill.

A flood of refugees from Berlin, unexpected and unwanted, began to stream into Paris. The city in the 1920s had already absorbed a wave of refugees from Soviet Russia after the Bolshevik revolution, and of blacks from the United States fleeing racial discrimination at home, but the original welcome had soured and the French no longer considered either émigré set chic.

Now Hitler was implementing and extending the draconian Nuremberg Laws by direct attack against the non-Aryan population of Germany. In one night of riot apparently instigated by storm troopers, but on signal from the Führer himself, Jewish shops were looted, the windows smashed, and the Jews physically assaulted. The night of the nightmare, because of the shattered windows, became known by the euphemism *Kristallnacht*.

SO ADMIRING WAS Lindbergh of the New Germany he called "the most interesting nation today," he had decided to move his family from the idyllic island retreat off the coast of Brittany to a house offered him in Berlin. The move was scheduled for the very day following *Kristallnacht*. Wisely Lindbergh changed his plans. His anti-Semitic sentiments "when there are too many" were well known, along with a confirmed racial bias favoring the white race over "a pressing sea of Yellow, Black and Brown"; and he could be certain—though he personally deplored *Kristallnacht*—that taking up residence in Berlin at this time would only add to the weight of the Albatross (Goering's medal) around his neck.

"I love France," Lindbergh declared, "second only to America," practically a refrain from Josephine Baker's theme song *"J'ai deux amours,"* but the Aryan air pilot and the black chanteuse were each singing of another Paris, a different United States.

Lindbergh settled himself and family in the fashionable 16th arrondissement of Paris at 11 bis avenue Maréchal Manoury in Passy on the edge of the bois de Boulogne. From this elegant home base the Lone Eagle (though often referred to as the Lone Ostrich when Lindbergh became associated with the American First movement) could partially satisfy his perpetual restlessness by frequent shuttle "diplomacy" between Orly Airport and Berlin's Templehof—with occasional concession to his wife's cultural interests and Left Bank ties by the purchase of paintings by fauve artist Maurice de Vlaminck. Lindy and Anne also took tea (once, and that may have been one time too many for Lindbergh) with fellow American expatriates Gertrude Stein and Alice Toklas.

The French geneticist Alexis Carroll was speaking not only for the scientific Right but for many Frenchmen, as well as for his good friend Lindbergh, when he declared: "A great race must propogate its own ele-

ments." This thesis was put into practice when the Nobel Prize winner
Albert Einstein, a refugee from Hitler's Germany, was initially offered
sanctuary in Paris with the chair of physics at the Collège de France,
but the outcry against émigrés, especially Jews, had become so shrill,
Premier Doumergue rescinded the invitation, a repeat of his travesty in
refusing Stravinsky the *Légion d'Honneur* because his name sounded
like "Stavisky."

FROM THE RUSSIAN community of exiles in Berlin, Vladimir Nabokov
was writing to friends outside Germany: "My situation has become so
difficult I have to search for any kind of work at all." The former aristocrat was subsisting hand to mouth by giving private lessons in English
and Russian, and the gleanings from an occasional lecture or even poor-
er pay from the publication of poems in émigré journals under his pen
name, Sirin. "I have a wife and child," his letters continued. ". . . In a
word my situation is desperate." Nabokov's desperation was compounded by the publication of the Nuremberg Laws and the appointment of
Goebbels as minister of culture. Nabokov's wife Verá was Jewish.

An even more pressing reason for an instant exit from Berlin was that
a certain Taboritsky had been appointed supervisor of émigré affairs.
Taboritsky in 1937 had just been released from a German prison for
complicity in a murder that took place at a political rally of the Russian
colony in Berlin. Vladimir Nabokov's father was shot and killed at the
rally. If Nabokov remained in Germany he would immediately fall under
the jurisdiction of his father's assassin.

A well-off friend in Paris, Ilya Fondaminsky, offered Nabokov temporary lodgings and the opportunity to join the Russian colony in
France, with the possibility (Fondaminsky would promote) of readings
and lectures to support himself and family. Vladimir would travel alone
and settle in Paris to prepare the way for Verá and son Dimitri to follow,
once a *permis de séjour* was in hand—a difficult visa to obtain when one
traveled on a Nansen passport (a "nonsense" passport, Nabokov called
it) issued to stateless persons.

From the gare du Nord, Nabokov went directly to Fondaminsky's vast
apartment in the upscale 16th arrondissement, at 130 avenue de
Versailles. Within almost an hour of his arrival Nabokov had met with
Russian literary friends in exile and bitterly quarreled with Mark
Aldonov—the Russian literary set in Paris, Nabokov discovered, was as

contentious as the coterie in Berlin—then fell out with Ivan Bunin, who had won the Nobel Prize but was envious of "Sirin's" reputation as the foremost Russian writer in exile.

Nabokov fared more amicably on the Left Bank under the aegis of Sylvia Beach at Shakespeare and Company, and with her friend Adrienne Monnier who introduced him to the leading French literary lights. Through Sylvia Beach, Nabokov was to discover a magician with words equal to his own literary sensibilities, James Joyce. Sylvia introduced him to the published portions of *Work in Progress* about to be named *Finnegans Wake,* but although recognizing the genius of *Ulysses*, like so many other admirers of Joyce, Nabokov became exasperated with the *Work in Progress*: "—the abstract puns, the verbal masquerade, the shadows of words, the disease of words . . . in the end wit sinks behind reason, and, while it is setting, the sky is ravishing, but then there is night."

Paul Léon was now entrusted with the thankless Joyce Industry and offered to arrange a meeting between the Russian and the Irish littérateurs, since Sylvia Beach was no longer involved with Joyce. But so many conditions were attached to the introduction that Nabokov declined "the honor."

When the two literary giants did meet, at the home of Maria and Eugene Jolas, Nabokov admitted after the brief encounter that he did not "shine"—nor did Joyce, who merely wanted from the Russian the recipe for *myod* (mead). Nabokov's only other encounter with Joyce was at a drafty meeting hall when Nabokov was lecturing on Pushkin to a meager audience of émigré friends: "a source of unforgettable consolation was the sight of Joyce sitting, arms folded and glasses glinting, in the midst of the Hungarian football team."

His wife Verá was slow to obtain an exit visa from Germany and Nabokov just as slow to establish a stable and salaried situation in Paris. He quarreled with Fondaminsky, so he took squalid lodgings on his own, still in the 16th arrondissement but in quarters so tiny he was obliged to write in the miniature bathroom, an ironing board across the bidet for a desk. Alone in Paris, essentially penniless (*"pas riche"* was his pun for the city's name in Russian, Parizh) and surviving under the cloud of morosity engendered by exile, Nabokov sought classic escape from melancholy by an impetuous romance.

This was a rekindled passion for an old flame, Irina Guadanini, also in Paris in exile from their prerevolutionary Russia. Irina's mother was aware that her daughter was still in love with the poet "Sirin," and in the romantic circumstances—lovers torn asunder by revolution, Nabokov's wife stranded in Berlin—Paris was the ideal setting for a reunion, an operatic backdrop for an affair, so the mother contrived to bring the lovers together. Nabokov would later characterize Irina's mother as a "procuress."

Less romantic than the setting and circumstances of the affair was Irina's employment as a poodle trimmer for a coiffeur of pets—but Russian aristocrats were reduced to ridiculous and desperate compromise in the narrow Paris market for émigré employment.

Vladimir had willingly allowed himself to be seduced, and eagerly continued the affair, though he was so stricken with guilt that he developed a disfiguring case of psoriasis. The émigré colonies in Paris and Berlin were in close touch, so it was not surprising that Verá began to receive anonymous notes in Cyrillic characters revealing Vladimir's renewed liaison with Irina. When Verá did at last obtain an exit visa for herself and son Dimitri and could join her husband in Paris, she confronted him with the rumors of his adulterous affair. Vladimir denied everything. This only compounded his guilt and misery, for he dearly loved his wife and not, he realized belatedly, Irina.

It was sometime during this period of frustration, remorse, and depression (though Nabokov thought it might have been during "a severe attack of intercostal neuralgia") that he ventured to the Jardin des Plantes where he might contemplate the celebrated ape in the Left Bank zoo said to be the first animal inveigled into producing a drawing that suggested human attributes.

"The first little throb of *Lolita* went through me . . . the impulse had no textual connection with the ensuing train of thought, which resulted, however, in a prototype [of *Lolita*], a short story of some thirty pages long."

The drawing the ape had sketched in charcoal "showed the bars of the poor creature's cage."

FOR REFUGEE ÉMIGRÉS like Nabokov, life in Paris in 1938–39 could be an existence in purgatory, and there were even worse-off exiles huddled in colonies along the ragged arrondissements of the city, the benighted regions untraveled by the respectable bourgeois (though explored in depth by subterranean forays of Henry Miller and Brassaï).

The colonies of refugees represented a second city, a Paris apart, where émigrés were associated by former nationality, a common language, and dependence on one another. These marginals were known to the police as SDFs (*Sans Domicile Fixe*, no permanent home) and were subject to expulsion for infractions of the *Code Civil*, and especially if they were judged a financial drain on the state.

As many discovered (Nabokov among them), a *permis de travail*, a work permit for foreigners, was almost impossible to obtain; nevertheless, in the cruel logic of officialdom, *l'étranger* was obliged to show proof of cash subsistence at any police inquiry.

Henry Miller could now count on Anaïs Nin's husband to vouch for him as financially stable (on Hugo's largesse), and Vladimir Nabokov could, in extremis (if Alexandra Tolstoy was agreeable), turn to the Tolstoy Foundation for support. At one point the owner of a Parisian cinema, Saveley Kyandzhuntsev, supported the Nabokovs with a stipend of one thousand francs a month.

THE HUNGARIAN-BORN Arthur Koestler, in exile from Germany (and more recently, from Spain), remembered that the German-speaking colony in Paris passed around a thousand-franc banknote from émigré to émigré, the symbolic note useful as instant proof of financial resource. Koestler, like so many of the foreigners in Paris, was unable to make social contact with Parisians. One managed a café acquaintance only: "A Frenchman would embrace you, then leave you shivering in the street, condemned to remain forever a permanent tourist or permanent exile, as the case may be."

Suffering the constraints of Paris in the 1930s to the point of desperation, Koestler was unable to envision any sign of hope for Europe, or for mankind, in the current downward spiral of events. He decided to commit suicide. There was a gas oven in his tiny living quarters, and that night he turned on the gas and stretched out on his bed stiffly in a preamble to rigor mortis, but his despondent gesture took a comic turn. The reverberation of the traffic outside his window, or the rumbling of the métro passing beneath his hotel, jostled a book from the shelf above the bed, which thumped down with a jolt on Koestler's head. It was an epiphany of sorts: of life yet to be lived, of events the significance of which was yet to transpire. He got up from his death-embracing pose, turned off the gas, and aired the room. Not long after the failed suicide,

Koestler was working on the manuscript of the book that revealed the grim truth of the totalitarian malaise that so oppressed him, *Darkness at Noon*.

AT FIRST THE Führer of Germany was best known to the French in caricature, an opéra bouffe Herr Schickelgruber portrayed by "Charlot" (Charlie Chaplin's *The Great Dictator*) or ridiculed in song by Edith Piaf in *"Il n'est pas distingué"*: "Me, I've got Hitler up my nose and can't sneeze him out," as newsreels were shown in Paris of the little man with abbreviated mustache. Did one take the bombast seriously? Adolf Hitler strutting across the political stage, his right arm thrust defiantly forward in the Nazi salute, screaming his demands in a saliva-spouting frenzy of menace.

Kristallnacht was but an inevitable reaction against the despised Jews, as the anti-Semitic *ligues*, and their sympathizers, interpreted that shattering crash of alarm. Another night's signal of horror to come, "The Night of the Long Knives," when Hitler so bloodily directed the slaughter of Nazi Party opponents, was considered an "internal affair," hardly of concern to a France riven by its own internecine struggle that same year, 1934.

When Hitler taunted France by deployment of troops in the demilitarized Rhineland, the French averted their gaze from the invasion. "The Germans are only invading Germany." Almost alone, Colonel de Gaulle deplored the French turning the other cheek. "They are," he said, "resting on the soft pillow of the Maginot Line."

Then Austria was "annexed" in an unchallenged takeover known as the Anschluss, and further demands for the recovery of German "living space" were being broadcast in near-hysterical terms by the Great Dictator next door to France.

Journalist Dorothy Thompson—wife of the novelist Sinclair Lewis (his *It Can't Happen Here*, translated into French as *Impossible Ici*)—was barred from the Adlon (Lindbergh's favorite hotel in Berlin) and expelled from Germany when her book *I Saw Hitler* was published. Such denigrating references as "[Hitler's] countenance is a caricature of a drummer boy risen too high" would have infuriated the Führer, alongside Thompson's more trenchant observations.

Equally prescient to the danger of the "drummer boy" of National Socialism was Janet Flanner's portrait *Führer* for her "Letter from Paris" in *The New Yorker.* But the French did not read *The New Yorker* or believe *Impossible Ici.*

GERTRUDE STEIN WAS writing to "Papa Woodjums" (Carl Van Vechten) about her new French poodle: ". . . it takes a lot of time to take baby Basket in and out and sit with him while he eats a bone . . . and there is lots going on." As an afterthought she wrote: "Hitler is certainly sending us a lot of people," referring to the streams of refugees from Nazi Germany into Paris and passing through the village where she spent summers. Her neighbor in Bilignin assured Gertrude that France could not possibly go to war with Germany, again, because (in French peasant's judgment, or Steinian rationale) "It is not logical."

If war should threaten, Gertrude found consolation in a nightly reading of prophecies derived from astrological signs, written by the abbé d'Ars, who became a saint. Gertrude Stein was at the time greatly attracted to saints, and had written an opera devoted to saints, *Four Saints in Three Acts,* with music composed by one of her favorite Young Men (though she quarreled with him, as she did with all her Young Men), the composer Virgil Thomson.

The abbé d'Ars conceded that a war with Germany would come about, but the Germans, Tuesday by Tuesday, would give way and eventually be overcome. The repetition of the word "Tuesday" in the abbé's prophecies offered a certain solace in an otherwise grim forecast, the repetition somehow comforting since repetition was one of the cornerstones of Gertrude Stein's literary style.

"SAW MORICAND LAST night and had a fine talk with him," Henry Miller informed Anaïs Nin. Miller was at last more concerned by the unsteady state of the Western world (Hitler's demands for Czech territory, and military buildup on the Czechoslovakian border) than his personal dilemmas, and turned to Moricand, an astrologer, for signs, forwarnings, and counsel. Conrad Moricand did horoscopes for a meager livelihood, supplemented by a small subsidy from Anaïs Nin.

" '*Le ciel chargé,*' [Moricand] says—but '*l augra les gains spirituels.*' " The astral sky was overcast and perturbed, but spiritual gains were in prospect. Miller, perpetually broke, took "spiritual gains" to mean money coming due.

Moricand's prediction was immediately confirmed by the arrival of a two-hundred-dollar check from the Gotham Book Mart representing under-the-counter sales of *Tropic of Cancer* (the book was banned in the United States but smuggling copies of *Tropic* became a specialty of tourists returning from Paris). The Sudetenland crisis was forgotten as Henry rejoiced in the windfall. He was so delighted, he even proposed to repay "the two or three thousand francs" [approximately 80 to 120 dollars] he owed Anaïs.

Moricand could be counted on for upbeat advice, and he assured Miller he was doing the right thing to accept the invitation from Lawrence Durrell to visit him and his wife at their island retreat on Corfu, in sun-blessed Greece, out from under the black *ciel chargé* of Paris.

At the time Miller was reading the theosophist Madame Blavatsky's *The Secret Doctrine*, as well as the I Ching and texts of Zen Buddhism for enlightenment. Also part of his reading was Durrell's *The Black Book*, in the style of Miller's own *Tropic of Cancer*, and riddled with augury of doom and destruction.

For a clue to the philosophy behind the present-day destabilized Europe, he even read *Mein Kampf* but found no evidence of a Second Coming in political terms, "though there are some profound truths in it."

He was eager to get in touch with Dr. de Fontbrune, in Montpellier, the noted Nostradamus scholar, who might provide succor and solutions to Miller's cosmological anxieties.

JAMES JOYCE'S SON Giorgio was persuaded by his American wife to leave Paris for the United States where he might revivify his dead-end singing career and, in any case, escape *mobilisation générale* if the French should begin to draft young men into the military.

Joyce professed horror of all things American, except the money coming to him from publication there, and naturally deplored his son's defection "across the water," always anxious to keep his family close at hand. "I love only my family," he once confessed to Samuel Beckett who was angling for an affection closer than their working friendship allowed. Finally Joyce shrugged off his son's abandonment of Paris, saying, "What can I honestly ask them to come back to? Paris is like myself a haughty ruin . . ." Ruin was the leitmotif of the moment: "If anything lies ahead of us except ruin I wish someone would point it out."

Someone might have pointed out the decision of Judge Woolsey to allow *Ulysses* to enter the United States at long last, but Joyce read the signs of promise differently. "There are not ten centimes of money in my work," he declared, despite the substantial advance offered by Benett Cerf of Random House now payable, since the work was free to be published. Joyce was more likely to be referring to *Work in Progress* as not representing ten centimes of money, but offers were coming in as well for that difficult and exasperating challenge of a novel.

Seeing all in shades of black was surely a result of Joyce's deteriorating eyesight and now almost constant abdominal pains, symptoms of an undiagnosed ulcer. His central anxiety, nonetheless, was his daughter Lucia's worsening mental state. Her condition so disturbed his peace of mind, the distraught father was rendered sleepless for nights at a time. For the stomach pains he could dose himself with laudanum, but not even his habitual concentration at the writing table could alleviate his mental anguish. During daylight hours he was tortured by bizarre auditory hallucinations, signals pertaining to he knew not what, sounds emanating from some unwholesome netherworld. Visual hallucinations accompanied the aural: "I can see nothing but a dark wall in front of me, a dark wall or a precipice if you prefer."

Essentially apolitical and ordinarily untroubled by news of the world, he did follow events in "Hitlerland" of late, and with growing alarm. Poland was threatened now and the wrangling over Danzig was more than a hallucination but an actual crisis. (Joyce was less dismayed by Mussolini's storm-trooper takeover of Italy, his former place of exile. "Mussolini's Italy is still Italy.")

In contrast to the ineffectual and corrupt leadership in France, Joyce cultivated a certain guarded admiration for "Hitler-Missler's" force of character and unifying instinct, and thought of him as a man of strength and determination France so sadly lacked. "Isn't this Hitler a phenomenon?" was an assessment more to taunt Nora, who despised the German dictator, than a statement of approval. "Think of getting a whole people behind you."

Outraged, Nora picked up a dinner knife and shouted back, "Jim, one more word about that devil and I'll murder you."

17

YUNG AND EASILY FREUDENED

we grisly old Sykos who have done our unsmiling bit on
'alices, when they were yung and easily freudened

— JAMES JOYCE, *FINNEGANS WAKE*

"C'EST MOI QUI *est l'artiste!*" Lucia Joyce screamed into the telephone, hysterical over the ceaseless calls to congratulate her father after *Ulysses* was cleared of obscenity charges. The calls continued until Lucia took scissors and cut the telephone line. Later, when the line was restored, the constant calls again infuriated Lucia. "*C'est moi, l'artiste!*" she insisted, and severed the line once more.

In the shadow of her father's fame, Lucia Joyce was desperate for some notice as an artist of sorts. She had been a talented young student of the dance until her mental instability forced her to abandon dancing. She was encouraged by her father to create a series of *lettrines*, ornate alphabet designs for *Chaucer's ABC*, which Joyce would pay to have published. The artwork was a temporary distraction from her phobias and served as a form of therapy.

To others Lucia often appeared to be lost in space, and a woman doctor seeing her in one of her trances remarked: "If I were the mother of

James Joyce's daughter and saw her staring off into space that way, I'd be very concerned about her."

Nora was at first more concerned about finding a suitable young man for her daughter, but then she too began to fear the worst. On the occasion of Joyce's fiftieth birthday Lucia hurled a chair at her mother and narrowly missed. She had the paranoid conviction that Nora was responsible for the breakup of her romance with Samuel Beckett, when actually the romance had been all on Lucia's side, and in her imagination.

Lucia's bizarre behavior and persistent melancholy became so obvious that hospitalization seemed inevitable, but Joyce would not hear of it. He followed up on whatever crank measures were suggested: ingestion of seawater was recommended. His patron Harriet Weaver recommended grapes, to which Joyce jocularly replied: "Thanks . . . [the grape] never had a more ardent disciple than I." When Lucia was twenty-five she received a series of injections meant to cure her "apathy." In 1935 Joyce decided to send his daughter to London for glandular treatment with bovine serum.

The symptoms of severe mental illness became evident to everyone but Joyce. That his daughter was depressed and subject to fits of hysteria he would admit—that she was insane he refused to believe.

When she was an adolescent Lucia's outbursts could be considered (as Joyce did) teenage tantrums brought on by the awakening of sexual awareness, but now in her twenties the bizarre episodes increased and Joyce was inclined to attribute the unsettling pattern of behavior to female temperament, the inexplicable nature of Woman. "*Subtile et barbare* person, my daughter." To Beckett Joyce confided the belief that Lucia's aberrant behavior must be due to an infection of the teeth.

Except for those Swiss doctors who treated and performed operations on his eyes, Joyce distrusted the medical profession and was particularly disdainful of psychoanalysis. He characterized the two leading analysts in a letter to Harriet Weaver as "a certain Doctor Jung (the Swiss Tweedledum who is not to be confused with the Viennese Tweedledee, Dr. Freud)." He preferred to treat Lucia himself, and at home. In one instance he gave her four thousand francs to buy a fur coat: "I think that will do her inferiority complex more good than a visit to a psychoanalyst."

"You've never really known your daughter," Nora once bluntly informed him.

"Allow me to say," replied Joyce, "that I was present at her conception." As if therefore he was qualified to know her troubled psyche.

But did anyone know her? When she was a baby her father sang an affectionate lullaby to her in Italian—now she sang lullabies to herself in any of the four languages she had picked up in her nomadic childhood. Sometimes Lucia stayed with Maria Jolas who described her as "sweet and Ophelia-like"—it is uncertain whether the reference was meant to suggest Ophelia's passive nature or her madness, or both.

The writer Thomas Wolfe observed the Joyce family on a tour bus in Belgium and commented on Lucia: "The girl was rather pretty—I thought at first she was a little American flapper." Indeed, Lucia was pretty, but did not think of herself as attractive. She was self-conscious about a small scar on her chin and almost pathologically sensitive about strabismus that afflicted one eye and caused a slight squint.

Nino Frank, Joyce's translator of *Ulysses* into Italian, wrote: "On the Champs-Elysées one morning about 1933, I ran into Lucia. I had never seen her so pretty, so gay, so strangely tranquil, then I watched her move off with a lithe, startling light step."

Within a short time Frank learned from Joyce himself that Lucia was in a sanatorium. The day he had seen her so gay and tranquil: "She was on the threshold of madness."

THE JOYCES WERE an exceptionally close-knit unit of four, the steadfast family bond something of a comfort and a defense against the alien cultures and desperate financial circumstances they had passed through. The French critic Louis Gillet noticed this strong family feeling: "Joyce was unusually attached to his own, and despite his terrific scepticism, he was a family man. In the chaos of the universe, the family was for him a sheet-anchor, a sacred ark . . ."

By the time Joyce settled his family in Paris (after Trieste, Rome, and Zurich) a certain stability was provided by an entourage of friends and supporters including Sylvia Beach, Ezra Pound, the Colums, and the Jolases. But even in Paris the nomadic shift from one unsatisfactory flat to another was a constant unsettling leitmotif of their existence. Nora was an indifferent cook, and the family took most meals together in restaurants, at les Trianons across from the gare Montparnasse where Joyce's favorite table was regularly reserved for them, or at Michaud's (in the 1920s) where, according to Ernest Hemingway, "the whole celtic crew of them" dined nightly.

Paris was something of a sanctuary, but Lucia and her brother Giorgio had been subjected to a challenging mix of language, interrupted schooling, and aborted childhood friendships in the peripatetic upbringing. Normal family life had been sacrificed to the scramble and demands of literary art, and Joyce was aware of the burden he had placed on his wife and children. He was deeply troubled by this and blamed himself for Lucia's increasingly unstable mental state, and for Giorgio's apparent drift and shiftlessness.

Joyce sang, and loved singing; he even went to great trouble and expense promoting the Irish tenor John Sullivan—once to the extent of crying out at the Paris Opera that he had regained his eyesight due to Sullivan's magnificent voice. Joyce may have wanted to sing professionally himself, and shifted this vague ambition onto his son when it was discovered that Giorgio had a fair and pleasing baritone voice. He urged Giorgio to study for the opera, and Giorgio did take training and eventually sang publicly on occasion. At his debut performance Giorgio was paid two guineas (about ten dollars), which happened to be the exact fee Joyce had earned for his one singing engagement onstage—an omen the superstitious Joyce considered propitious. But it was not. His son was unprepared for any such disciplined endeavor; though Giorgio sang professionally in a marginal way, he lacked the drive and spirit (and probably the voice) for a successful operatic career—and was subject, moreover, to stage fright.

Brash, outspoken Nora Joyce could always complain—good-naturedly enough, but with more than a sigh—of her husband's eccentric ways and evident failings (a weakness for drink foremost) that misdirected their family life. She loved her "Jim," for there was not another like him, and loyally followed along his foresworn and erratic path to fame, sharing his life in uncertain exile. There was his genius to respect and his celebrity to bask in, if she had been the respectful type or one to bask, but Nora hardly shared the limelight her writer husband enjoyed (and detested). Unable to comprehend his work, she was reluctant even to read him.

"Well, Jim, I haven't read any of your books but I'll have to someday because they must be good considering how well they sell."

But why didn't he write books that people could understand?

As Joyce stood by, amused, Nora commented to a friend, "I've always said he should give up writing and take up singing."

In turn Joyce showed another friend, with Nora present, a sample of the sentimental romances his wife read. The two took amiable and malicious delight in flaunting their opposing natures and contrasting tastes. According to Sylvia Beach, "Joyce enjoyed being called a good-for-nothing by Nora; it was a relief from the respectful attitude of others."

And they loved each other for all their differences and dislikes; James and Nora Joyce had been through too much together to give up on each other.

It is impossible to know what sustained Nora during the grim times and tides of fortune, but for Joyce there was always the escape from reality into his *Work in Progress*—not even failing health and dimming eyesight could keep him from the labor over an obscure linguistic experiment and convoluted labyrinthine text for as many as twelve hours daily. Respite came in the dark evening with bottles of Swiss white wine, drinking until his cigarette burned down to his fingers.

Of Joyce's last masterpiece of his career many considered it a protracted joke (Joyce himself insisted that *Finnegans Wake* was pure comedy, "not a serious line in it"), an extravagant piece of folly.

Ezra Pound who had so diligently championed Joyce in the 1920s for his *Ulysses,* now in the thirties said of *Finnegans Wake*, "Nothing so far as I can make out, nothing short of divine vision or a new cure of the clapp can possibly be worth all the circumambient peripherization."

Harriet Weaver, loyal patron still, continued her support of Joyce despite her "perplexity" over his *Work in Progress*.

By some, Joyce was considered insane, and his madness handed down to the daughter.

Richard Ellmann, Joyce's eminent biographer, expressed the father-daughter madness theme more charitably: "It seemed to [Joyce] that her mind was like his own, and he tried to find evidence in her writing and drawing of unrecognized talent." Joyce believed, or tried to believe, that his daughter was a "tortured and blocked replica of genius."

NORA HAD DELIVERED Lucia at a pauper's ward in Trieste, and the delighted father expressed his enchantment at the birth:

Rosefrail and fair—yet frailest
A wonder wild
In gentle eyes thou veilist
My blueveined child

In July of 1933 Lucia was diagnosed by Professor Hans Maier as schizophrenic (hebephrenic psychosis with serious prognosis) who counseled that she be placed under the care of Dr. Oscar Forel at Les Rives de Prangins clinic in Nyon, Switzerland.

Three years earlier, after her mental breakdown in Paris, Zelda Fitzgerald was committed to the same institution with approximately the same diagnosis, having danced herself into dementia from the same yearning ("for something of her own," Fitzgerald said of his frustrated wife) as Lucia's craving to be the artist with a gift equal to her father's. It was a dramatic and contemporary theme Fitzgerald could draw from for his long-blocked and -delayed novel *Tender Is the Night,* art inspired from a pitiable source and at a terrible price.

Joyce was still convinced that Lucia should neither be placed under treatment nor confined to an institution. "She behaves like a fool very often," he admitted, "but her mind is as clear and unsparing as the lightning."

Doctors disagreed. Although Dr. Forel pronounced the schizophrenia as being with pithiatric elements (subject to cure), Joyce was disatisfied with treatment at Les Rives de Prangins and withdrew Lucia from the clinic—perhaps as much because doctors recommended that Lucia be kept from her parents, and also because Dr. Forel advised Joyce to give up drinking altogether, for his daughter's sake.

By September 1933 Lucia was at home, but intractable even under the care of a nurse-companion. In January of 1934 she fled from home and Joyce was obliged to turn to the French police to negotiate her return. At home she passed through a series of phases from schoolgirl tantrums to seizures to clearly intelligent intervals that encouraged Joyce to say, "She'll get all right they say." He did not specify who said this. "One needs Job's patience with Solomon's wit and the Queen of Sheba's pin money thrown in."

It was decided to try a *"cure libre"* with Dr. Loz in Geneva, but before the treatment was initiated Lucia set fire to her room at the clinic and had to be transferred to the dread Burghölzhi in Zurich (Lucia remembered the asylum's reputation from her childhood). At Burghölzhi the blood expert Professor Naegeli was to treat Lucia's condition in the hope that a physical cure would restore her to sanity.

"Why did you set fire to your room at Prangins?" asked Professor Maier, and Lucia replied (but only later, to a nurse), "Because my father's face is very red and so is fire."

Joyce took little enough notice of political upheaval and apparently none at all at the turbulent French political scene of 1934. By November of that year Lucia had been treated by twenty-four doctors and under the care of a dozen nurses and eight "keepers." In 1935 Joyce wrote to his all-suffering benefactor Harriet Weaver: "My daughter is in a madhouse where I hear she fell off a tree." In another urgent plea to secure funds beyond his allowance, he wrote: "I have to pay the following bills immediately if not sooner—" and supplied a list of five doctors (one he listed as "Keeper of the madhouse") with their corresponding accounts for a total of nearly twelve thousand francs.

No sooner did a treatment begin than Joyce more often than not frustrated its course by withdrawing Lucia from the establishment. He could not bear to think of his daughter "locked away" and in one instance was so opposed to her confinement that he smuggled Lucia "out of the clinic, through Paris and to Austria . . . whether my plan in double-crossing three doctors succeeds or fails I shall be blamed—"

Since Harriet Weaver was almost alone in holding out hope for Lucia's sanity, Joyce poured out his confessions of frustration and misery to her. Miss Weaver was as sensitive to Joyce's state of mind during the unending ordeal as she was concerned over Lucia's mental illness. Joyce's letters sometimes took on a bitter, jaunty tone, and in one letter he attempted to convince Harriet Weaver that his daughter was a gifted clairvoyant, citing instances proving Lucia's extrasensory perceptions.

More to the point, he penned an abstract diagnosis of Lucia's psyche to Giorgio: "[Your sister] has sometimes the wisdom of the serpent and the innocence of the dove."

"I HATE WOMEN who know anything," Joyce once complained of Mary Colum when she insisted he acknowledge his debt to Freud and Jung for the psychological insights apparent in *Ulysses,* and particularly his use of *monologue intérieure* suggested by the Freudian "free association" technique encouraged of patients undergoing psychoanalysis. Actually Joyce had been influenced by the French novelist Edouard Dujardin in the use of interior monologue, and he was altogether disdainful of the discoveries and theories of both the "Tweedledum and Tweedledee" of the psychiatric profession.

Joyce was further annoyed by Maria Jolas when she implored him to seek treatment for Lucia from Carl Jung. Joyce had a personal aversion to Jung dating from Jung's introduction to the German translation of *Ulysses,* objecting to certain references to the novel's style and content. He referred to Jung as someone who "amuses himself at the expense (in every sense of the word) of ladies and gentlemen who are troubled with bees in their bonnets."

Joyce reserved his most antagonistic attitude toward women, especially those women who had sacrificed most to support him and his work, devoting themselves tirelessly to the "Joyce industry." Ironic that the great celebrant of the feminine mystique—loving creator of Molly Bloom in *Ulysses* and Anna Livia Plurabelle in *Finnegans Wake*—would in the final decade of his life develop so strong a streak of misogyny—though the tendency was always there, seasoned by a steady resentment of dependency on women. He had already broken with Sylvia Beach and Adrienne Monnier in a manner that at least allowed for courteous exchange at cool distance, but now Joyce suddenly lashed out at Beach, saying that she had been poisoned against him for ten years, and against Lucia for the past two. It was a final unfair accusation meant to end whatever friendly remembrances of the twenties lingered on: the two devoted associates from that era, as close friends as Joyce would allow, were never to meet again.

Even the complaisant Harriet Weaver who graciously submitted to Joyce's constant demands and extended her purse at every excessive request became a target of his sarcasm. Weaver loyally sided with him on the issue of Lucia's hospitalization, and went so far as to volunteer the care of Lucia in her own home. Having underestimated the state of Lucia's disturbed mind—Joyce in his letters was inclined to present his daughter in hoped-for rather than in actual terms—the therapeutic visit was a disaster. The generous-spirited, tender-hearted Harriet Weaver was not capable of dealing with a sometimes violent and always capricious in-house patient. Lucia would disappear from the premises or impulsively leap aboard a bus during a promenade with a nurse, once requiring the help of the London police to track down the fugitive.

In his displeasure over Harriet's failure to handle his daughter Joyce wrote: "Possibly Lucia, not having been brought up as a slave and having neither Bolshevik nor Hitlerite tendencies [Harriet Weaver was about to join the Communist Party], made a very bad impression on you and she certainly does not flatter . . ."

Any occasion Joyce interpreted as unacceptable attitude by well-meaning women friends, Lucia as catalyst, brought on the defensive father's vindictive response.

According to Richard Ellmann, the James Joyce of the 1930s "thought of women more and more [as] dolls, unfortunately not mindless." His wife could be indulged in her feminine "doll-state" by encouraging her extravagance in hats by Agnès, gowns designed by her wealthy daughter-in-law's dressmaker, or a shopping spree at Lelong, Marlene Dietrich's couturier on the avenue Matignon.

"La femme c'est rien," Joyce told Stuart Gilbert, and when another male friend, Arthur Power, asked what he thought of Italian women, Joyce declared, "Cold, like all women."

Lucia was excepted from the sour contempt Joyce felt toward women, his daughter placed in a special category of protectiveness and paternal understanding of her extraordinary nature. He dreamed up more instances of her clairvoyance: she was a mystic, not a madwoman. He sought every excuse to explain her bizarre actions as manifestations of creative inspiration, relative to his own, and if Lucia needed psychiatric care then so did he. Ellmann expressed this associative father-daughter defense as: "[James Joyce's] defiant attitude was that she was no madder than her father. But he was bitterly sane, and foolish fond like Lear."

The excessive and unbalanced father-daughter relationship was considered dangerous by doctors, and both parents were warned away from contact with their daughter. Nora, constant target for Lucia's hostility, complied; Joyce was unable to do so. (When her father did absent himself, Lucia became all the more depressed or violent.) Lucia was deeply attached to her father, and he—now in her mental turmoil—to her. Because of their close relationship and from speculation arising out of explicit fantasies in Ulysses and again noticeable in Work in Progress, absurd and unpleasant gossip began to circulate among Left Bank Joycean friends. When the suggestion of incest reached Richard Ellmann, he blithely replied that James Joyce was not highly enough sexed to transfer incestuous fantasy to act.

AFTER REREADING THE Molly Bloom sequence in *Ulysses,* Jung revised his opinion of that work in a way that was certain to flatter the author.

"I suppose the devil's grandmother knows so much about the real psychology of women," wrote Jung. "I didn't."

When this insight from Jung was read aloud to Nora Joyce, she delivered the outspoken opinion: "He [Jim] knows nothing about women."

It is tempting to believe that Jung's flattering reaction to *Ulysses* finally convinced Joyce to entrust his daughter's damaged psyche to the doctor's care. More likely, Joyce by now had nowhere else to turn. Lucia was admitted to a private sanatorium at Küsnacht where Jung was on the staff and would personally attempt to treat Joyce's daughter—the twentieth doctor to do so. (Joyce complained of the expense, the clinic at seven thousand francs per month, another thirty-six hundred francs to Jung.) Lucia did at first relate unexpectedly well to the eminent Dr. Jung—so seldom did she submit to such doctor-patient sessions with any ease or candor—and appeared happy with arrangements at Küsnacht, and even began to gain weight, taken by Joyce as a good sign.

But Lucia's positive response to Jung may have been no more than a sly schizoid deception on her part, or a display of cooperation meant to impress her father, for she later expressed a more heartfelt assessment of her doctor: "To think that such a big fat materialistic Swiss man should try to get hold of my soul!"

Jung had already ruled out psychoanalysis in the case of schizophrenia, and when the initial rapport with his patient declined he became less sanguine that Lucia was curable—dashing Joyce's hopes once again. Jung then made the tactical error of diagnosing James Joyce (from evidence in his work) as also manifesting schizoid elements, then further exceeded his mandate by suggesting Joyce's eccessive drinking was a factor in both father-daughter pathologies, thus ending any consideration that "the reverend Dr. Jung" (as Joyce referred to him afterward) was meant to be his daughter's savior.

The ill-considered venture to send Lucia abroad when the Jungian therapy failed was partly at Lucia's urging, for Samuel Beckett happened to be in London at that time and Lucia, still obsessed with her phantom lover, hoped to meet him there (perhaps the reason for her evasion from Miss Weaver's care).

Lucia visited Joyce's widowed sister in Ireland for a sojourn as catastrophic as the earlier visit with Harriet Weaver: she started a fire on the bungalow floor so that she might smell the odor of burning turf.

When Lucia returned to Paris Maria Jolas offered hospitality to Joyce's daughter at her home in Neuilly, a doomed attempt at home care for the hopeless case. Lucia became hysterical and had to be taken to a clinic at Vésinet in a straightjacket, but was refused admission there and was eventually confined to a *maison de santé* in Ivry. What Joyce had dreaded had finally come to pass: Lucia was institutionalized for the rest of her life. Her father visited at one hospital or another (Lucia once attempted to strangle him), but Nora was never to see her demented daughter again.

18

LAST DANCE

But Society's finished, there are no longer any rules, any proprieties, in conversation anymore than in dress. Ah, mon cher, it's the end of the world.

—BARON CHARLUS, IN MARCEL PROUST,
REMEMBRANCE OF THINGS PAST

THE EDITOR OF *Paris Soir* described the comtesse Hélène de Portes (born Rebuffel) as having been born *"au milieu des caisses de savon,"* in the middle of soap boxes, and designated her as *"la première"* of a pair of infamous mistresses of the two most powerful political leaders of France. The second, the marquise Jeanne de Crussol (born Beziers) "was born amidst sardine tins."

When Jeanne Beziers, daughter of a sardine canning magnate from Normandy, became the marquise de Crussol, her elevation in society invited the invidious pun: the sardine who believed herself a sole [*crue sole*].

Her aspirations grew far beyond the title by marriage of marquise; she intended, like Hélène de Portes, to manipulate by way of a political lover the destiny of France.

Both women were aware that the essential setting for their grandiose ambitions required a salon, and one frequented by a key political figure through whom—if only behind the damask draperies of a salon—she could influence affairs of state.

The establishment of a distinguished salon called for a noblewoman at its head, and the way to a title for a daughter of the bourgeoisie was by marriage to an aristocrat. Jeanne Beziers targeted for marriage the marquis de Crussol, grandson to the Duchesse d'Uzes, who responded to the beauty from Normandy (perhaps more so to the Beziers fortune in fisheries) and soon made her his wife and marquise. The marquis himself, an indifferent marriage partner and avid clubman, was neither threat nor hindrance to his wife's salon ambitions or to her calculated adultery. She took as a lover Edouard Daladier, "the bull," known for his top-heavy physique and blunt peasant manner, *"Daladier d'abord en salon, puis en chambre"* as the Parisian wit would express the liaison: "Daladier at first in [Jeanne's] salon, then in her bedchamber."

The seduction bred mutual benefit. Though Daladier enjoyed a certain Leftist patronage at the polls, his connection to the aristocratic marquise did no damage to that image and enhanced his reputation in the public eye as a statesman on the rise. A popular song of 1935 was *"Tout va très bien, Madame la Marquise,"* and for the marquise de Crussol, all went exceedingly well indeed. She had succeeded in two of her primary goals by way of shrewd alliances, and now enjoyed the promise of the third, that Daladier would become premier again. (Edouard Daladier served as French premier for nine months in 1933, something of a record in the 1930s when the average survival rate of a premier's cabinet was three months before the government inevitably fell.)

Arch-rival to the marquise was comtesse Hélène de Portes, née Rebuffel, whose father was a wealthy shipping magnate in the Midi, thus heiress to a fortune that entitled Hélène to an aristocratic marriage as well, hers to comte Jean de Portes, son of the marquis de Portes and the Duchesse de Gadagne, which automatically bestowed upon Hélène the title of comtesse. The comte was equally indifferent to his wife's role as society adventuress, with (as it turned out) even more sinister aspirations than had the marquise de Crussol.

Madame de Porte's choice of pilot fish into the domain of political power was Paul Reynaud, about whom Princesse Marthe Bibesco early on advised Hélène: "Listen, the Marshal Lyautey [of the radical Right] admires him . . . he even said to me, 'Take notice of this little man. He's over fifty years old but it's now he will begin to grow.'" Hélène de Portes did take notice. Reynaud attended her salon almost on tiptoe, to appear taller, his thumbs hooked into his vest, known to be a formidable orator—

no small gift in the articulate circles of Parisian society, and could compensate for a diminutive stature—and a growing reputation as statesman. Taking as his mistress the beautiful, now titled, Hélène de Portes was another addition to the self-conscious Reynaud's stature. Madame de Portes instinctively recognized her value to him, as well as his to her, and played out the seduction to advantage much in the way of Wallis Simpson who succeeded so completely with the besotted Edward VIII.

THE CRUSSOL SALON, featuring Daladier as its drawing card, appeared as "liberal" as the Right can lean; the de Portes salon, promoting the fortunes of Paul Reynaud, catered to the extreme Right (though the label was not altogether applicable to Reynaud), since Mme. de Portes's sympathies lay in that direction, appreciably fascistic. She admired "strong men" like Hitler and Mussolini, and favored their ruthless policies—yet Reynaud, who showed instances of strength, was dominated even in his finest hours by his much stronger-willed mistress. Reynaud's vanity made him compliant to his mistress's wishes; he took measures to appear taller than he was, and dyed his hair to look younger than he was, all for love of "la belle Hélène," or so he believed.

It was said that the plutocracy of not more than two hundred families "ran" France, or at least the politics and commerce, and it was as true in the 1930s, as in the 1890s Banquet Years. Proust's Baron Charlus described this milieu as "a middle-class circle cross-bred with minor nobility, where people who are very rich and connected by marriage with an aristocracy the higher aristocracy does not know."

HOSTESSES TOOK PRECAUTIONS to invite either Madame Crussol or Madame de Portes to their parties, but never the two together—though inadvertently, at Madame Paul de Beaumont's soirée, the two women did appear and in the course of the evening the mistresses of "the two most important political figures of France" engaged in a snide encounter that began with insulting remarks and ended when the two woman had to be physically pulled apart.

Both husbands of these two ambitious socialites allowed their wives *"une grande libérté sociale"* and seldom accompanied either the comtesse

La comtesse Hélène de Portes (right).

Mme. de Portes (fourth from left) at the Beaumont costume ball, June 1939.

or the marquise to social functions—the lovers, Daladier and Reynaud, taking precedence as escorts, an arrangement perfectly acceptable to all concerned.

The Crussol-Daladier alliance and, more important, the Mme. de Portes liaison with Paul Reynaud, was to affect the destiny of France in its most troubled hour, but in the beginning merely drove a wedge between two powerful political figures who should have been united in efforts to support a nation on the brink of crisis.

AN OMNIPRESENT FIXTURE at parties and balls given by the "two hundred" was a rather sinister presence, Otto Abetz, often accompanied by his consort, the Baroness von Einem, assumed to be his lover but whose background was as shadowy as that of Abetz. Despite their obscure origins, the two Germans blended ideally with the titled families who tended to live in the enclave of ancient town houses in the faubourg St. Germain and were known as the faubourg society of aristocrats. Abetz had been introduced into this exclusive milieu by the Duke and Duchess d'Harourt, a pro-Nazi couple whose political coloration was shared by many in that set. Ostensibly Abetz was in Paris to promote the Comité Franco-Allemagne, an organization seeking to establish friendly relations between the two historic enemies. The impeccable dress and manner of the baroness and the amiable social finesse of Abetz convinced many of the committee's benevolent intent. Actually the two German socialites were espionage agents of Nazi Germany's Abwehr.

Director of the Far Right journal *Gringoire,* Horace Carbuccia was an ardent supporter of Abetz, and to honor the German "friend of France" he gave a lavish party for him, inviting the cream of Parisian society. The honored guest, however, had been under surveillance by French Intelligence for some time; when the party ended Abetz was politely approached by a young man with an envelope for him—the man was an Intelligence officer, and the envelope contained a one-way ticket to Berlin. No exchange between the two was necessary: Otto Abetz was being expelled from France.

That same night Sûreté agents appeared at the door of the Baroness von Einem—Abetz enjoyed diplomatic immunity, but the baroness was subject to arrest—and when they inquired were informed that Madame had already fled.

JANET FLANNER NOTED in her *Letter from Paris* that the city was having a fit of prosperity, gaiety, and hospitality: "the first good time since the bad time started at Munich last summer. It has taken the threat of war to make the French loosen up and have a really swell and civilized good time."

Flanner was at hand to record the "civilized" gaiety of Paris, and Elsa Maxwell to mastermind the late season's parties. The Smart Set of American expatriates flourished in a world apart from the "higher aristocracy" of the faubourg St. Germain; the ubiquitous Americans with their wayward dollars and democratic bonhomie were social anarchists, no awareness of caste or standing, the dressy Duchess of Windsor their sole showpiece.

Never mind, was Elsa Maxwell's opinion, who stopped catering to aristocrats anyway: the show of deference required of them would "kill" a party. If her friends among the expatriates were not invited to the faubourg affairs, she need not include aristocrats on her guest lists for the theme parties: Come as Somebody Else, Come as the Person You Like Best or Least, Come as You Were When the Autobus Arrived (bus transport for the party calling at the addresses of the guests, which gave the invited a chance to attend in provocative deshabille). Who wanted haughty French aristocrats at a scavenger hunt anyway?

At the Ritz and the Crillon and Meurice hotels, an air of insouciant high living persisted despite the news of Germans now massing tanks on the frontier of Poland. (Elsa Maxwell's invitations now read ICNW instead of RSVP—In Case No War.) The Ritz Bar won out over the Crillon because Paul the concessionaire was reputed to serve the best cocktails in Paris, and the Ritz appealed to the live-for-the-moment set. Elsa Maxwell staged some of her most extravagant in-house parties at the Ritz, and at one such affair the hefty Elsa took it upon herself to eject an obnoxious drunk; she personally led him by the scruff of his dinner jacket to the taxi ramp on the place Vendôme. Having organized the affair at the behest of the man's wife, when she returned to the bar she was informed that she had kicked out the host.

The carefree gaiety that prevailed among the Ritz crowd was enlivened by the hijinks of Noel Coward—over from London, attached to a branch of British Security—and of his bosom companion, Cole Porter, in what Elsa Maxwell called the Lavender Element. Cole Porter regaled the drinking set with comic tales of his heroics during World War I (Noel Coward, his straight man), even to the Croix de Guerre he had been awarded, elaborate fictions all.

A fan of Porter's Broadway musicals awarded him (no Croix de Guerre) a gift pair of garters with gold elastic bands that Cole donned in the bar at the Ritz, hiking his pants for all to admire and tossing his old set of garters to Claude the barman. Gold was "in." (It had always been in with the French, who traditionally hoarded gold as a reserve currency to see them through national catastrophe.) A few doors from the Ritz, Cartier was selling yo-yos in gold to take advantage of the latest craze, and the sophisticates were spinning these trinkets in public as if counting prayer beads against disaster.

THAT THE ARISTOCRATIC stock of the "two hundred" was in decline was exemplified by the aging, eccentric, habitually reclusive marquise Casati, who would on impulse throw a lavish party that only hastened the diminishment of her limited means. The sine qua non of her soirées was a party of parties meant to begin with a fanfare of trumpets and end the marquise's entertaining for all time.

The Casati town house was not sumptuous enough to accommodate a masquerade ball of such historical extension, grandiose in theme ("famous couples throughout history"), so the marquise rented the former pink marble pavilion of comte Montesquiou: its formal gardens perfect for an alfresco fête, the ideal setting for the dream finale of a fading socialite before the curtain fell.

Costuming by Chanel or Schiaparelli, with suggestions from Dalí or Bébé Bérard (who often furnished inspiration for such theatrical affairs, or for the theatre itself), or the guests might devise costumes themselves from an historical era of choice, as far back in time as the Garden of Eden—"Eve" being reserved for the marquise Casati herself. The favorite period, naturally, was the reign of Louis XVI, which offered the greatest lavishness of dress and coiffure (requiring eighteenth-century wigs, the lacquered specialty of coiffeur Antoine) and the reign of the Sun King was a perfect frame in which the titled guests, whose titles in Republican France showed less and less luster, might disport themselves in fairy-tale display.

Daisy de Segonzac chose to attend as Marie Antoinette on the arm of her lover in history, comte d'Artois (enacted by Meyer, the musical revue star). Marie Antoinette, at the time of a general strike in Paris, was an unfortunate choice.

The entire evening was a misconceived event, ill-timed, when working-class Paris was most agitated and resentful of the privileged "patricians" parading through their neighborhood. In its day the quarter of le Vesinet had been an upper-class stronghold, but by the 1930s Montesquiou's elegant grounds were situated in a suburb populated by laborers; the pink marble pavilion was an almost comic anomaly against a backdrop of anonymous gray façades on either side.

The arrival of these fantastically garbed bluebloods in that particular neighborhood, at that significant moment, aroused angry resentment along with amused scorn. Here was a symbolic insult to everything the *grève générale* represented, the idle gentry cavorting among them dressed as their oppressors of 1789, the loudest hoots and jeers reserved for Marie Antoinette and consort (taken for Louis XVI himself, and not her lover) the royalty France had rid itself of (by beheading) on the place Royale . . . attended by just such a mob as now gathered round the pavilion Montesquiou. The local proles even took front-gallery seats along the low wall surrounding the formal gardens, to observe the fête at close quarters, intending to be entertained.

Meanwhile the guests at the outdoor affair wandered the gardens in disconsolate confusion. They had been promised a trumpet fanfare on arrival (but had been booed by a rowdy crowd instead). Where was the orchestra? Where was the hostess to greet them? The crowd could have informed the guests that the musicians were probably on strike. But where was the marquise Casati? When was the ball to be inaugurated?

The marquise intending to appear as Eve surely had second thoughts upon examining her costume, or lack of one, in a full-length mirror. Unlike her friend Lady Mendl who kept herself in pristine shape in her eighties (she could still stand on her head, and did so publicly on every possible occasion), the form and flesh of marquise Casati had given way to time and gravity. Moreover, her hired "Adam" rebelled at carrying the live snake the marquise had presented him. (She kept a private menagerie of wild animals, as did Josephine Baker, a publicity stunt in Baker's case, for the marquise a neurotic indulgence.) While the assembled guests wandered the gardens like untethered livestock, deprived of an orchestra, no hostess in sight, the crowd on the wall and from upper-story windows applauded the fiasco as if staged for their benefit.

The folly culminated in a sudden downpour that scattered guests and audience alike, the costumed women lifting the mille-feuilles skirts of their ball gowns as they ran shrieking for the shelter of cars and carriages to end the night's misbegotten affair.

Next morning a team of bailiffs arrived to confront the absentminded marquise at the behest of her debtors, but there was nothing in the way of collateral to offer them except Eve's papier-mâché fig leaf and the somnolent snake "Adam" had refused to carry to the garden party.

PARTIES AND BALLS followed one after the other throughout the fall and winter of 1939, though the gaiety was tempered with all the tension implicit in the term "at war." On September 1 Germany broke trust in the Munich accords signed the year before and attacked western Poland, while its new ally Russia attacked and occupied eastern Poland. Three days later England declared war on Germany; France reluctantly announced its own declaration of war, obliged to support its British ally. No fighting ensued, and the period became known as the *"drôle de guerre"* (the Phony War), wartime conditions prevailing, no enemy in sight.

As he took most calamities outside his immediate domain, James Joyce considered the outbreak of war a personal affront, and included the Phony War as part of fate's conspiracy against him. During the holiday season of '39, Joyce remained morose and silent for the most part, a figure of woe with his pirate's eye patch . . . but suddenly, at a Christmas party, he became quite animated. He went over to Maria Jolas twirling his ashplant cane and asked her to dance.

"Come on, then. You know very well it's the last Christmas."

19

DEBACLE — I

*T*HE SALON OF the marquise de Crussol was swept into glowing regard when its stellar attraction, Edouard Daladier, became premier at a critical moment in the nation's history. The threat of Europe plunging toward another disastrous conflict called for a French premier of cool-headed determination, capable of adaptable strategy in foreign affairs and a resolute policy in dealing with Hitler—none of which applied to Daladier.

The marquise may well have influenced his foreign policy, for Daladier satisfied the appeasement crowd completely. The faubourg set could only applaud the appointment (except, of course, Hélène de Portes, who seethed in the shadows offstage while her despised rival enjoyed her shallow triumph). The comtesse de Portes would await her hour, hovering in the wings, prepared to push Paul Reynaud into the spotlight as soon as Daladier took a pratfall.

Daladier's first opportunity to fail came at the Peace Conference in Munich in September 1938. The French premier stood beside Neville Chamberlain, prime minister of England, in a three-way confrontation stage-managed by the German Führer. The Munich Conference was less about "peace in our time" (Chamberlain's phrase) than Hitler's insistent demands, his insatiable appetite for Germany's "vital living space."

Flaunting his trademark umbrella, symbol of mild-mannered respectability (and naïveté), Chamberlain assumed he was signing a gentleman's agreement in signing away Czechoslovakia as a sacrifice to peace. The passive response of both England and France over Hitler's escalating demands could only cause Hitler to rub his hands. He was assured conclusively of the fecklessness of his powerful opponents to the west. For even the bumptious "bull of Vaucluse," the new premier of France, proved to have the horns of a snail.

In his memoirs Daladier admits to the shameful backing-down at Munich that only postponed the inevitable. He would have to answer to France for his faint-hearted surrender; therefore, on his return from Munich he eyed with trepidation the crowds gathered at Le Bourget to greet his return.

As he stepped from the plane Daladier turned up his collar in antic-ipation of a barrage of rotten eggs being hurled at him by the irate citi-zens he had so clearly betrayed. He was expecting a shrill *sifflement* (the whistling that expressed a crowd's disdain), but . . . bizarre . . . instead he heard the cry, "Vive Daladier!" from all sides. Instead of eggs, flow-ers were tossed at him, and his craven behavior at Munich was reward-ed with applause. Jeanne de Crussol beamed at him from the crowd gathered along the runway.

If the newspaper reviews of Daladier's performance at Munich were any barometer of popular sentiment, the premier had "saved" France. Even the opposition leader on the Left, Léon Blum, offered Daladier "a just tribute of gratification." Blum declared that war was averted and now "Man can take up his work again, can sleep at night, can once more enjoy the beauty of the autumn sun."

Indeed, the autumn sun of that year in France shone resplendently; the crisp clear days beside the Seine, rare in Paris, offered a setting con-ducive of hope. In the shadows, and out of power, were those who real-ized that Munich merely purchased for Hitler the advantage of a further buildup of arms and construction of planes for the lightning attacks of the Luftwaffe.

Charles de Gaulle impatiently paced the corridors of the Ministry of War, and in England Winston Churchill observed the downward spiral of events with horror—the two intrepid warriors awaiting a call to arms.

BY NOVEMBER 1939, the sun still smiling unseasonably on Paris, Warsaw had surrendered and Poland was occupied by German troops.

During the wartime somnolence of the *"drôle de guerre"* in Paris preparations were in effect to arouse an indifferent populace to the fact that France was truly at war.

At noon on Thursdays the air-raid sirens were tested. Underground shelters were designated across the city where during drills neighbor met neighbor (many for the first time) with a handshake and an *"Enchanté."* Gas masks had been issued at the time children were being evacuated from the city. The masks were distributed free of charge, though Sylvia Beach was informed that she, as a foreigner, would be obliged to pay for hers. (She would not in any case have donned such a grotesque apparatus, unable to relate poison gas to the vicinity of Shakespeare and Company, and her friend Hemingway, an expert on modern warfare, had told her that gas would not be used in combat this time—it was too expensive.) In combat, she mused . . . she and her bookshop were"in combat" with no one.

Women were advised not to wear mascara under a gas mask as it would irritate the eyes and cause the wearer to remove the mask at her peril. In shop windows on the place Vendôme and the place de la Madeleine mannequins were shown with colored bows at the neckline of their gas masks, a quaint touch of chic to that gruesome protective device. A confectioner on the avenue de l'Opéra was selling chocolates in boxes shaped like gas masks.

Food rationing was minimal and only fitfully observed. A war correspondent (with no war yet to document) described his first meal on a return to Paris from the garrisoned Maginot Line: "a choice of seven kinds of oysters, six or seven kinds of fish including bouillabaisse, no butcher's meat (veal, mutton, beef) and no sausages, 'only' rabbit, chicken and curry . . ."

A. J. Liebling, correspondent for *The New Yorker,* also noticed that food was still plentiful, "but people got thin worrying . . . The cheekbones, the noses, and the jaws of all Paris were becoming more prominent."

Café waiters no longer allowed saucers to accumulate: patrons were asked to pay when served; at any time an air-raid siren might empty the tables instantly.

Restrictions and halfhearted security measures had been put into effect two months before the Poland crisis: crossword puzzles in *Marianne* were discontinued in case they contained code. Leaves of absence in the military were canceled as the German panzer divisions turned westward toward the Low Countries, and the pace of mobilization stepped up, the raw recruits queuing up unhappily at the gare de l'Est.

"Every day somebody said good-bye to me," wrote A. J. Liebling. "[Those who remained] seemed to congregate on the boulevards. It gave them comfort to look at one another . . . You could get a table at a sidewalk café only with difficulty, and the ones that had all-girl orchestras did particularly well." (Male musicians had been drafted into military bands.) No curfew had as yet been imposed so the Folies Bergère and Casino de Paris attracted an overflow; the popular song of the moment was *"J'attendrai,"* meant to be a love ballad but could as well mean "I will wait" for the Germans.

AFTER HAVING BLUDGEONED Poland into surrender, German troops overran tiny Denmark almost as an afterthought, then invaded Norway. Holland resisted for three days only, then succumbed to the powerful German onslaught, with no help from France, and the only effective aid from Britain was a gunboat dispatched across the Channel to evacuate Queen Wilhelmina of the Netherlands.

Chamberlain had sadly rolled his symbolic umbrella and retired from the world stage; a statesman of opposite temperament replaced him, Winston Churchill, who was to become Britain's new symbol of bulldog determination as the Phony War became the real one.

The day of the collapse of Poland, the Duke of Windsor was an honored guest at the Marigny Theatre charity ball for the war effort. His wife, the Duchess, was at the Ritz organizing a bandage-rolling circle there; the dilemma of a dress code for the organization was posed, whether to wear Red Cross uniforms, or to dress fashionably "to keep up morale."

As obsolete royalty living in Paris, there was the touchy issue of how to respond to the expatriated Duke's entreaty for an official function of wartime usefulness—more to the question was the public friendship the Duke and Duchess exhibited for Adolph Hitler and his regime— which effectively canceled out their equally warm relationship with the new prime minister Winston Churchill. Churchill found a compromise assignment in sending the Duke on an inspection tour of the Maginot Line (the prime minister had already inspected the line himself, and drawn his own gloomy conclusions). The Duke reported favorably enough on France's first line of defense, a marvel of military engineering, but the Duke, among others (including Churchill) questioned the effectiveness of these extensive defenseworks if the Germans (as on two earlier historical occasions) chose to strike at France through the kingdom of Belgium, where the Great Wall ended quixotically at the Franco-Belgian border.

THE GENERALISSIMO CHOSEN by Premier Daladier for the ultimate defense of France was Maurice Gamelin, sometimes known as "Gagamelin" for his near-senile insistence on fighting World War I over again, the war in which he had distinguished himself as a strategist. Gamelin was convinced the German army would revert to the notorious Schlieffen Plan, which had served von Molte with such success in 1914. But Gamelin was counting on the Ardennes mountain range to block progress of German motorized tank units bound for the French frontier with Belgium.

In France the seige mentality prevailed. No one in power— certainly not Daladier or Gamelin—seemed to recall Napoléon's famous warning against trust in fixed fortifications. A defensive garrison strategy, in warfare as in chess, inevitably invited defeat.

GAMELIN WAS CORRECT in one assumption, that the German military would again launch an attack through Belgium so as to strike at the capital city of Paris. The Deuxième Bureau was receiving intelligence reports that an attack through Belgium was imminent, a report confirmed by an eye-witness account of Antoine de Saint-Exupéry (author of Le Petit Prince) flying reconnaissance missions over Belgium. The intrepid (and reckless) French pilot flew over German panzer divisions throwing up pontoon bridges substantial enough to accommodate heavy tanks crossing rivers and streams along Germany's border with Belgium.

Preceding the German advance was a stream of refugees, "like an interminable treacle, moving toward a ghostly terminus."

If General Gamelin received any of these communications—intelligence communiqués did not always get through to the general staff at Versailles—he did not act on the information.

RIGHTISTS IN PARIS nurtured the perpetual dread of an uprising on the Left to take advantage of instability and national crisis, but so far the only notable rebellion was by a determined legion of concierges, the city's most independent-minded citizens. These guardians of the city's multiple-dwelling residences had never unionized but were allied by common traits of character and traditional duties and responsibilities. They were the foremost quartier gossips, and their news spread as quickly as the postal system of *pneumatiques* (and far superior to the intelligence communiqués of the military). When trucks from the sanitation department unloaded neat piles of sand in front of apartment buildings, the sand was to be carried to attics or to the topmost floor of the building to help prevent the spread of fire from incendiary bombs. This was no part of duties expected of a concierge, and there was wholesale refusal to carry buckets of sand up so many flights of stairs. The sandpiles remained at curbside for the few children left in Paris to play in, or for the convenience of stray cats as feline *pissotières*.

THROUGHOUT THE "PHONY War" the Académie Française continued its costumed tradition of formal conferences on Wednesday afternoons to determine which words were acceptable for entry into the classic *Dictionnaire Larousse,* and at the time of King Leopold's capitulation of the kingdom of Belgium, the Académie was engaged in determining whether a chicken wing was a limb or a muscle.

20

EXODUS

Paris is melting away as if infected with consumption.

— ARTHUR KOESTLER

TUESDAY BY TUESDAY, just as the abbé d'Ars predicted, disaster came to pass (and not just on Tuesdays—any day of the week could be bad-news day), to Gertrude Stein's increasing anxiety and dismay. Who would have expected a pact between Hitler and Stalin to divide the spoils of the Polish conquest? The Republic of Spain was no more and the pathetic little kingdom of Belgium in abject surrender after the German blitzkreig. Lately Gertrude turned to a favorite saint for enlightenment, Saint Odilie, who promised "that the world would go on and there would come the worst war of all and the fire would be thrown down from the heavens [but] that Paris which was in the greatest danger would be saved because of the holiness of its holy women." Gertrude and Alice were far from the holiest of women, but if the world was to go on, so would they. They were engaged in arrangements to leave the city.

The dealer Kahnweiler was in charge of storing Gertrude's valuable collection of modern art; they took with them only the portrait of

Gertrude by Picasso and a single Cézanne. Alice loaded the car with all the practical things they would need at their summer home in Bilignin in central France, including their poodle Basket's pedigree papers (and of course the dog's ration card, for Gertrude had wangled a ration card for Basket along with cards for herself and Alice)—where they would wait out these suspenseful events in the tranquillity of village life where one Tuesday was like another and no more disastrous than Tuesday last.

In those few hours in Paris for last-minute arrangements and final packing-up Gertrude realized that, though Paris was and always would be her "home town," the country was a better place than a city in wartime: "They grow things to eat right where you are, so there is no privation . . ." In that, Gertrude seemed for once to be as sensibly pragmatic as Alice.

EXCEPT FOR THE late revels of the socialites, the city closed down edgily at-nightfall behind floor-length drapes of partial blackout—called "blueout" at first because of its negligible application, impossible to impose stringent and universal precautions and expect skeptical Parisians to comply. To submit to ritual discipline was not in the French character (a trait of the French Lindbergh so deplored, and admired the opposite in the Germans). The end-of-summer skies were particularly unclouded and empty of threat. There was a passive acceptance of preliminary precautions—*mobilisation générale* the most grave—while otherwise Paris succumbed to numb resignation that war most likely would someday come to pass, for many remembered the conflict of only twenty years before. So far hostilities were in suspension, and Paris performed exercises of a theatrical nature: certain remembered restrictions (three meatless days a week, no hard liquor served in restaurants . . . but champagne still permitted), as if in rehearsal for the zeppelin attacks of 1914–18.

At dark shopkeepers slammed down their metal shutters with a finality suggesting that there would be no opening on the morrow—but open they did next morning, for the hoarding season was on, and the occasion to inflate prices (and for many *commerçants* this represented the heady anticipation of black market prices ahead, come what may). Candles were at a premium and sold one at a time.

"I WAS SO sure there was not going to be war," groaned Gertrude Stein en route for Bilignin. The roads south were crowded, but mostly with refugees from Holland and Belgium, so far. "And here it was, it was war, and I made quite a scene."

But was it war?

True, raw conscripts were queued up at the gare du Nord and the gare de l'Est with their sad civilian valises to be exchanged for uniforms and backpacks when they reached their units in the northeast. There they would dawdle in limbo. Nothing to occupy the literary imagination of one, Jean-Paul Sartre, recently mobilized, brooding on the fall of Madrid and the shameful haste to recognize the Franco regime by both Paris and London . . . and wait, while avoiding or enduring the more obnoxious of his fellow conscripts. When Simone de Beauvoir visited the grim philosopher at his post near Strasbourg, she found him resigned but convinced of a *drôle* concept of this *drôle de guerre:* it would be, he said, a bloodless conflict. "Sartre is persuaded that there will be no fighting, that it will be a modern war without massacres as modern painting is without subject, music without melody, physics without matter."

That was Sartre's existential summary of the crisis, but at the same time the sculptor Ossip Zadkine suggested a less sanguine outcome, recording in his diary: "The cord draws tighter and tighter around the neck and one notices in the smallest village something is broken in France."

Picasso wasted no time in analysis of impending cataclysm, but to continue painting he would have to seek a sunnier clime than the gloom that obsessed Paris, and set forth for the Riviera where the sun was an uncertain barometer of current mood, but offered warmth and light to paint by.

To escape France altogether, Salvador Dalí headed for his native province of Catalonia, having no quarrel (as did Picasso) with Spain under fascist rule.

ON THE WAY to see Kahane his publisher in the place Vendôme, Henry Miller could not fail to have noticed, and considered the significance of, public monuments sandbagged at the base: "Cleopatra's Needle" poking through its layer of sandbags at the place de la Concorde, at place des Pyramides a gilded equestrian Jeanne d'Arc reinforced with wooden scaffolding, and above all the Vendôme column sandbagged heavily to support the effigy of Bonaparte aloft in case of ground-shaking bombardment. All of which contributed to Miller's desperation and determination to move on. Kahane would surely advance funds sufficient for his author to escape Paris.

The war was not the only reason driving Miller to Kahane's office. Paris was no longer the abode of Miller's head and heart, nor cherished headquarters to a literary career. Only a year ago he was made euphoric beyond reason to pass a bookshop window on the rue Castiglione filled with copies of *Tropic of Cancer*. The books were piled around a bust of Henry Miller . . . well, a photograph of a bust of him (the bust by a Czech sculptor of Miller's acquaintance). Lately, after a decade of exile here, the charm and excitement of Paris had lost its edge; the flighty betrayals of Anaïs Nin hardly mattered anymore. A sharper edge and more immediate demand was that of Paris in imminent peril; a need to flee the city replaced the earlier sense of adventure and romance.

Another need seethed inside Miller, that of recognition as an artist of merit and daring in his own country, to achieve acceptance as an important literary figure and not just as the author of a famous d.b. (dirty book) for the tourist trade. Kahane, Anaïs, and Lawrence Durrell (and not just friends and cronies, either) pronounced *Tropic* a masterpiece, so why not let the world know?

Of primary concern, however, was to escape the doomed city. Anaïs was in London with Hugo, so he would have to turn to Kahane for help. First he would go to Greece; any avenue of departure was worth taking, with apocalypse just around the next corner.

As he walked along rue de Castiglione he replayed another mind trip he had considered. He thought of entering a Buddhist monastery in Tibet, and had actually made serious inquiries to that end. Brassaï declared that he already looked the part—almost totally bald, his remaining tonsure of white hair like a fallen halo. .

But first, why not explore southern France, a region of no strategic military interest and therefore safe? The landscapes of the Midi were unfamiliar to him except by way of paintings by Cézanne and Van Gogh at the Jeu de Paume museum . . . a tour of the Mediterranean—after all these years confined to the urban landscape of Paris.

Then he would set sail for the Aegean, having replied positively to Durrell's invitation to visit him in Corfu, concluding his letter with the habitual entreaty, "Send Dough!" An idyllic sojourn in Greece would prepare his mind and heart for a return to the States. He would write

Anaïs in London for money if Kahane didn't come through. Nin was in England seeking a British publisher for her diaries, as unlikely a prospect as Henry Miller becoming a Buddhist monk.

On the same side of the place Vendôme as Kahane's Obelisk Press was the salon display window of Schiaparelli, featuring her Cash-and-Carry line of parachute-shaped dresses (another reminder of the war), ample dresses with pockets everywhere in case of air raid for a woman "to pack" and dash for a shelter. (Schiaparelli's entire fall line reflected the patriotic motif, colors in Foreign Legion red, airplane gray, Maginot Line blue.)

Kahane was always good for a modest "advance" since *Tropic* had become a trophy item for tourists to smuggle back to the States, and was selling at rare-book prices. The editor promised to send Miller a monthly stipend in Greece; Anaïs Nin sent money for train fare to the Midi, and promised to meet Miller in Aix-en-Provence. Two hundred dollars came through from Frances Steloff for books smuggled by a sailor into New York—but the package destined for the Gotham Book Mart was misaddressed and fell into the hands of Customs, then promptly confiscated. Henry promised to replace the contraband books, or refund Frances the two hundred dollars . . . whenever, and discounting the apocalypse.

"I am poised," Miller wrote to his benefactors, "like a bird, not certain in which direction to take off."

MOBILISATION GÉNÉRALE HAD drastically reduced the city's population of young men of military age, but the most notable absence in Paris was that of children, gone from the weekend Guignols in the Luxembourg Gardens (now showing to adults, featuring marionettes of Hitler and Stalin), and also the eager children with their sailboats at Lenôtre's circular *bassin* in the Jardins de Tuileries, coaxing their toy boats to safe harbor at the *bassin*'s rim, now sent to safe harbors themselves, in Brittany or to the Midi. The mass evacuation counted some 16,500 children sent away.

IF JAMES JOYCE was aware of the absence of children, or of the designated air-raid shelter at his local metro stop, he gave no serious consideration to its implications. He was absorbed in revising the final pages of *Wake*, with the drive to finish, in spite of stomach pains, war drums in the background. The threat of war engaged Joyce's thoughts only peripherally; as he told Danish journalist Ole Vinding (who broke through Joyce's guard against interviewers by posing as an artist): "Isn't it better to make a great joke instead [of making war], as I have done?" Joyce considered his latest work and final masterpiece a triumph of humor, but many, including those who supported him in the writing of it, thought if the book was meant to be funny, the joke was on Joyce. The *Work,* or the *Wake* (when the title was at last divulged) was the only sustaining element to his life of late, and reviewing the galleys he sometimes laughed to himself aloud. It was the only time he laughed now.

If the Parisian mystique had faded for Henry Miller, it had never occurred to James Joyce; the city represented little more to him than a place to get on with his literary endeavors, which were coming to an end with *Finnegans Wake*. Paris for two decades had been for Joyce a locale conducive to the "silence, exile, cunning" necessary to the gargantuan task. As for the charm and beauty of Paris, he was more than satisfied with its conveniences for work and attracted to its restaurants (though an indifferent gourmet) and to the middle-class accommodations in the quieter neighborhoods, provided him by patrons and friends. He might as well have dwelt on the banks of the Liffey in Dublin (and might have done so if not for his longstanding feud with Ireland) rather than beside the Seine. He wrote nothing about Paris. If he saw the city of light at all (with his execrable eyesight, and inattention to setting), it was only to travel in Nora's wake from flat to flat, the more resemblant to rooms in Dublin the better.

Joyce may not have noticed the steady exodus from the city, but Nora was aware of the migration of Parisians elsewhere and a great many apartments now available. She discovered an ideal one in the posh neighborhood of Passy on the rue des Vignes, after turning down another flat as "not fit to wash a rat in."

Giorgio and his wife Helen were back in Paris, Giorgio under threat of military call-up, his wife suffering a series of "breakdowns" her husband (as dismissive of the frailty of women as his father was) attributed to hysterics. Helen, like Lucia, would eventually have to be hospitalized. The hospital in Brittany where Lucia was confined had been taken over by the military, so new arrangements would have to be made for his daughter, which further unnerved Joyce.

The abdominal pains that plagued Joyce periodically were more intense than ever, and he was urged by a doctor to submit to X ray, but

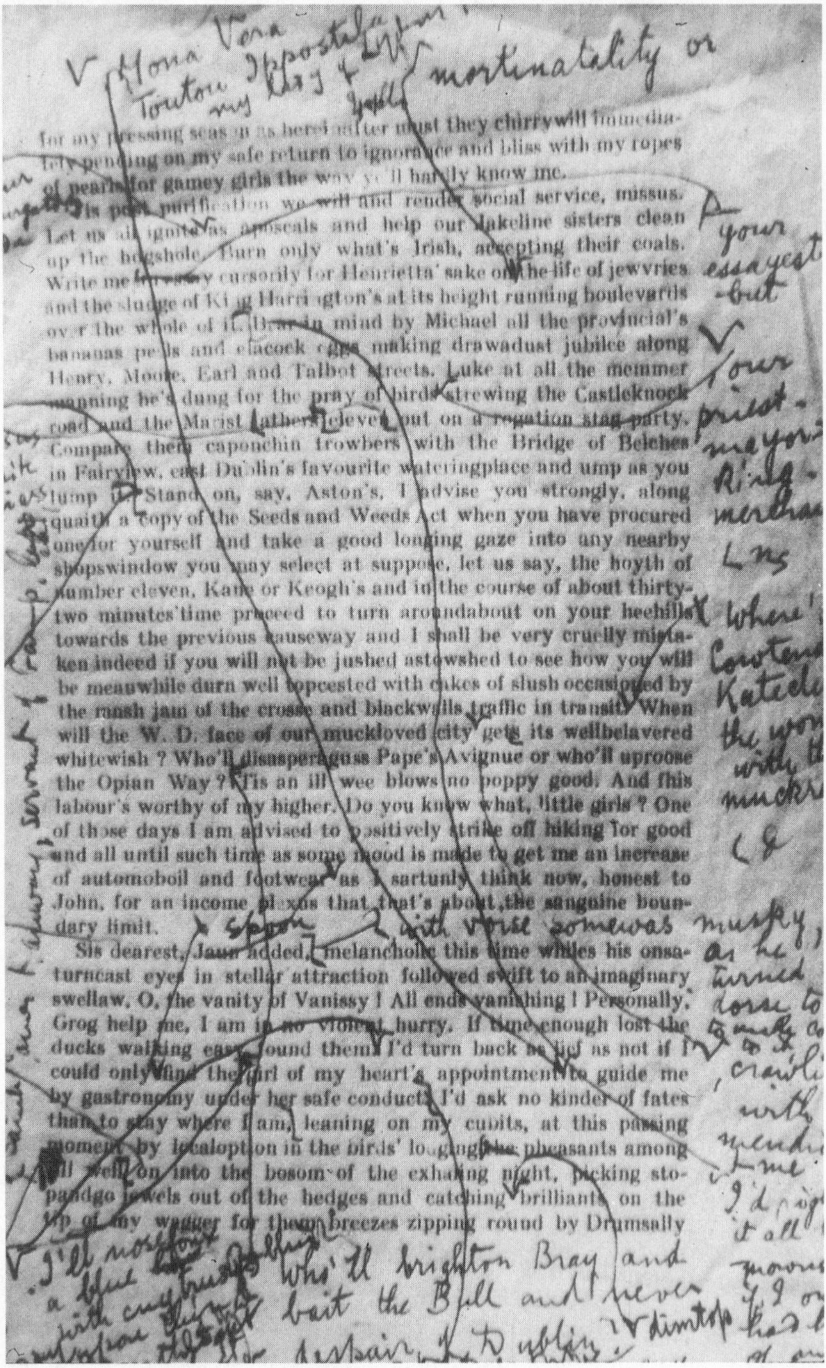

for my pressing season as hereinafter must they chirrywill immediately pending on my safe return to ignorance and bliss with my ropes of pearls for gamey girls the way you'll hardly know me. This post purification we will and render social service, missus. Let us all ignite as aposcals and help our lakeline sisters clean up the hogshole. Burn only what's Irish, accepting their coals. Write me ... cursorily for Henrietta' sake on the life of jewvries and the sludge of King Harrington's at its height running boulevards over the whole of it. Bear in mind by Michael all the provincial's bananas peels and peacock eggs making drawadust jubilee along Henry, Moore, Earl and Talbot streets. Luke at all the memmer manning he's dung for the pray of birds strewing the Castleknock road and the Marist fathers eleven out on a rogation stag party. Compare them caponchin trowbers with the Bridge of Belches in Fairyview, east Dublin's favourite wateringplace and ump as you lump it. Stand on, say, Aston's, I advise you strongly, along quaith a copy of the Seeds and Weeds Act when you have procured one for yourself and take a good longing gaze into any nearby shopswindow you may select at suppose, let us say, the hoyth of number eleven, Kane or Keogh's and in the course of about thirtytwo minutes'time proceed to turn aroundabout on your heehills towards the previous causeway and I shall be very cruelly mistaken indeed if you will not be jushed astowshed to see how you will be meanwhile durn well topcested with cakes of slush occasioned by the ransh jam of the crosse and blackwalls traffic in transit. When will the W. D. face of our muckloved city gets its wellbelavered whitewish ? Who'll disasperaguss Pape's Avignue or who'll uproose the Opian Way ? Tis an ill wee blows no poppy good. And this labour's worthy of my higher. Do you know what, little girls ? One of those days I am advised to positively strike off hiking for good and all until such time as some mood is made to get me an increase of automoboil and footwear as I sartunly think now, honest to John, for an income plexus that, that's about the sanguine boundary limit.

Sis dearest, Jaun added, melancholic this time whiles his onsaturncast eyes in stellar attraction followed swift to an imaginary swellaw, O, the vanity of Vanissy ! All ends vanishing ! Personally, Grog help me, I am in no violent hurry. If time enough lost the ducks walking easy found them I'd turn back as lief as not if I could only find the girl of my heart's appointment to guide me by gastronomy under her safe conduct I'd ask no kinder of fates than to stay where I am, leaning on my cubits, at this passing moment by localoption in the birds' lounging the pheasants among all well on into the bosom of the exhaling night, picking stopandgo jewels out of the hedges and catching brilliants on the tip of my wagger for them breezes zipping round by Drumsally

Page proofs from *Finnegans Wake* with Joyce's corrections.

he neglected to do so. Nerves, he believed, was his problem—and the postpartum depression that overcame the writer at the completion of a major work—the same symptomatic disorder had occurred when Joyce wrote Molly Bloom's final resounding "yes" in *Ulysses*.

He had yet to reveal the title *Finnegans Wake* (suggested by the Irish legend of a hod-carrier who dies and is resurrected by the smell of whiskey at his wake) to anyone; not even his publisher Faber and Faber could get the title from him, as if he were saving the revelation as a punch line to what he believed were the comic adventures of Shem and Shaun. Though sometimes a slip of the tongue or a ditty being sung or an educated guess (by Eugene Jolas, in one instance) almost revealed the secret. When the Russians attacked Finland, and that tiny nation bravely resisted invasion, Joyce (who referred every earthshaking event only in terms of his *Work*) quoted his own pun from the text that gave the title: "the Finn again wakes"—but no one, of course, caught it.

With the *Work* completed, Joyce complained to Samuel Beckett that he would have to turn to teaching again to make a living (since there was not "ten centimes" of prospective income from *Finnegans Wake*), and Beckett proposed he apply for a lectureship in Italian that was opening at the University of Capetown. Joyce seriously considered the opportunity, then told Beckett that he had heard thunderstorms were frequent in South Africa and he would not apply. Joyce was as afraid of thunder as he was of dogs.

LIVING IN THE same Passy neighborhood as Joyce, though the two writers did not meet, Vladimir Nabokov endured the same uncertain circumstances as the troubled Irishman. Then came an unexpected but timely check for six hundred dollars from the American publishers Bobbs Merrill for an early novel *Camera Obscura*, now retitled *Laughter in the Dark*. The new title was apt, and applicable to the times: by September 1939 the blackout was fully enforced. (Nabokov remarked on the ornate street lamps "under veils.") At last there was something to laugh about. "We're rich!" he declared to Verá.

But the laughter faded as the war situation worsened, their own situation desperate when the Bobbs Merrill advance evaporated in living expenses while the Nabokovs made the rounds of crowded ministries (the streets were mostly empty, but the embassies full) soliciting the necessary stamps, documents, and visas required for permission to travel to the United States. The process was wretchedly slow, complicated because the Nabokovs were traveling on the Nansen passports issued refugee exiles from Sovietized Russia. French bureaucrats distracted by problems of their own had little sympathy to spare for the stateless Russian family stranded in Paris. Even if and when the visas came through, the Nabokovs needed $560 for transatlantic steamer accommodations.

Incredibly, Nabokov continued to write during this stressful episode. German tanks were moving into northeastern France in a double-pronged assault toward the seacoast and in the direction of Paris; young Dimitri had been sent to safety with friends in Deauville but might now be in more danger than if he had remained in Paris. Now that the British forces had been evacuated at Dunkirk and French divisions were in retreat, where would the Germans strike next?

Meanwhile Nabokov wrote, while his wife Verá trekked from embassy to ministry, pursuing every avenue of hope with persistence and determination.

Again, fellow Russian émigrés came to the rescue. Rachmaninoff sent Nabokov the loan of twenty-five hundred francs, and Alexandra Tolstoy provided the money from the Tolstoy Foundation for passage aboard the *Champlain*. (Visas were cleared when Nabokov paid a two-hundred-franc bribe to an official to recover a "lost" Nansen passport at the *préfecture*.)

The sailing of the *Champlain* had to be transferred from Le Havre to St. Nazaire when the port of Le Havre was threatened by advancing troops. Before the Nabokovs were to board, Dimitri was discovered to be feverish, running a temperature of 104°F. It seemed they would have to return to Paris and try for a later sailing, but the ship's doctor administered sulfamide tablets every four hours, Dimitri's fever subsided, and the *Champlain* got under way. An exciting surprise to the weary trouble-buffeted refugees was that they were given first-class accommodations, a luxurious surprise gift of the Tolstoy Foundation.

Unaware of what fortune had in store for them in the New World, but lucky to have left the Old, the Nabokovs actually escaped Paris with their lives. Soon after they left their last Paris lodging on the rue Boileau, that building was demolished in an aerial bombardment; and their vessel to the safety of the United States, the *Champlain*, was torpedoed and sunk by German U-boats on its very next sailing from France.

It was as if the fates had played so unfairly with the Russian family, the Nabokovs were now entitled to reprieve from oppression. Passing through Customs and Immigration on arrival in New York, the only ill luck was the minor loss of their key to a steamer trunk due for inspection. An aloof customs official blithely applied his jimmy to the trunk, and the lid popped open. There were two pairs of boxing gloves packed at the top of the trunk (Vladimir had been teaching young Dimitri to box), and the customs official put on one pair, joined by another official who donned the other, to start a mock boxing match. The Nabokovs could laugh again, furnished an astonishing first spectacle of how light-hearted life in America could be.

AN EQUALLY FARCICAL turn took place at the port of New York when the *Excambion* docked, with Salvador Dalí aboard. Reporters were on hand to interview celebrities, and Dalí was known to them from his previous New York visit as a shameless show-off and good for a story. When Dalí disembarked he was wearing a baguette of French bread strapped to his head with a belt, a startling image with his long surrealist twists of mustache.

"What's the bread all about?" asked one reporter. The bread, he declared, symbolized the starving masses of Europe.

Fellow surrealist Man Ray and the composer Virgil Thomson had traveled aboard the *Excambion* with Dalí, all three obliged to share the ship's library (where Man Ray's camera was stolen), sleeping on the floor since no berths were available. Embarrassed by Dalí's exhibitionist press conference, his reluctant shipmates managed to slip away unnoticed, blending anonymously with the crowd of debarking passengers at the pier.

AT THE TIME the Phony War was declared, Ambassador Bullitt called on all Americans to return to the United States. Bricktop's response was: "even after I knew what I should do, which was to get out, I didn't. I realized there was really nowhere for me to go . . . [Paris] had become my home. Returning to America had no appeal to me . . . so I stayed in Paris."

Bricktop expressed the common dilemma of the diehard expatriates, both black and white. Josephine Baker also realized that she "belonged" to Paris, all the more so since her disastrous attempt to stage a comeback on Broadway, a humiliation and rejection she had never had to endure in France. Now when Baker sang her theme song "*J'ai deux amours*" she was really emphasizing the phrase: "*Paris* est *mon pays*" rather than "*Paris* et *mon pays*." She would stay on until Paris became impossible; then she would join the Free French movement, traveling between Marseilles and North Africa, carrying coded messages between the lyrics of her sheet music.

Nightclub custom fell away when the blackout was imposed and killed most of Paris After Dark. Black performers were moving on as their engagements were canceled, though music hall attractions remained well attended, "La Miss" (Mistinguett) and Maurice Chevalier as popular as ever.

Bricktop missed the cabaret crowds and all-night clubbing of yester-year, the sound of a solo jazz trombone instead of an air-raid siren—she began to seek solace in the bottle, often alone. During one air-raid drill Bricktop was so drunk she had to be carried into an air-raid shelter in Montmartre. By the end of 1939 when the real air raids began, Bricktop knew the party was over and she would have to leave: "On the boat train I met four American musicians who, like me, were among the last entertainers to leave, and we shared our fears about going back to a country we hadn't seen for years and where we would be strangers."

JANET FLANNER BOOKED passage on the *Manhattan* not long after King Leopold surrendered Belgium to the invading German forces. She promised to return in three weeks—Paris, after all, was her adoptive turf and the central topic of her *Letters* to the *New Yorker*. When she did not return, her replacement for the *New Yorker* profiles, A. J. Liebling, took her to task as "a reporter coming away from a story just as it broke."

Liebling was unaware of Flanner's guilt about not being in Paris in its hour of jeopardy, and moreover for abandoning a lesbian triangle of lovers that included Solita Solano and Noël Murphy (sister-in-law to Gerald Murphy, the model for Dick Diver in F. Scott Fitzgerald's 1930s novel *Tender Is the Night*). Noël Murphy remained behind in Paris to transport pregnant women from the city by ambulance.

What Liebling could not have known, and Noël and Solita to learn, was that Janet Flanner in the emotional chaos of wartime displacement had met and fallen in love with a beautiful Italian émigrée in New York, Natalya Danesi.

■ ■ ■

WITH GERMAN TROOPS approaching Paris and the first aerial bombing of the city, James Joyce did finally decide to leave, and traveled to central France as far as Saint-Gérand-le-Puy in the vicinity of Vichy. In considerable abdominal pain, he moped about the country village, taking long lonely walks (Nora did not like to walk) in the ragged countryside, his pockets weighted with stones, like a suicide, but stones he meant to throw at the stray dogs he had always feared and detested.

For those like Joyce who intended to leave France but remain in Europe, Switzerland was the destination of choice. Joyce had already spent time in Switzerland, in Zurich, waiting out World War I and thought to do so again. The neutral Irishman assumed that the neutral Swiss would welcome him once more (and would provide sanctuary for Lucia at some psychiatric establishment in Zurich), but the situation had changed. The Swiss were refusing to admit more refugees, and to cross the Franco-Swiss border had become a tightrope walk, especially for citizens of the belligerent nations. Joyce thought he was certainly exempt from that category. He was wrong: when he applied for a visa at the Swiss legation in Vichy, he discovered he was applying as a British citizen because of his British residency declared in London when he married Nora there. Furthermore, he was considered a Jewish émigré—because someone at the legation had no doubt read *Ulysses* and confused the visa applicant with his creation, Leopold Bloom.

"C'est le bouquet, vraiment!" [It's the last straw, really.] In the prose style of *Finnegans Wake* Joyce replied: "I am not a Jew from Judea but an aryan from Erin."

Waiting, he walked the country roads throwing stones at the canine offspring of Cerberus, the many-headed dog guarding Hades. He might have been throwing stones at the offending Germans who had displaced him and his family (and were the reason *Finnegans Wake* would receive no notice and go unread) with the Western world engaged in war. When he declared, "They have no souls," Joyce could have been referring either to the dogs or to the Germans.

GEORGES BRAQUE AT his studio in Varengeville north of Paris learned of the German approach and ceased to paint on a canvas only just begun. He cleaned his brushes thoroughly, carefully stacked his canvasses in the car, and fled with his wife to Castillon in the Midi.

The painter Balthus was married to a Swiss national, therefore qualified for émigré status in Switzerland. En route for the Franco-Swiss border Balthus passed through Bilignin and visited Gertrude Stein and Alice Toklas in their mountain village redoubt. Gertrude was sawing wood: "I had to saw wood . . . there was plenty of wood to be had, but no man to saw it." Balthus and his wife had traveled from Paris in the outflow of refugees "sleeping two days in their little car, and they were going to their summerhouse in Savoy."

Gertrude and Alice were urged by Balthus to leave for Switzerland, and family and friends wrote to them to return to the United States. To such urgent entreaties, Gertrude's reply was vague: "Well will we come or not it is for you to say . . ."

The local officials and their neighbors in Bilignin insisted they stay. "Everybody knows you here," the doctor assured them. "Everybody likes you; we all would help you in every way. Why risk yourself among strangers?"

Despite the constraints of country life, the sawing of wood, and lack of stimulating Parisian society, Gertrude (unlike Joyce, who was miserable) was enjoying life "in the real country."

As a practical gesture—proposed by Alice, who decided that sooner or later "we would have to go"—they set off for Lyon in Gertrude's Ford roadster with a picnic lunch prepared by Alice to Gertrude's taste, who was "awfully fussy" about food. They were not the only picnickers at roadside, and as they drove on they found the thoroughfares near Lyon too crowded for driving comfort so they returned to Bilignin without getting their passports in order at the American consulate, and were still undecided about what to do.

When they thought of attempting to drive to Lyon again, neighbors continued to offer help in every way if they would stay on. Alice prepared another picnic lunch for roadside dining. But when about to embark on the trip, Gertrude discovered that the Ford had a flat tire. "You see," she said, "even the car does not want to leave."

The final decision was: "Here we are and here we stay."

MORICAND'S PARTING HOROSCOPE for Henry Miller was an evocation of a water creature plunging to the nethermost depths of the sea: "to bring back to the surface the trophies of an unknown world." This was entirely propitious to Miller's arrival in Marseilles, ready to make the plunge to the Aegean Sea, then across the Atlantic for whatever trophies the New World would yield to him. Anaïs was at dockside to see him off. They had met in Aix as she had promised, to play out their ceremony of farewell, a sentimental occasion mixed with nostalgia and regret after a last sweaty session of lovemaking at the hotel.

Since Anaïs Nin had joined him, Henry Miller had carried on a nonstop disparagement of Paris, vowing never to return to that "city of sewers"—his way of psychologically divorcing himself, as Anaïs intuited, from the city that had been Miller's great good place for a decade.

At first (even making love to her in Aix) he may have thought of Anaïs in those same terms of severance, justified by a mental catalog of her temperamental infidelities with both himself and Hugo—and who knew, except as phantom lovers in her diaries, how many others?—but suddenly, in a complete reversal of mood, he could not let go of her. She must come with him aboard the *Théophile Gautier,* sail with him to Corfu for the one possible interlude of peace before the world went to hell.

Then they would marry, live in the United States—California!—at the rosy dawn of a new life together!

Governed as Anaïs was by careless impulse and romantic extravagance, she for once replied, "No." She could not abandon her husband, the one stabilizing factor in her life—and she did, truly, love Henry as well—though she had been recklessly unfaithful to Hugo all along (and to Henry, but that went without mention). (In subtext to Nin's farewell speech was the coincidence of her current lover, Gonzalo Moré, making vague uncertain plans to leave France from Marseilles, and by some grotesque fate might take the same transatlantic steamship as Henry, the two rival lovers sailing to the States together—though this did not happen.)

In lieu of pledging herself to Henry forever, Anaïs pressed upon him a wad of cash, a ritual offering that had dominated their relations from the beginning. Clearly their *au revoir* was an *adieu.*

They would of course meet again—and under less pressing circumstances than Paris offered—in the New World. For now, all passion spent and tears aside, it was the farewell of two lovingly devoted soul mates at the end of an excessively concupiscent pairing, a romantic adventure only Paris could inspire. They concluded on a note of enduring friendship, an abatement representing a rarer sentiment than many long-committed lovers would ever know.

21

DEBACLE—II

Had [Paul] Reynaud been three inches taller the history of
the world might have been changed.

—HAROLD NICOLSON, *DIARIES*

A N OMINOUS CLOUD blackened the sky above Paris like
the *ciel chargé*, the overcast sky predicted by Moricand in
Henry Miller's horoscope—but this was an actual cloud
of smoke obscuring the white alabaster domes of the Sacre Coeur as the
cloud reached the summit of Montmartre. Many believed the smoke
was a screen behind which French troops were retreating, others that a
smoke screen covered an advance panzer unit thundering toward Paris.

Actually the smoke was from oil reserves burning along the Basse
Seine at St. Cloud and St. Denis, to keep the precious fuel from falling
into the hands of the enemy. Also smoke from individual bonfires at
embassies choked the narrower streets and billowed across the Seine
from ministry courtyards where officials were burning sensitive files
before personnel were to be evacuated to Tours.

"Who ordered this?" screamed Hélène de Portes.

Her luggage had been piled on the steps of the circular staircase as if she and her belongings were being evicted from the palais de l'Elysée where she had been in residence since Paul Reynaud had been made premier. (Her husband comte Jean de Portes was serving at the front; Reynaud's wife had volunteered as a nurse with the Flying Ambulance Corps.)

The comtesse de Portes was further incensed to learn that she would not be riding in the premier's limousine with Reynaud, but traveling separately in the government convoy to Tours, with her excessive baggage. She was used to the role of command, but now with the government in extremis, moving like a gypsy caravan out of Paris, she feared losing control.

GAMELIN HAD LOST battle after battle in the northeast, and now the capital itself was threatened. Since Gamelin had been appointed by Premier Daladier, and consistently was supported in his blunders by the premier, Daladier was held responsible for the generalissimo's incompetence. Gamelin was replaced by an even older commander in chief, General Weygand, who accepted the post with an initial burst of optimism—the French army was the greatest military force in the world, he declared, with the highest morale—but now sided with the defeatists in the camp of Mme. de Portes . . . proponents of armistice.

Hélène de Portes, in formal dress at a dinner party at the Ritz, leaned over to Anatole de Monzie, a fellow advocate of capitulation: "It's high time these war-mongering campaigns [by the Left, and diehards like Churchill] were silenced. Since Hitler is evidently the strongest, the best thing is to give in to him, *c'est tout.*"

"What would Paul Reynaud say, if he heard you say that?" de Monzie exclaimed.

"*Zut!*" Madame de Portes answered. "I tell him that every day. I'll surely convince him in the end."

THE WEAK-WILLED president of the republic, Albert Lebrun, was a vacillating head of state subject to nervous fits, tics, and uncontrollable weeping—and there was much to weep about during his tenure as president. When Daladier's government fell, Lebrun appointed "the little fighting cock" Paul Reynaud as the new premier. (Reynaud was afflicted with a nervous tic of his own: his head twitched spasmodically when events ran ahead of him and his confidence suffered.)

In public the new premier appeared certain of himself and maintained a deliberate poise to belie his diminutive height. He actually felt self-consciously taller in the company of his demanding mistress; he dyed his hair to appear younger than sixty-two (twice the age of Hélène de Portes) and played the gallant attentive lover to assure her constant favor. She used him shamelessly to her own ends (which became increasingly sinister as the military situation deteriorated); he knew it, and he adored her nonetheless.

Reynaud did not command a majority in the Chamber or the Senate, and he was unable to form a government without the help of the outgoing premier Daladier. He could hardly approach his defeated rival directly to ask for the support of Daladier's adherents in Parliament, but a trade-off was arranged behind the scenes—a compromise of noblesse oblige between the faubourg salons of Madame de Portes and *her* rival, the marquise de Crussol. With no little irony, the inept Daladier, a proven fool in military affairs, was awarded the cabinet post of Minister of Defense.

AS SOON AS her lover became premier, Hélène de Portes placed herself at the center of command: "smoking cigarette after cigarette . . . sitting picturesquely on the [chef de Cabinet's] table-desk. She is having all the news flashes brought to her as they come in."

A news flash that would have been read by the comtesse before reaching the premier was a vivid firsthand account of the German breakthrough in the northeast. The novelist Joseph Kessel reported to the editor of *Paris Soir* that the Germans were here:

"Here? What do you mean? Where?"

"Not far from Paris. I don't know how I got through. For kilometers on end I didn't see a single French soldier who had kept his arms, who wasn't fleeing in wild panic from the attacks of the dive bombers, from the waves of tanks. They were terrified, above all, because they felt lost, abandoned, without orders, without leaders. I saw them looking up into the sky for a sign of Allied planes, and along the roads for the tanks, for the replacements that never came . . ."

FRENCH ARMY UNITS were essentially leaderless, floundering and out of touch with central command at Versailles. The replacement of Gamelin by General Weygand did nothing to ameliorate the situation:

the so-called Weygand Line collapsed along the extended northeast perimeter. Lack of communications was critical—there were officers who lamented the obsolescence of carrier pigeons used in the Great War—and what news did reach Weygand's headquarters was of fresh disaster. French and British troops were trapped with their backs to the English Channel at Dunkirk awaiting air cover and reinforcements.

Winston Churchill was making frequent shuttle flights at great personal risk to meet with Reynaud and General Weygand. At the time of the German encirclement of troops along the coast at Dunkirk, Churchill demanded of Weygand: *"Où sont les réserves stratégique?"*

"Aucune," replied the general. There are no strategic reserves.

Churchill was stupefied. He had been promised by the French (but that was when Gamelin had been commander in chief) a large force of reserve troops kept in readiness for just such an emergency.

With Weygand's *"aucune"* still ringing in his ears, the British prime minister ordered the evacuation of the British Expeditionary Force from Dunkirk by whatever means possible—which meant a heroic flotilla of ferries, troopships, small craft, and pleasure boats, whatever vessel could navigate the Channel, to evacuate Britain's remnant army before the Germans closed in.

In the ranks of the French at Dunkirk was the complaint that British soldiers were given precedence for being taken aboard rescue craft.

SOON AFTER BECOMING premier, Paul Reynaud came down with a case of influenza. The journalist Pierre Lazareff did not know of the premier's illness and arrived at the Hôtel Matignon for a scheduled interview. "I found Hélène de Portes sitting at Paul Reynaud's desk. She was presiding over an assorted gathering of generals, high officers, members of the Parliament, and officials. She was talking in a peremptory tone of voice, giving advice and orders left and right. Every once in a while she would open the door and step into the next room. One could hear her say: 'How are you, Paul? Now just relax and take it easy. Don't worry about a thing. We're working.' "

ONE AFTER THE other the approaches to Paris were breached and the defenses overwhelmed as the blitzkreig moved in ominous rattling tank treads toward the capital. All the old place names from 1914–18—Amiens, Ypres, the Somme and Marne Rivers—were recalled as battlefront milestones in the relentless parade of defeat. Perhaps the most significant and symbolic German victory was at Sedan, a reenactment of the Prussian breakthrough in the Franco-Prussian War when Napoléon III was captured and France forced to capitulate. Now the German troops were triumphant at Sedan once again and, for the third time in half a century, Paris was under threat of capture.

Despite catastrophe on all sides, General Charles de Gaulle—made brigadier general on a temporary appointment (the "upstart and political meddler" assigned a field command to remove him from the war office and out of Paris)—comported himself admirably as commander of a tank division at the Battle of the Somme. For that engagement de Gaulle was written up in praiseworthy terms by *Le Soir* and decorated by the government—to the disgust of Marshal Pétain, who detested him.

In another echo from the past, in the interests of morale, Marshal Pétain was recalled from his post as ambassador to Spain. Pétain, the "hero of Verdun," had rallied the nation at that decisive battle in 1918; now the aged hero confided to Franco before he left Madrid, "They are calling me home to lead France." He soon became part of Madame de Portes's cabal of defeatists working toward armistice and terms with Germany.

Before the government fled Paris for Tours, Premier Reynaud, accompanied by his generals Weygand and Pétain, attended solemn mass together at Notre Dame cathedral to pray for deliverance from the enemy. The bishop of Paris called upon the patron saints of France, Sainte Genevieve, Saint Louis, Saint Denis—above all, the martyred saint Jeanne d'Arc—to intercede once again to protect beleagured Paris. Perhaps their prayers were intended to bring to pass another Miracle of the Marne when taxicabs, not saints, delivered reserve troops to the battle and saved Paris from the German assault. General Charles de Gaulle, who in any case did not believe in miracles, was not invited to pray with them.

"ADRIENNE . . . AND I went over to the Boulevard Sebastapol," wrote Sylvia Beach, "and, through our tears, watched the refugees moving through the city. They came in at the East Gate, crossed Paris by way of the boulevard Saint Michel and the Luxembourg Gardens, then went out through the Orleans and Italie gates: cattle-drawn carts piled with household goods; on top of them children, old people and sick people, pregnant women and women with babies, poultry in coops, and dogs and cats. Sometimes they stopped at the Luxembourg Gardens to let the cows graze there."

Observers in mourning silence stood beside Sylvia and Adrienne at curbside as the grim parade filed past. It might have been a funeral cortège, for indeed a convoy of hearses passed, though the passengers sat upright and alive; they were the elderly being evacuated from nursing homes and patients from the mental institutions in suburban Vincennes. Fiacres of second-empire vintage creaked past full of antique belongings, most of the cars with protective mattresses roped to the roof in case of strafing by German patrols; one low-riding auto with extra cans of gasoline attached to the running boards had a canoe on the roof.

There was a jaunty note in that teenage cyclists were weaving in and out of the traffic stream of woebegone refugees on foot, beeping their bicycle horns gaily, excited, happy at the prospect of whatever adolescent adventure, like a summer holiday, lay ahead. A chartered busload of Les Petits Chanteurs, the famous choral group of St. Eustache cathedral, turned onto the boulevard at rue Turbigo singing out the windows to the crowds, as jubilant as the cyclists, but Adrienne and Sylvia were unable to share in that sole moment of uplift, depressed beyond measure.

PEGGY GUGGENHEIM WAS determined to linger in Paris until the last moment, part of the Elsa Maxwell coterie seeking sanctuary at the Ritz (though Elsa had departed Paris for the Riviera). Wealth from her trust fund came through in dribbles due to the wartime restrictions at the Banque de France, but Peggy still had sufficient funds to buy up the works of departing painters at "bargain prices," now that the artists were desperate.

She was living on the place Vendôme in the apartment where Chopin died, and was in fact remodeling the premises (though warned by the owner that the Germans were coming) to better exhibit her collection of mostly surrealistic works. Peggy trekked from studio to studio making last-minute transactions for artworks. She paid Picabia three hundred dollars for his *Very Rare Picture Upon This Earth* and for fifteen hundred dollars bought Georges Braque's *La Valse* before he left Varengeville for the Midi. Peggy strode into Fernand Léger's atelier and came away with his *Men in the Town* for one thousand dollars. For months she had beseiged the sculptor Brancusi at his garage-shed studio in the impasse

Ronsin, disputing the price for his *Bird in Space*, which Brancusi did not want to sell and Peggy coveted. She finally succeeded in acquiring the sculpture, and at her price.

Peggy was less fortunate hoping to purchase a Picasso. When she tried to meet the painter at a gathering in his studio, Picasso pointedly ignored her until she approached him directly, when he curtly informed her: "Lingerie is on the next floor."

In all, Peggy Guggenheim paid $40,000 for her most important acquisitions, $250,000 for the entire collection she had accumulated over the decade. Eventually the collection would be worth $40 million, but when Peggy begged for a cubic meter of storage space at the Louvre (at Léger's suggestion, when the Germans were at the gates of Paris), the conservative French museum curators advised her that her collection was not worth saving, and refused to consider her request.

At the same time Sylvia Beach was watching the sad procession of refugees passing along the boulevard Sébastopol, Peggy Guggenheim was at the Dôme drinking champagne with her latest lover (on a day when hard liquor was forbidden). Guggenheim commented on the tragedy of the miserable hordes pouring through Paris and out the city gates leading south: "I can't imagine why I didn't go to the aid of these unfortunate people. But I just didn't; instead I drank champagne with Bill."

ON HER TERRACE overlooking the place Vendôme, Peggy Guggenheim kept a private hoard of gasoline, emergency fuel she was certain to need when she too would be obliged to flee Paris. She had heard gasoline supplies were limited and on the southern roads was sold at exorbitant prices. Even water was at a premium. At a roadside stand one enterprising farmer was selling water at ten sous per glass; to fill a canteen he charged two francs, as if peddling holy water at the shrine in Lourdes.

Not all those who lived along the sad route leading south were profiteers. The French actress Corrine Luchaire arrived at her farm in Nantes to discover that the farmhands had abandoned the place and left the cows groaning with painful unmilked udders. She set about to milk the cows herself, then stood at the roadside offering milk to passing children.

Cars broke down en route, repairs or replacement parts unavailable, vehicles abandoned then pushed into ditches not to impede the flow of

Portrait of Peggy Guggenheim by Alfred Courmes.

traffic. At one bottleneck of stalled cars, a limousine chauffeur brandished a pistol to assure his right of way; but at another bottleneck a Rolls Royce was attacked by thugs who made off with the vehicle, leaving the passengers stranded.

Jean Cocteau on his way to Cannes noticed the large number of nuns on the road. He heard that at one village a nun had been arrested; she had turned out to be a man, and a German spy.

Small village shops were often broken into and looted. The *gardes champêtres* had been advised not to risk assault by arresting the vandals, but to take down license numbers of suspects, for later judicial pursuit, "when things got back to normal."

Of course the greatest tragedy was the frequent unchallenged air raids, German planes that swept down on the defenseless slow-moving "treacle" of refugees, strafing the hapless travelers at random.

TRAVELING IN THE opposite direction to the tide of southbound refugees was a brothel keeper named Bordier who managed to hitch a ride with a British officer returning, like Bordier, to Paris. Bordier had heard that the Germans were already at St. Cloud and he was beset by second thoughts about his place of business . . . he intended to collect the silver he had hoarded in his office safe and empty the slot machines in the corridor of his *maison de passe* before the Germans got to his treasure.

IN CENTRAL FRANCE some two thousand graves had been dug and left exposed in the fields around a small church. A solitary airman detached from his unit, having parachuted into the macabre landscape, walked through the field of open pits to the small parish church in the center of this preliminary graveyard. He entered the church and went to the organ, placing his silk parachute like a bundle of laundry beside the foot pedals of the instrument, sat down, and began playing the Bach chorale: *A Mighty Fortress Is Our God*. In the otherwordly evening stillness of the field of open graves, a parish priest had seen the airman enter the church, then heard the solemn organ notes resounding over the field. He did not know if the organist-pilot was French, English, or German.

TO COMPLEMENT THE anticipated use of prepared graves, more than a million "instant" burial forms were printed and stored at local town halls, requiring only name, date, and cause of death to certify official burial.

Thus the classic governmental scenario of administration continued in robot fashion: the invisible but pragmatic bureaucracy plodded along in the pedestrian routine of turning out instant burial forms and arranging for mass burial sites, with no apparent directive from above. At its highest levels of power, the Third Republic—Premier Reynaud, the weeping president Lebrun, General Weygand, and above all Reynaud's mistress urging appeasement in her shrill, demanding voice—was incapable of command, blundering backward and forward in indecision and divisiveness Left versus Right. By contrast, the petty administration of bureaucratic *fonctionaires* could at least give the appearance of keeping the moribund body of state alive.

"The more Paul Reynaud drifted toward the Left," noted the editor of *Paris Soir*, "the more Hélène de Portes pulled to the Right." The comtesse had a staunch ally in the defeatist general Weygand, when Reynaud considered the option of moving the government to North Africa and continuing the war from Algiers. Weygand urged the premier not to leave "the sacred soil of France" but to end the war and seek terms with Germany, reminding Reynaud (in the words of the philosopher Quintus Ennius): "Conquered Greece tamed her brutal conqueror."

"Terms?" Reynaud was reminded of the terms offered Prince Leopold when Belgium capitulated: unconditional surrender. Weygand had arrived at his insight by reading Quintus Ennius, but had he read *Mein Kampf*?

France and her ally England, Reynaud insisted, will hold out to the bitter end. "This *is* the end," countered Weygand, reporting that by the time the government had evacuated to Tours, General Rommel had taken forty thousand French prisoners, twelve of them generals.

A compromise was proposed to Paul Reynaud by General de Gaulle that became known as the Breton Redoubt, whereby the remaining French forces in the north would be concentrated in Brittany, and the government join its army there, a holding position that would keep the Third Republic on French soil and possibly stave off invasion of Britain. The retreat to Brittany required the cooperation of Admiral Darlan, who would deploy the French fleet from Toulon and the Mediterranean to Breton ports and furnish ten troopships to transport some thirty thousand men in the first wave of transport. Darlan was known as a rue

258

Royale sailor (the address of the Ministry of Marine) and had so far kept the fleet from active engagement. He was also a defeatist in the camp of Marshal Pétain, and both Pétain and Darlan intended to keep the French fleet as a bargaining chip in armistice negotiations with Hitler. Resistance to the plan was immediate (and in some respects justified, for the large-scale maneuver would expose troops and ships to attack by the Luftwaffe) and Darlan expressed his outrage: *"C'est une blague!"* "It's a joke!"

In the end neither Brittany nor Algiers became the next provisional captital of the Third Republic. The lovely Gallo-Roman city of Tours came under aerial attack by German stukas passing blithely over the "impregnable" Maginot Line to raid the vulnerable eastern flank of central France, strafing the refugees along the open roads when no military target presented itself—until the bombardment of Tours offered grand sport.

The gypsy caravan of government was obliged to decamp and take to the road once again, this time to Bordeaux, a port city on the Atlantic that offered an escape route by sea if Algiers became the next desperate "provisional" destination. Alas for those who hoped France would fight on: Bordeaux was under the scheming fascist-minded disciple of Hitler and Mussolini, mayor Adrien Marquet, close friend to the treacherous Pierre Laval. The mayor of Bordeaux was now host to a divided Third Republic in a city of chaos, teeming with refugees, embassies, and legations overwhelmed with requests for visas to Spain, Portugal, and the United States.

Bordeaux's equivalent to the Paris Ritz was the Hôtel Splendide, and Marquet was delighted at the opportunity to exercise his sympathies by assigning accommodations according to prejudice. Naturally Hélène de Portes was given a two-room suite at the Splendide; her co-conspirator Laval was installed in the royal suite after Marquet evicted the former queen of Portugal. President Lebrun, still supporting Reynaud's policy of continuing the struggle (however uncertain he was about all else), was assigned a room at police headquarters.

If Bordeaux had any *place* to equal the place Vendôme in Paris, it would have to be the cours de l'Intendance that attracted the wealthier displaced Parisians, its restaurant the Chapon Fin frequented by the elite set of defeatists, centered around Pierre Laval who dined there daily, always with his trademark white tie beneath a pudding face, dangling over his "black heart." Laval was Pétain's front man and evil genius, spewing out plots to undermine Reynaud and the Third Republic between sips of his consommé. His dinner companion was most often the comtesse Hélène de Portes.

General Spears, Churchill's liaison officer in Bordeaux, summed up the atmosphere: "As if all the sewers of France had burst and their nauseating mess was seeping into the beautiful city like a rising flood of abomination."

TO CHURCHILL IT was imperative that France continue to stand fast against Germany and maintain strict adherence to its alliance with Britain. If France should falter and give in, England was sure to be invaded soon after. He must contact Reynaud again, even risking a flight to Bordeaux, to put before him a plan that might strengthen the alliance and put iron in Reynaud's backbone.

On one such flight to confer with the French premier, Churchill made the crossing in an unescorted Flamingo aircraft and narrowly missed being shot down on the French side of the Channel coast; but the Germans were too busy firing at suspect fishing vessels in the water to notice the small plane flying overhead with its sole passenger and critical target, the prime minister of England aboard.

In Bordeaux, Churchill knew of the malign influence Reynaud's mistress cast over the premier, and he diplomatically confronted Hélène de Portes first, to comply with the pun on her name that she was the *porte à côté*, the side door by which one gained access to Paul Reynaud.

They conferred in French, since the comtesse did not speak English, though Churchill's French, of which he was inordinately proud, was faulty.

"Mon pauvre pays," she began, "is bleeding to death . . ." to which Churchill replied in sympathy and politesse, *"Je comprends."* He repeated *"Je comprends"* to each of the arguments Hélène de Portes presented for France to capitulate and seek a separate peace outside the alliance with Britain. Each time Churchill uttered *"Je comprends,"* he meant to express a simple, "I understand," though in French, in another sense, the statement could have meant "I agree"—which was the meaning Mme. de Portes chose to broadcast among the deputies and senators who had managed to make their hazardous way to Bordeaux, that England now agreed to France seeking a separate peace.

When word got back to Churchill he was outraged, and went directly to Reynaud this time to insist England hold France to its bond. Furthermore he presented the newest alternative to a craven defeat, that Britain and France not only continue the war together but that their alliance be strengthened by a most extraordinary pact, a veritable Declaration of Union, a forging of the two nations into one indivisible sovereign country. Britons and Frenchmen would enjoy the benefits of mutual citizenship, their armies forged into a single powerful monolith capable of resisting the military machine of the Third Reich.

Pétain and Pierre Laval in 1934.

General Spears prepared a translation to be presented to Reynaud and his cabinet, and as he was showing a copy of the Declaration of Union to one member: "There stood the inevitable Mme. de Portes. As I handed a secretary the pages she stepped behind him and read over his shoulder, holding his arm to prevent his turning the pages too fast for her to read them. It was difficult to tell from her expression whether rage or amazement prevailed."

The comtesse immediately went to work behind the scenes to discredit the proposed union—an easy accomplishment with so many of the deputies who either distrusted or detested their ally across the Channel. England had after all been the traditional enemy and rival of France long before a confederated Germany existed.

Reynaud was naive to believe that "the great secret" he was about to reveal to his cabinet would now resolve the crisis facing France by a flourish, a signature, and a vote of confidence. He had no idea that his conniving mistress had already exposed and spoken against the proposal for union. When Reynaud read aloud the Declaration of Union to his cabinet, he did so with enthusiasm and confidence, but the declaration provoked the greatest uproar he had encountered so far at a cabinet meeting. Reynaud was completely nonplussed at this violent reaction—his head began to shake left and right under emotional stress.

In the resistance group Reynaud still had loyalist Georges Mandel, Secretary of State, on his side, and the wavering weak-minded support of President Lebrun among others, but true confidence in his continued premiership was dwindling—with doddering, aged Pétain waiting in the wings, promoted by his treacherous henchman, Pierre Laval. In a conciliatory gesture, Lebrun offered to meet with Churchill to discuss a revision of the declaration, but a deputy shouted him down: "No need to go on. We have no intention of becoming a dominion of the British Empire." When Mandel cried, "Would you rather be a German district than a British dominion?" [the deputy] shouted back, "Yes! Better be a Nazi province. At least we know what that means."

The Right considered the declaration preposterous, and General Weygand called the union *une blague*, a joke. As the deputies wrangled on, it became apparent that not only would France and England never become one sovereign nation, but that Paul Reynaud's tenure as premier was approaching its finale.

■ ■ ■

WHY DID SHE do it? Many who knew the premier and his mistress would ask why Hélène de Portes, who conspired to place Paul Reynaud in the position of premier, would then practice every underhanded maneuver to undermine his power while in office. Charitable observers of the match credited the comtesse's great love for France, a greater love than for her lover, as the motive for serial treacheries—but that would not explain the last inadvertent but criminal embarrassment she had cast upon the premier. Hélène de Portes had dispatched to Spain, with two unsuspecting aides of Reynaud, a fortune in gold and jewelry, plus eighteen million francs, from the "secret funds" of the French treasury. The contraband she intended to smuggle out of France included bundles of foreign office documents she had hoarded during Reynaud's time in office. At the Spanish border the booty was discovered by customs officials and reported to Franco who sent the treasure back to Bordeaux.

The ends Hélène de Portes had worked for would succeed almost by default. At a private meeting with President Lebrun, the now desperate Reynaud blurted out in reply to a faint challenge by Lebrun: "Then let Pétain form a government!" (According to Reynaud's memoirs, he had meant the suggestion sarcastically, for Pétain was prepared to seek an armistice with Germany as soon as he had the power to do so.) But the fateful words were uttered, Paul Reynaud resigned, and the Hero of Verdun sued for peace with Germany as the new premier of France.

The government would move one last time, to the famous spa of Vichy where the aged and ailing took the waters, an appropriate capital city for Marshal Pétain, on the brink of senility, given the illusion of power and manipulated by the puppetmaster Laval, to reign over half the territory of France unoccupied by German troops.

IN POSTSCRIPT THERE was no further political role for Reynaud and his mistress to play in the Vichy regime—a tentative offer by Pétain to appoint Reynaud as ambassador to the United States had delighted Mme. de Portes but was rescinded by Laval.

Paul Reynaud and Hélène de Portes planned to marry as soon as their divorces came through. The comtesse had contrived, when

Reynaud was in power, to have his Minister of Justice, Georges Bonnet, reduce the legal waiting period for remarriage from three years to one. With the happy thought of marriage at last, the couple set off for the Riviera in a near-to-honeymoon mood. They were on their way to Sainte-Maxime and thence to Spain, on the same picturesque road the Duke and Duchess of Windsor had traveled when Churchill refused the Duke's request to send a gunboat to evacuate the Windsors from Cap Ferrat. The Grande Corniche highway was carved out of the cliffside banking the Mediterranean shore, known for its abrupt and perilous curves. Paul Reynaud, like many vain Frenchmen, was notoriously reckless behind the wheel of a car, inclined to make up for poor judgment by excessive speed. Taking one curve on the Corniche too fast, he crashed into a roadside tree, badly injuring himself; the excess luggage spilled forward on impact, smashing into the back of his companion's head and killing her instantly.

When Paul Reynaud regained consciousness at the hospital in Nice, he was told that Hélène de Portes was dead. Weeping, he struggled to pronounce the epitaph for his mistress the comtesse: *"Elle était la France."* She was France.

22

THE FALL

The German night has swallowed up the country . . . all that is over now. France is nothing but a silence; she is lost somewhere in the night with all lights out.

—Antoine de Saint-Exupéry,
open letter to *The New York Times*

SYLVIA BEACH WATCHED the beginning of the formal entry of the victorious troops of the Third Reich marching into Paris "on a lovely June day," but nothing else about the day was lovely. Most shutters were closed against the sight of the parade of troops filing into the city along the northern and eastern boulevards, Sylvia part of a scattering of crestfallen Parisians witness to the humiliating march. There was no expressing the depth of her sorrow as "an endless procession of motorized forces: tanks and armored cars and helmeted men with arms folded" rumbled past. "The men and machines were all a cold gray, and they moved to a steady deafening roar." From that time on, the color of metallic gray would represent to Sylvia the spirit of the Occupation of Paris by the Germans.

German tanks entering Paris.

■ ■ ■

THE TANKS LED the way like lead-colored automatons, four abreast in a relentless show of mechanized force. At the Champs-Elysées soldiers on foot directed the advance with red-tipped monitor batons while French police, as part of the Open City stipulations, lined the sidewalks with their white batons unsheathed to maintain order.

The advance column reached pont Alexandre III and crossed the extravagantly sculpted and gilded bridge to the esplanade des Invalides where mighty Napoléon lay in his marble catafalque. A young German officer racing ahead of the mechanized column hurriedly pulled down the banners marking French victories over the Germans in previous conflicts.

PRESIDENT ROOSEVELT HAD ordered the American ambassador to leave Paris, but William Bullitt thought it his greater duty to serve as neutral mediator between France and Germany in handing over the city officially.

Bullitt asked the distinguished brain surgeon, Dr. Thierry de Martel, to remain behind also. Martel was director of the American Hospital in Neuilly; he would be needed. He sent Bullitt a *pneumatique*: "I promise you to remain in Paris dead or alive . . . Adieu, Martel." When his message had been dispatched, Dr. Thierry de Martel went into his *cabinet de medicaments* and administered to his arm a lethal dose of strychnine.

GENERAL VON STUDNITZ requisitioned the Prince of Wales' suite at the Hôtel Crillon as his headquarters, and prepared immediately for the meeting with the American ambassador by donning his dress uniform with an array of medals across his chest, jackboots polished, and monocle in place. The American embassy was just across the rue Boissy d'Anglas from the Crillon, but von Studnitz chose to traverse the mere fifty yards in his large black Mercedes. The general was met in the embassy courtyard by Ambassador Bullitt, who accepted the treaty of terms for the occupation of Paris, and who would in turn present the treaty to the French military commander, General Dentz, who would abide by the terms outlined by the Germans. The ceremony of handing over Paris to the Germans was chillingly formal and lasted no more than ten minutes.

As part of the agreement to declare Paris an open city, General Dentz was to insure that no "enemy action" took place, or immediate reprisal would be visited on the civilian population. Von Studnitz considered the burning of the fuel tanks at St. Cloud clearly an act of military sabotage, in violation of the agreement, but Dentz presented von Studnitz a map of the area, pointing out that the fuel tanks were in St. Cloud, and St. Cloud was outside the city limits, therefore not covered by the agreement. It was the German general's first taste of the specious reasoning of the Cartesian French, and an early example of the petty exasperations Parisians were prepared to inflict on their conqueror.

ANOTHER ACT OF sabotage was the dismantling of the Eiffel Tower elevator meant to prevent the Germans from replacing the French flag with the swastika, but this was only a delaying tactic for the determined Germans carried their flag up the 1,671 steps to the summit, took down the French tricolor, and attempted to hoist the German swastika in its place, but discovered that the flag was too large for the staff at the top of the tower, so they descended for a smaller flag and doggedly climbed the 1,671 steps once more to hoist their banner of victory over Paris for the benefit of the officers assembled on the Champ de Mars at the foot of the Eiffel Tower with their cameras at the ready.

AMBASSADOR BULLITT HAD been greatly shaken by the ceremony of handing over Paris to the Germans, more despondent than diplomatic reserve allowed him to express. The sight of the German swastika flying from the top of the Eiffel Tower was another grim indignity to endure on this black day—but Bullitt was not about to allow German incursion on American embassy grounds.

Not long after General von Studnitz departed, a team of German soldiers arrived, with ladders and tools and rolls of telephone wire. They scrambled up the sides of the embassy building to the roof where they were about to install a private telephone line from von Studnitz's headquarters at the Crillon for direct access to Berlin. The ambassador was outraged at this arrogance; he abandoned his professional cool to shout at the Germans on the roof to come down immediately "or you will be fired upon!" Bullitt was flanked by two U.S. Marine guards prepared to fire on command.

The Germans descended and brought down their equipment with them. They retreated from the embassy compound and did not return: a first American-German encounter, a small prelude in anticipation of conflict to come.

EPILOGUE

GHOSTS

"I never left Paris," Sylvia Beach explained, "—hadn't the energy to flee, luckily, as nothing happened to us nor to the other monuments."

THE DAIMLER-BENZ with outrider on a motorcycle effectively blocked the narrow rue de l'Odéon from number 4 (where a plaque attested to Thomas Paine's residence there in 1792) to number 12 at the threshold of Shakespeare and Company, the motorcycle parked but rumbling ominously, impatiently, as Sylvia Beach attempted to explain to the outrider's Brigadeführer—who did not deign to enter the celebrated bookshop but remained seated stiff-backed in his Daimler—that there was only one copy of *Finnegans Wake* on the premises; the book belonged to herself, and was not for sale.

Sylvia Beach's defiance may have been the officer's first setback in a painless campaign to dominate the "open city" of Paris. He was visibly angered at Sylvia's refusal to sell him the latest, and last, volume by James Joyce. Icily in perfect English the German informed the proprietor he would return. He was to have a copy of *Finnegans Wake* "or else." The inference was that Shakespeare and Company would be closed down and her entire stock confiscated, if "Madame" denied him his purchase.

The threat was clear, but Sylvia did not for a moment regret her determined stand against the German officer (what did the *boche* want with *Finnegans Wake* anyway?—the works of James Joyce were declared decadent and no doubt banned in Germany . . . it must be the attraction of "forbidden fruit" and the belief he was to have another *Ulysses* and not the incomprehensible final work Joyce loved more than life itself), for despite Sylvia Beach's obliging nature and ladylike New England demeanor, she could be obstinately contrary in such instances of what she thought "right."

Would that she could have sold the arrogant *Brigadeführer* a copy of Thomas Paine's *Common Sense*—did he realize that his thuggish outrider had parked his motorcycle, and noisily so, the motor thundering, beneath the window where Paine had contemplated this same tranquil thoroughfare when writing his *Age of Reason*? Sylvia tried to think what age Thomas Paine would call today's.

The rue de l'Odéon immediately reverted to its country village aspect when the Daimler-Benz and the motorcycle departed, but Sylvia could not regain her composure. She knew now her beloved bookshop, failing to find customers in any case (her mainstay, Americans in Paris, were no more), would have to close. The proprietor of the building offered Sylvia a room on the fourth floor, rent free. It would serve as a secret storage place for the duration.

Adrienne Monnier would help her move, but Sylvia would begin the transfer of books at once. The Germans would not close down Shakespeare and Company; Sylvia would do so herself.

First she would take down the William Shakespeare effigy that had served from the beginning as the identifying logo of the bookshop. (The famous sign had three times been stolen and each time replaced until Sylvia decided to bring the sign inside at night.) Now the sign was down for good.

Next Sylvia must find a safe place for Joyce's *Finnegans Wake*. She carried her only copy to the fourth floor and stuffed the volume into a mattress, the way French peasants had always done to hoard their gold in troubled times. To his infinite delight, Joyce would have made much (if only she could have told him the story) of her audacity in the face of the German conqueror by hiding the *Wake* in a mattress.

■ ■ ■

PAUL LÉON, JAMES Joyce's "seeing eye" and secretary after the rup-
ture with Sylvia Beach, performed one last fateful errand in the Joyce
business. He traveled to Paris from Joyce's temporary sanctuary in
Saint-Gérand-le-Puy, though Joyce begged him not to place himself at
risk. Léon, in any case, was sick of village life and badly missed Paris,
where he tried to collect Joycean memorabilia and belongings. Joyce's
former landlord had sold the furniture for back rent due, and much else
at auction, so the original purpose of Léon's errand ended in frustration.

Long after the Russian Jew should have fled Paris, Samuel Beckett
was shocked to meet Léon in the street. He urged him to quit the Nazi-
occupied city, but Léon told Beckett he wanted to see his son receive
his *baccalauréat*. Léon was arrested by the Germans and sent to a concentration camp, where he died.

In Saint-Gérand Joyce was, as ever and all the more, in need of
money—fifty thousand Swiss francs required of aliens seeking refuge in
Switzerland who might otherwise become wards of the state. The "guarantee" was an impossible sum for Joyce to imagine, much less produce
(with patrons out of touch, and Harriet Weaver become a Communist
now!). Nevertheless a dedicated banker friend in Zurich, Paul Ruggiero,
arranged to have the guarantee reduced to twenty thousand francs and
had the generous impulse to provide the bond himself.

James Joyce, with Nora and Giorgio, at last gained admission into
Switzerland, made welcome by the mayor of Zurich, but Joyce suffered
the guilt and misery of having to leave Lucia behind in France. It was
impossible to obtain a Swiss visa for a mentally ill émigrée.

Joyce was in constant pain and became increasingly impatient with his
benefactor Ruggiero who, like Beckett, Léon, and others of his devotees,
wanted to spend as much time as possible in the enlightened company of
the Irish genius. Ruggiero would drop in at the Hôtel Pension Delphin
uninvited and unannounced, invariably tossing his hat on the bed. Didn't
the man know that a hat on the bed meant somebody was going to die?

EACH VOLUME SYLVIA Beach carried to the fourth floor was like a
person, the book's author, being sheltered and kept hidden until . . .
well, until a new Age of Reason. (She placed Hemingway's *Men
Without Women* and Katherine Anne Porter's *Pale Horse, Pale Rider* in

opposite corners of the room, since the two authors had refused to meet despite Sylvia's attempt to introduce them.)

Pale Horse, Pale Rider was one of the last books Sylvia received from the States before transatlantic shipping had become too hazardous, and the book in her hand, the last novel published by Thomas Wolfe.

In her memory's eye Sylvia could see the oversized southerner stalking around her bookshop and gesturing so largely he was liable to knock the books from their shelves, or smash the miniature bust of Shakespeare on the mantel, with his big hands thrown upward for emphasis to his drawling monologues. Sylvia hadn't taken to the giant (in literary stature as well as in physique), but now mourned his passing. He had died, she heard, at the age of thirty-eight, and the book she carried upstairs was published posthumously. *You Can't Go Home Again*. Well, you can't.

Sylvia could never return to the United States any more than Joyce could go back to Dublin, though Joyce may have wanted to see Dublin more than in his writer's eye. Sylvia had received word of Joyce's death from Maria Jolas, who was now in the States but kept in touch with the Joyce family in Zurich. A Swiss doctor had finally convinced Joyce to submit to X ray, and it revealed a life-threatening perforated duodenal ulcer. After a consultation with specialists, an immediate operation was advised: Joyce was somehow cheered, momentarily, by the offer of two stalwart Swiss soldiers from Neuchâtel to give blood in case of a transfusion. It was a good sign, Joyce thought—hadn't he always enjoyed Neuchâtel wines?

Nora shared his confidence: "Jim is tough," she said. But not tough enough to survive: Joyce lapsed into a coma after the operation and died. He was buried in Zurich not long into the New Year of 1941. When Lucia was finally told of her father's death, she could not at first believe that he had died. Then she thought his burial a great joke: "What is he doing under the ground, that idiot? When will he decide to come out? He's watching us all the time."

THE RUE DE L'ODÉON was surely haunted, for Sylvia could verily hear Joyce's ashplant tap-tapping down the street, the near-blind author making his uncertain way to Shakespeare and Company—but this evening it was another cane tapping, the "staff of Diogenes," carried by Raymond Duncan, looking ghostly indeed in his flowing Greek toga.

Duncan had adopted the Greek motif from his sister, the famous dancer Isadora, and after her death settled in Paris and opened a gallery, a handicraft atelier on the rue de Seine, continuing the Greek tradition by dressing the part his sister played and fashioning sandals at his little shop, the Akademia, in the Greek style—Gertrude Stein had always worn a pair of Raymond's Greek sandals.

The Germans considered Raymond Duncan harmlessly insane, and there would be no threats to close his Akademia down . . . it was an advantage, during the Occupation, to be an eccentric. The Germans only laughed at Raymond.

(Duncan dreamed of a "New Paris York" as he called his vision of a new Atlantis, and proposed that transatlantic passengers—and the *Normandie* and *Mauretania* would surely sail again, with Americans bound for Paris—drop stones from the ships' decks at a halfway point across the Atlantic: "Thus in time will the new city rear its glorious head above the waves." The new city was to be free of taxes, free of any strictures whatsoever, which, Sylvia concluded, is exactly what Americans had expected of Paris all along.)

It grew dark early in that first winter of the Occupation, and Sylvia, watching from behind the blackout curtain on the fourth floor, followed Raymond Duncan's promenade for a few more steps in the direction of the place de l'Odéon, fearful for Raymond that it might be past curfew and he risked arrest. But the early dark was deceptive, and people were still out and about. Two students Sylvia recognized from the Foyer des Étudiants (where she and Adrienne sometimes took a two-and-a-half-franc evening meal) came up to the door of Shakespeare and Company. They had been walking hand in hand, and the boy carried a book he was returning to Sylvia's now nonexistent lending library. There was a note on the door, in English and French, that any returned books could be taken across the street to Adrienne's La Maison des Amis des Livres at 7 rue de l'Odéon. The students started across the street, hand in hand still, then paused in the middle of the street and in the veiled lamplight (Sylvia saw only the shadows of the two) embraced.

That, too, was what Americans expected of Paris.

The students stood kissing at the very spot where Sylvia and Adrienne had met so many years before. *"J'aime beaucoup l'Amérique,"* Adrienne had announced, and Sylvia's reply was, *"J'aime beaucoup la France,"* and the pledge had endured, as had their love for one another.

(Adrienne had fallen in love with the photographer Gisèle Freund during one heartbreaking interval, but that was past—Gisèle, a Jew, had fled Paris for South America—and Sylvia and Adrienne now continued their devoted liaison.)

James Joyce, in the portrait by Gisèle Freund, did seem, as Lucia believed, to be watching Sylvia all the time, until she took the photograph, and all the other portraits of authors she had known, to the fourth floor, and painted the empty downstairs walls white. Sylvia had the feeling the German officer would not be back, and she was right. In any case the books—almost five thousand volumes—were safely out of sight, the shelves removed (even the light fixtures were stored) and the legend on the outside wall painted over: "Bookshop-librarie." Beloved spirits haunted Shakespeare and Company still. The vacant premises were filled with phantoms only.

NOTES AND SOURCES

*I*N RESEARCHING *The Twilight Years,* it occurred to me how like those of a novel were the events and characters I discovered in the formal histories of the era, and how naturally the period 1930 to 1940 follows a dramatic plot line. Since I am a novelist, I was delighted to uncover a ready-made story in the material under study, and where possible I have endeavored to emphasize the story quality of a decade that has always fascinated me, by means of a selective process with the dramatic elements in mind. In some few instances I applied my imagination to scenes that would otherwise go unrecorded. I could not know, nor could anyone know, the thoughts of Jules Pascin just before his suicide, but having lived on Pascin's sad and sordid boulevard Rochechouart and now having studied his life and work and attitudes, I believe I can reconstruct Pascin's last tragic promenade as closely as the "facts" allow.

CHAPTER 1: ENTER LAUGHING, TRISTE ADIEU

I

Baxter, Annette Karr. *Henry Miller, Expatriate*. Pittsburgh: University of Pittsburg Press, 1961.

Dearborn, Mary V. *The Happiest Man Alive*. New York: Simon & Schuster, 1961.

Ferguson, Robert. *Henry Miller*. New York: W. W. Norton, 1991.

Martin, Jay. *Always Merry and Bright*. Santa Barbara, Calif.: Capra Press, 1978.

Miller, Henry. *Black Spring*. New York: Grove Press, 1963.

———. *The Henry Miller Reader*. Ed. Lawrence Durrell. New York: New Directions, 1959.

———. *Letters to Emil*. Ed. George Wickes. New York: New Directions, 1989.

———. *Tropic of Cancer*. Paris: Obelisk Press, 1934.

Verbatim quotations are from Miller's letters to Emil Schnellock and from Miller's *Tropic of Cancer*.

II

Bay, André. *Le Roman de Pascin*. Paris: Albin Michel, 1948.

Brodzky, Horace. *Pascin*. London: Nicholson & Watson, 1946.

D'Ancona, Paolo. *Modigliani, Chagall, Soutine, Pascin*. Milan: Edizioni del Milone, 1953.

Hemingway, Ernest. *A Moveable Feast*. New York: Scribners, 1964.

Jianou, Ionel. *Zadkine*. Paris: Arted, Editions d'Art, 1964.

Kessel, Joseph. *Kisling*. New York: Harry N. Abrams, 1971.

Kiki. *Kiki's Memoirs*. New York: Ecco Press, 1996.

Kluver, Billy, and Julie Martin. *Kiki's Paris*. New York: Harry N. Abrams, 1989.

Warnod, André. *Pascin*. Monte Carlo: Editions du Livre, 1954.

Werner, Alfred. *Pascin*. New York: Harry N. Abrams, 1962.

The quotations are translations from the French in *Le Roman de Pascin*, the Hemingway-Pascin dialogue from *A Moveable Feast*.

CHAPTER 2: BEACHHEAD IN BOHEMIA

Antheil, George. *The Bad Boy of Music*. London: Duckworth, 1976.

Beach, Sylvia. *Shakespeare and Company*. New York: Harcourt, Brace, 1956.

Ellmann, Richard. *James Joyce*. London: Oxford University Press, 1959.

Fitch, Noel Riley. *Sylvia Beach and the Lost Generation*. New York: W. W. Norton, 1983.

Givner, Joan. *Katherine Anne Porter*. New York: Simon & Schuster, 1982.

Joyce, James. *James Joyce's Letters to Sylvia Beach, 1921–1940*. Ed. Melissa Banta and Oscar A. Silverman. Bloomington: University of Indiana Press, 1987.

Lidderdale, Jane, and Mary Nicholson. *Dear Miss Weaver*. London: Faber and Faber, 1970.

Monnier, Adrienne. *The Very Rich Hours of Adrienne Monnier*. Trans. Richard McDougall. New York: Scribners, 1976.

A reproduction of the contract between James Joyce and Sylvia Beach appears in the section "Flowers of Friendship Fade" (Fitch's *Sylvia Beach*).

Quotes concerning the Ulysses contract are from Ellmann's *James Joyce*. Sylvia Beach's own quotations from her memoir *Shakespeare and Company* and from Fitch's *Sylvia Beach*.

CHAPTER 3: PARIS BY NIGHT

I

Brassaï. *Brassaï*. Intro. Lawrence Durrell. New York: Museum of Modern Art, 1968.
————. *Henry Miller, the Paris Years*. New York: Arcade Publishing, 1995.
————. *Le Paris Secret des Années 30*. Paris: Gallimard, 1976.
Miller, Henry. *Black Spring*. New York: Grove Press, 1963.
————. *The Henry Miller Reader*. Ed. Lawrence Durrell. New York: New Directions, 1959.
————. *Letters to Emil*. Ed. George Wickes. New York: New Directions, 1989.
————. *Remember to Remember*. London: The Grey Walls Press, 1952.
————. *Tropic of Cancer*. Paris: Obelisk Press, 1934.
Nin, Anaïs. *The Diary of Anaïs Nin, 1931–1934*. New York: The Swallow Press/Harcourt Brace & World, 1966.

In *Remember to Remember* Miller looks out from a W.C. he describes as a cell-like oubliette: "The vista was so sweepingly soft and intoxicating it brought tears to my eyes." Anaïs Nin's statements are from her diary.

CHAPTER 4: PARIS BY NIGHT

II

Baker, Josephine, with Jo Bouillon. *Josephine*. Paris: Editions Laffont, 1976.
Bricktop, with James Haskins. *Bricktop*. New York: Atheneum, 1983.
Flanner, Janet. *An American in Paris*. New York: Simon & Schuster, 1940.
McBride, Bunny. *Molly Spotted Elk*. Norman, Oklahoma: University of Oklahoma Press 1995.
Stovall, Tyler. *Paris Noir*. Boston: Houghton Mifflin, 1996.
Weber, Eugen. *The Hollow Years*. New York: W. W. Norton, 1994.
Wiser, William. *The Crazy Years*. London: Thames and Hudson, 1983.
————. *The Great Good Place*. New York: W. W. Norton, 1991.

Quotes by Josephine Baker are from *Josephine*. Quotes by Bricktop from *Bricktop*. Quotes by Molly Spotted Elk from the McBride biography.

CHAPTER 5: THE SIBYL OF MONTPARNASSE AND THE BOOTBLACK OF MONTMARTRE

Gertrude Stein

Brinnin, John Malcolm. *The Third Rose*. Boston: Little Brown, 1959.
Mellow, James R. *Charmed Circle*. New York: Praeger Publishers, 1974.
Stein, Gertrude. *The Autobiography of Alice B Toklas*. New York: Harcourt Brace, 1933.
————. *Everybody's Autobiography*. New York: Random House, 1937.

Pablo Picasso

Brassaï. *The Artists of My Life*. New York: Viking, 1982.
Chipp, Herschel B. *Picasso's Guernica*. Berkeley, Calif.: University of California Press, 1988.
Daix, Pierre. *Picasso Créature*. Paris: Editions du Seuil, 1987.
Fermigier, André. *Picasso*. Paris: Le Livre de Poche, 1969.

Flanner, Janet. *Men and Monuments*. New York: Harper and Row, 1957.

Raynal, Maurice. *Picasso*. Geneva: Skira, 1953.

Read, Herbert. *Histoire de la Peinture Moderne*. Paris: Editions Aimery Somogy, 1960.

Stein, Gertrude. *Picasso*. Camera work. August 1912.

Warncke, Carsten-Peter. *Picasso 1881–1973. Tome II Les oeuvres de 1937 à 1973*. Munich: Benedict Taschen Verlag, 1922.

Wineapple, Brenda. *Sister Brother*. New York: Putnam's 1975.

Picasso's poems appeared in *Les Cahiers d'Art* with an introduction by André Breton comparing his poetry to painting.

Dora Maar, when Picasso left her for Françoise Gilet, had a nervous breakdown, then became a recluse. Marie-Thérèse Walter survived Picasso by four years: she committed suicide at Cap d'Antibes in 1977.

Gertrude Stein's quotations are from her works cited above.

CHAPTER 6: UN BEAU CRIME, S.V.P.

Crosland, Margaret. *Simone de Beauvoir*. London: Heinemann, 1992.

Dearborn, Mary V. *The Happiest Man Alive*, New York: Simon & Schuster, 1961.

De Beauvoir, Simone. *La Force de l'Age*. Paris: Gallimard, 1960.

Ferguson, Robert. *Henry Miller*. New York: W. W. Norton, 1991.

Flanner, Janet. *The Murder in Le Mans* From *Paris was Yesterday, 1925–1939*. New York: Viking Press, 1972.

Genet, Jean. *The Maids*. Les Bonnes, M. Barbezat Decines, isere 1963

Lacan, Jacques. "*Motifs du Crime Paranoiaque*." *Minotaure* 3–4 (12 December 1933).

Martin, Jay. *Always Merry and Bright*. Santa Barbara, Calif.: Capra Press, 1978.

Miller, Henry. *Letters to Emil*. ed. George Wickes. New York: New Directions, 1989.

Tharaud, Jerome/Jean. *Paris Soir* 28, 29, 30 September; 8 October 1933.

White, Edmund. *Jean Genet*. New York: Knopf, 1993.

In Genet's play *The Maids* the horror of eye-gouging is omitted, as in the tradition of classic Greek theatre (the self-blinding of Oedipus takes place offstage so as not to appal the audience), but in the modern sense much is made of the sexual union of the two protagonists and the master-slave relationship of that union.

Henry Miller's teaching stint in Dijon is referred to in the Dearborn, Ferguson and Martin biographies, but most vividly in the exaggerated sequence from *Tropic of Cancer*.

CHAPTER 7: THE CATALYST FROM CATALONIA

Ades, Dawn. *Dada and Surrealism Reviewed*. London: Arts Council of Great Britain, 1978.

———. *Dalí*. London: Thames & Hudson, 1982.

Brandon, Ruth. *Surreal Lives*. New York: Grove Press, 1999.

Brassaï, *The Artists of My Life*. New York: Viking, 1982.

Breton, André. *La Clé des Champs*. Paris: Editions Pauvert, 1953.

Cowles, Fleur. *The Case of Salvador Dalí*. Boston: Little Brown, 1959.

Dalí, Salvador. *The Secret Life of Salvador Dalí*. New York: Dial Press, 1942.

Johnson, Douglas and Madeleine. *The Age of Illusion*. New York: Rizzoli Publications, 1987.

Morse, A. Reynolds. *Salvador Dalí/Pablo Picasso*. Cleveland, Ohio: The Salvador Dalí Museum, 1973.

Orwell, George. *Dickens, Dalí & Others*. New York: Harcourt Brace, 1973.

Picon, Gaëton. *Surrealists and Surrealism*. New York: Rizzoli Publications, 1983.

Weld, Jacqueline Bograd. *Peggy, The Wayward Guggenheim*. New York: Dutton, 1986.

Dalí's quoted comments are from his autobiography *The Secret Life*. Brassaï's descriptions of Gala and Dalí are from *The Artists of My Life*.

CHAPTER 8: A PAWNSHOP SCAM THAT ROCKED THE NATION

Bald, Wambly. *On the Left Bank 1929–1933*. Ed. Benjamin Franklin V. Athens, Ohio: Ohio University Press, 1987.

Bernier, Olivier. *Fireworks at Dusk*. Boston: Little Brown, 1993.

Bourdel, Philippe. *La Cagoule*. Paris: Editions Albin Michel, 1970.

Chavardès, Maurice. *La Droite Française at le 6 Fevrier 1934*. Paris : Flammarion, 1970.

Daudet, Léon. *Magistrats et Policiers*. Paris: Bernard Grasset, 1935.

Flanner, Janet. *Paris Was Yesterday 1925–1939*. New York: Viking, 1972.

Miller, Henry. *Letters to Emil*. Ed. George Wickes. New York: New Directions, 1989.

———. *Tropic of Cancer*. New York: Grove Press, 1961.

Shirer, William. *The Collapse of the Third Republic*. New York: Simon & Schuster, 1969.

Weber, Eugen. *The Hollow Years*. New York: Norton, 1994.

Werth, Alexander. *France in Ferment*, Gloucester, Mass.: Peter Smith, 1968.

———. *The Twilight of France 1933–1940*. New York: Howard Fertig, 1966.

The conversation between Wambly Bald and Ernest Hemingway concerning passage to America was told to Benjamin Franklin V by Bald and appears in the preface to *On the Left Bank*.

CHAPTER 9: STREET SCENE

Bald, Wambly. *On the Left Bank 1929–1933*. Ed. Benjamin Franklin V. Athens, Ohio: Ohio University Press, 1987.

Bernier, Olivier. *Fireworks at Dusk*. Boston: Little Brown, 1993.

Bourdel, Philippe. *La Cagoule*. Paris: Editions Albin Michel, 1970.

Chavardès, Maurice. *La Droite Française at le 6 Fevrier 1934*. Paris : Flammarion, 1970.

Daudet, Léon. *Magistrats et Policiers*. Paris: Bernard Grasset, 1935.

Flanner, Janet. *Paris Was Yesterday 1925–1939*. New York: Viking, 1972.

Miller, Henry. *Letters to Emil*. Ed. George Wickes. New York: New Directions, 1989.

———. *Tropic of Cancer*. New York: Grove Press, 1961.

Shirer, William. *The Collapse of the Third Republic*. New York: Simon & Schuster, 1969.

Weber, Eugen. *The Hollow Years*. New York: Norton, 1994.

Werth, Alexander. *France in Ferment*, Gloucester, Mass.: Peter Smith, 1968.

———. *The Twilight of France 1933–1940*. New York: Howard Fertig, 1966.

The proclamation by the Duc de Guise is from Shirer's *The Collapse of the Third Republic*. Janet Flanner's summary of French newspaper headlines is from *Paris Was Yesterday* "Bloody Tuesday 1934."

CHAPTER 10: THE SCENT OF PRINCESSES

Flanner, Janet. "Perfumes and Politics." From *An American in Paris*, ed. pp. 121–134. New York: Simon & Schuster, 1940.

Gregory, Alexis. *Paris Deluxe*. New York: Rizzoli Publications, 1997.

Irvine, Susan. *Perfume*. New York: Random House, 1995.

Lazareff, Pierre. *Deadline*. New York: Random House, 1942.
Morris, Edwin T. *Fragrance*. New York: Scribners, 1984.
Weber, Eugen. *The Hollow Years*. New York: W. W. Norton, 1994.
Werth, Alexander. *France in Ferment*. Gloucester, Mass: Peter Smith, 1968.

CHAPTER 11, CHAPTER 13: PLACE VENDÔME

I and II

Baudot, Francois. *Elsa Schiaparelli*. Paris: Editions Assouline, 1997.
Bernier, Olivier. *Fireworks at Dusk*. Boston/New York: Little, Brown, 1993.
Charles-Roux, Edmonde. *Chanel and Her World*. Paris: Hachette-Vendôme, 1981.
Deslandres, Yvonne. *Poiret*. New York: Rizzoli Publications, 1986.
Flanner, Janet. *An American in Paris*. New York: Simon & Schuster, 1940.
Gregory, Alexis. *Paris Deluxe: Place Vendôme*. New York: Rizzoli Publications, 1997.
Madsen, Axel, *Chanel*. New York: Henry Holt, 1990.
Rubinstein, Helena. *My Life for Beauty*. London: The Bodley Head, 1965.
Schiaparelli, Elsa. *Shocking Life*. New York: Dutton, 1954.
Shaplen, Robert. *Kreuger, Genius & Swindler*. New York: Knopf, 1960.
Steele, Valerie. *Women of Fashion*. New York: Rizzoli Publications, 1991.
Wiser, William. *The Great Good Place*. New York: W. W. Norton, 1991.
Schiaparelli's encounter with Paul Poiret and her comment on "the human body" are from *Shocking Life*. Ivar Kreuger's comment on building his "enterprise" is from Shaplen's *Kreuger*. Mary Cassatt's advice to James Stillman is from *The Great Good Place*.

CHAPTER 12: THE WOMAN WHO WOULD BE QUEEN

Bloch, Michael, ed. *Wallis and Edward, Letters 1931–1937*. New York: Summit Books, 1986.
Channon, Henry. *Chips: The Diaries of Sir Henry Channon*. London: Wiedenfeld & Nicholson, 1967.
Higham, Charles. *The Duchess of Windsor*. New York: McGraw Hill, 1988.
Murphy, Charles J. V., and J. Bryan III. *The Windsor Story*. New York: Morrow, 1979.
Simpson's confession ". . . the minute I put my foot inside France" is from *The Windsor Story*.

CHAPTER 14: WIDENING CIRCLES

Bair, Deirdre. *Anaïs Nin*. New York: Putnam's, 1991.
Brassaï. *Henry Miller (Grandeur Nature)*. Paris: Gallimard, 1975.
Fitch, Noel Riley. *Anaïs (The Erotic Life of Anaïs Nin)*. Boston: Little, Brown, 1993.
Miller Henry. *Black Spring*. New York: Grove Press, 1963.
———. *The Henry Miller Reader*. Ed. Lawrence Durrell. New York: New Directions, 1959.
———. *Letters to Emil*. Ed. George Wickes. New York: New Directions, 1989.
———. *Tropic of Cancer*. Paris: Obelisk Press, 1934.
Nin, Anaïs. *Fire, The Unexpurgated Diary of Anaïs Nin 1934–1937*. New York: Harcourt, Brace, 1995.
———. *The Diary of Anaïs Nin 1931–1934*. Ed. Gunther Stuhlmann. New York: Harcourt, Brace, 1966.
———. *Recollections of Anaïs Nin*, Ed. Benjamin Franklin V. Athens, Ohio: Ohio

University Press, 1996.

Nin, Anaïs, and Henry Miller. *Henry and June*. New York: Harcourt, Brace, 1986.

———. *A Literate Passion*. Nin/Miller Letters, ed. Gunther Stuhlmann. New York: Harcourt, Brace, 1987.

The dialogue at the bordel in rue Blondel is from Nin's diaries. Brassaï's description of June is from his *Grandeur Nature*.

CHAPTER 15: LIAISONS DANGEREUSES

Bair, Deirdre. *Anaïs Nin*. New York: Putnam's 1995.

Ellmann, Richard. *James Joyce*. New York: Oxford University Press, 1982.

Maddox, Brenda. *Nora, the Real Life Story of Molly Bloom*. New York: Houghton Mifflin, 1988.

Martin, Jay. *Always Merry and Bright*. Santa Barbara, Calif.: Capra Press, 1978.

Nin, Anaïs, and Henry Miller. *Henry and June*. New York: Harcourt, Brace, 1986.

———. *A Literate Passion*. Nin/Miller Letters, ed. Gunther Stuhlmann. New York: Harcourt, Brace, 1987.

Quotations are from the Ellmann biography of James Joyce.

The quotations of Henry and June Miller are from the Martin biography *Always Merry and Bright*, and from Bair's *Anaïs Nin*, as well as *Henry and June* and *A Literate Passion*.

CHAPTER 16: PORTENTS AND ALARMS

Berg, A. Scott. *Lindbergh*. New York: Putnam's, 1998.

de Gaulle, Charles. *Memoires de Guerre (L'Appel)*. Paris: Plon, 1954.

Field, Andrew. *VN, The Life and Art of Vladimir Nabokov*. New York: Crown, 1986.

Hamilton, Ian. *Koestler*. New York Macmillan, 1982.

Kemp, Anthony. *The Maginot Line*. New York: Stein & Day, 1982.

Lazareff, Pierre. *De Munich à Vichy*. New York: Brentano's, 1944.

Lottman, Herbert R. *The Left Bank*. Boston: Houghton Mifflin, 1982.

Mellow, James R. *Charmed Circle*. New York Praeger, 1974.

Shirer, William L. *The Collapse of the Third Republic*. New York: Simon & Schuster, 1969.

Stein, Gertrude. *Everybody's Autobiography*. New York: Random House, 1937.

———. *Paris, France*. New York: Scribner's, 1940.

———. "The Winner Loses." *Atlantic Monthly* (November, 1940).

Ward, Charles A. *Oracles of Nostradamas*. New York Modern Library, 1940.

Werth, Alexander. *France in Ferment*. Gloucester, Mass.: Peter Smith: 1968.

———. *France and Munich*. London: Hamish Hamilton, 1939.

The individual quotations by Joyce, Koestler, Lindbergh, and Nabokov are from their separate biographies listed above. Nabokov's remarks on the genesis of *Lolita* appear in the afterword to that novel.

Gertrude Stein's quotations are from her *Paris, France* and *The Winner Loses*.

CHAPTER 17: YUNG AND EASILY FREUDENED

Ellmann, Richard. *James Joyce*. London: Oxford University Press, 1959. From previously cited references to James Joyce and quotations from the Ellmann biography.

CHAPTER 18: LAST DANCE

Bernier, Olivier. *Fireworks at Dusk*. New York: Little, Brown, 1993.

Ellman, Richard. *James Joyce*. London: Oxford University Press, 1959.

Faucigny-Lucinges, Prince Jean-Louis. *Fêtes Memorables*. Paris: Hersher, 1987.

Flanner, Janet. *An American in Paris*. New York Simon & Schuster, 1940.

———. *Paris Was Yesterday*. New York: Viking Press, 1972.

Lazareff, Pierre. *Deadline*. New York: Random House, 1942.

———. *De Munich à Vichy*. New York: Brentano's, 1944.

Maxwell, Elsa. *RSVP*. Boston: Little, Brown, 1954.

Morella, Joseph and George Mazzei. *Genius and Lust*. New York: Carroll & Graf, 1995.

Schwartz, Charles. *Cole Porter*. New York: The Dial Press, 1977.

Smith, Jane S. *Elsie de Wolfe*. New York: Atheneum, 1982.

Stovall, Tyler. *Paris Noir*. Boston: Houghton Mifflin, 1996.

Weiss, Andrea. *Paris Was a Woman*. New York: Harper, 1995.

Wiser, William. *The Crazy Years*. New York: Atheneum, 1983.

As editor of *Paris Soir*, Pierre Lazareff followed the rise of Hélène Rebuffel who became comtesse de Portes, and of Jeanne Beziers who married into the title of marquise de Crussol. He also reported on the career and exposure of Otto Abetz, spy for the German Abwehr. When the armistice was signed with France, Hitler appointed Abetz ambassador to France.

Joyce's quote at Christmas party is from *James Joyce*.

CHAPTER 19: DEBACLE

I

Carley, Michael Jabara. *1939*. Chicago: Ivan R. Dee, 1999.

Churchill, Winston. *The Second World War. Vol. II Their Finest Hour*. Boston: Houghton Mifflin, 1949.

de Gaulle, Charles. *Memoirs de Guerre*. Paris: Plon, 1954.

Lazareff, Pierre. *De Munich à Vichy*. New York Brentano's, 1944.

Liebling, A. J. *Liebling at the New Yorker*. Albuquerque, N. Mex.: University of New Mexico Press, 1994.

———. *The Road Back to Paris*. New York: Doubleday, 1944.

Micaud, Charles A. *The French Right and Nazi Germany 1933–1939*. New York: Octagon Books, 1972.

Saint-Exupéry, Antoine de. *A Sense of Life*. New York: Funk & Wagnalls, 1965.

———. *Wartime Writings 1939–1944*. New York: Harcourt, Brace, 1986.

Sartre, Jean-Paul. *Les Carnets de la Drôle de Guerre*. Paris: Gallimard, 1983.

Shirer, William. *The Collapse of the Third Republic*. New York: Simon & Schuster, 1969.

Weber, Eugen. *The Hollow Years*. New York: W. W. Norton, 1994.

Werth, Alexander. *The Twilight of France, 1933–1940*. New York: Howard Fertig, 1966.

Liebling's quoted impressions of Paris during the Phony War are from his letters to the *New Yorker* (*Liebling at the New Yorker*).

CHAPTER 20: EXODUS

Baldwin, Neil. *Man Ray*. New York: Clarkson N. Potter, 1947.

Ellman, Richard. *James Joyce*. London: Oxford University Press, 1959.

Field, Andrew. *VN, The Life and Art of Vladimir Nabokov*. New York: Crown, 1986.

Knowlson, James. *Damned to Fame, The Life of Samuel Beckett*. New York: Simon & Schuster, 1996.

Nin, Anaïs, and Henry Miller. *Henry and June*. New York: Harcourt, Brace, 1986.

———. *A Literate Passion*. Nin/Miller Letters, ed. Gunther Stuhlmann. New York: Harcourt, Brace, 1987.

Stein, Gertrude. *Everybody's Autobiography*. New York: Random House, 1937.

Wineapple, Brenda. *Genet, A Biography of Janet Flanner*. New York: Ticknor & Fields, 1989.

The quotations of Gertrude Stein are from her previously cited works: *Paris, France, Everybody's Autobiography* and *The Winner Loses*.

Joyce's quotes are from the *James Joyce*. The Miller/Nin parting scene based on *Henry and June* and *A Literate Passion*.

CHAPTER 21: DEBACLE

II

In addition to the works cited for Chapter 19, the following books were consulted:

Barber, Noel. *The Week France Fell*. New York: Stein & Day, 1976.

Beach, Sylvia. *Shakespeare and Company*. New York: Harcourt, Brace, 1956.

Beaufré, André. *Le Drame de 1940*. Paris: Plon, 1960.

Bernier, Olivier. *Fireworks at Dusk*. New York: Little, Brown, 1993.

Nicolson, Harold. *Diaries 1930–1964*. Ed. Stanley Olson. New York: Atheneum, 1980.

Pertinax (A. Geraud). *Gravediggers of France*. New York: Doubleday, 1944.

Shirer, William. *The Collapse of the Third Republic*. New York: Simon & Schuster, 1969.

Spears, Sir Edward. *Assignment to Catastrophe*. 2 vols. London: Heinemann, 1954.

Weld, Jaqueline Bograd. *Peggy, The Wayward Guggenheim*. New York: Dutton, 1986.

Zay, Jean. *Carnets Secrets*. Paris: Les Editions de France, 1942.

The newspaper correspondent Geraud ("Pertinax") wrote extensively of the failings of Gamelin, Daladier, and Reynaud, and the treachery of Pétain and Laval.

Sir Edward Spears was liaison officer between Churchill and Reynaud; the firsthand observations of Hélène de Portes are primarily his, plus impressions by Harold Nicolson who also dealt with Mme. de Portes during the debacle. Further reports on the behavior of the countess are from Shirer in his *Collapse of the Third Republic* and from Barber's *The Week France Fell*, as well as quoted remarks. All sources are agreed on the disastrous influence on Reynaud of Mme. de Portes.

Peggy Guggenheim's remark about refugees is from Weld's *Peggy*. Sylvia Beach's quoted report on the flow of refugees through Paris is from her *Shakespeare and Company*.

CHAPTER 22: THE FALL

In addition for works cited in Chapters 19 and 21, the following was consulted:

Bullitt, William C. *For the President: Personal and Secret*. London: Andre Deutsch, 1973.

The *pneumatique* sent to Ambassador Bullitt by Thierry de Martel just before his suicide is from Barber, *The Week France Fell*.

EPILOGUE: GHOSTS

Beach, Sylvia. *Shakespeare and Company*. New York: Harcourt, Brace, 1956.

Ellmann, Richard. *James Joyce*. London: Oxford University Press, 1959.

Fitch, Noel Riley. *Sylvia Beach and the Lost Generation*. New York: Norton, 1983.

Monnier, Adrienne. *The Very Rich Hours of Adrienne Monnier*. Trans. Richard McDougall. New York: Scribner's 1976.

Root, Waverly. "Montparnasse Memories." *The International Herald Tribune* (Paris). 17–18 July 1982.

The death of James Joyce is reported in *James Joyce*, and Lucia's remark is from the same source.

Raymond Duncan's idea for "New Paris York" and his quotation are from the article by Waverly Root.

INDEX

('i' indicates an illustration)